Building A Writing Community:
A Practical Guide

by
Marcia S. Freeman

MAUPIN

HOUSE

Maupin House Publishing

Building a writing community : a practical guide
© Copyright 1995 Marcia S. Freeman

Book design by Anthony Johnson

Freeman, Marcia S. (Marcia Sheehan), 1937-
Building a writing community : a practical guide / Marcia S. Freeman
p. cm.
Includes bibliographical references (p.)
ISBN 0-929895-13-4 (alk.paper)

1. English language—Composition and exercises—Study and teaching (Elementary)—United States—Handbooks, manuals, etc. I. Title.
LB1576.F728 1995
372.6'23'044—dc20   95-23882
                                     CIP

Printed in the United States of America
10 9 8 7 6 5 4 3 2 1

Maupin House Publishing
P. O. Box 90148
Gainesville, FL 32607
1-800-524-0634.

CONTENTS

Dedication

To my inspiration; young writers

Acknowledgments

My thanks to Dr. Frank Fahy, Assistant Superintendent (retired of the West Caldwell/Caldwell School District in New Jersey for bringing Donald Graves to Caldwell and for his subsequent support of the teachers who embraced the writing process approach to teaching children to write. Thank you, Donald Graves, for the inspiration.

My appreciation goes to Frank DiSessa, Lincoln Elementary School principal, who encouraged me and gave me great latitude during my early attempts to understand and implement the writing process in my classroom. Teresa Matrisciano, master kindergarten teacher at Lincoln Elementary, shared her enthusiasm and knowledge, for which I thank her.

I am grateful to Wendy Kasten, Ph.D., Associate Professor, Literacy Education, Kent State, Ohio, for her confidence in me and for recommending me to school administrators seeking assistance in upgrading their writing instruction programs. I also thank Dr. Katherine Gottschalk, of the John S. Knight Writing Program at Cornell University, and poet Brod Bagert for encouraging me in my writing.

I appreciate the many generous teachers who have given me the opportunity to work in their classrooms and who have contributed or validated many of the ideas in this book. I could not have written this book without the help and support of my husband, Mike, who acted as peer responder, editor, and computer consultant.

Most importantly, I want to thank all the children with whom I have learned how to build a classroom writing community.

Preface

As a writing education consultant, I conduct workshops about the writing process for elementary teachers. The question they most frequently ask me is, "What, exactly, should I do in the classroom to make this work?"

The answer can be found, in part, in the myriad of books about the writing process and children as writers. Graves, Routman, Calkins, Butler and Turbill, Atwell, and Parry and Homsby provide a wealth of information and inspiration. Teacher's journals and magazines offer lessons and creative ideas as well.

Notwithstanding, many teachers have said to me, "I have read some of these books and I've been to workshops, but I still need specific things to do that will work in my classroom. Can you show them to me?" It is for these teachers that I have written this book.

A number of years ago I remember having the same questions and need. Two days before the start of a new school year, Donald Graves, children's writing researcher and professor of education at the University of New Hampshire, addressed the district faculty in Caldwell, New Jersey where I taught a combination fourth and fifth grade class. He exhorted us to teach children to write as real writers do, using a process that includes time to think, write a rough draft and revise, and the opportunity to publish. For those of you who have not had the opportunity to meet or hear him, Donald Graves is awesome and inspiring. Over the next two days I threw away my language arts plans, hastily made a batch of small blank books, set up writing folders, rearranged my room, and brainstormed briefly with a kindred spirit on our faculty.

I plunged headlong into the Writing Process. With the help of a copy of Grave's *Writing: Teachers and Children at Work,* the support of a group of teachers similarly inclined, the encouragement of a principal who fostered creativity, and the enthusiasm of my 29 fourth and fifth graders, I made it through that first year. I floundered sometimes, but I was regularly rewarded by the results and struck by the possibilities.

Today, my enthusiasm for the process approach to teaching writing continues unabated, if not unbounded. My evolution from classroom teacher to writing education consultant has allowed me to see the impact that writing process has on writing instruction in classroom after classroom. I have watched any number of teachers, initially skeptical of the philosophy, try some of the techniques and lessons I provided. The immediate positive results were enough to convince them of the possibilities, and they, too, have become enthusiastic devotees of the writing process workshop classroom.

These successes gave me the impetus to write this book. It is a compilation of specific information, models, practical strategies, and detailed lessons that will help elementary teachers implement and manage the writing process, encourage young writers, and teach writing skills. It presents procedures and practices to create a classroom environment that will support and sustain young writers as they develop their writing craft.

Most of the ideas presented in this book are ones that I have devised and used in my classroom, in writing workshops for children, and with classroom teachers to whom I serve as consultant and mentor. Classroom teachers and young writers themselves have contributed the rest. These ideas share two traits. They all have been tested in classrooms of 25 to 31 children. And, they all work.

Marcia S. Freeman
April 1995

Chapter I

Introduction

What is the Writing Process?

The writing process is how we translate ideas into written text. It starts with an idea in our head and the need to develop it, communicate it to an audience, and preserve it.

Every writer goes through a process to achieve these ends. The process includes thinking, rehearsal, planning the presentation, drafting, reading and listening to the text, revising it, polishing it for publication, and publishing. Between drafting and publishing a writer cycles back through thinking, writing, and listening any number of times — the more times, the better the quality of the final product.

For instructional purposes, these stages are commonly labeled Prewriting, Drafting, Revising, Editing, and Publishing. I include an additional stage, Response, that comes between Drafting and Revising. Young or developing writers use peers, parents, and teachers to hear their texts and to help them revisit their manuscripts. Response and Revision are closely related in the same way as are Editing and Publishing. In the former two stages, the writer focuses on clarity, meaning, and interest. In the latter two stages, the writer focuses on convention and form, preparing the manuscript for an audience.

This book devotes a chapter to each stage. The accompanying procedures, models, lessons, and information are designed to help teachers and developing writers through the respective stage.

Implementing writing process strategies and practices alone does not guarantee a successful writing community. The use of Author's Chair does not qualify you for Writing Process Teacher of the Year. For this you must also be well read in the underlying philosophy. Most important of all, you must be well versed in, and constantly teach, writing content.

What is Writing Content?

An effective writing curriculum must provide the tools, techniques, and information that young writers need to ply their craft. Writing, as does science, social studies, music, math, and art, contains a body of knowledge. That content — style and genre characteristics; organization, composing, and literary skills; and writing conventions — should be the basis of an elementary school writing curriculum and should be taught through the use of the writing process.

The writing process facilitates writing content instruction. It provides a powerful learning vehicle. Learners learn best when need drives their acquisition of knowledge and skills. Learning through application is one of the underlying philosophies of the writing process approach — learn by doing, learn to write by writing.

Using the writing process without teaching content, however, is an ineffectual exercise. It is equivalent to presenting kids with the rules and process of conducting a game of baseball, having them play, but never teaching and coaching the skills of hitting, throwing, catching, pitching, base running, bunting, and fielding.

Because content and skills play such a large role, I have devoted a substantial portion of this book to them. You will find this information in the Writing Content chapter and in the Process chapters as well. The subject of writing skills far exceeds the scope of this book. The material included here represents only the tip of the writing content iceberg — but it is a place to start.

You will want to increase your knowledge about writing as your classroom writing community prospers. Your students will expect you to know it and will look to you as a resource for this information. Chapter II contains a list of books about writing that both you and your students will enjoy. Additionally, books pertaining to specific genre and skills are cited in Chapter IX, Writing Content.

Structure and Choice

Throughout this book, I stress procedures and practices that encourage independence and give young writers a high degree of choice. At the same time, I describe and promote procedures and practices that create a highly structured environment. These two emphases may appear to be contradictory. They are not. A successful writing process workshop provides the structure young writers need in order to take risks and learn their craft.

The importance placed on giving young writers choices must not be interpreted as letting them do anything they like. Their choices and independence must operate within clearly established parameters of curriculum, instruction, and workshop procedures. Requiring young writers to demonstrate the use of a specified writing skill(s) — within a genre and topic that they select — is an example of balancing structure and choice.

When we tell children, "You're the boss of your writing," or "You are the author and you make the decision to revise or not in response to comments or suggestions," we are talking about their maintaining control of the message, style, and content of their piece; we are talking about them retaining authorship and ownership of their piece. Teaching them composing skills and modeling the techniques of accomplished writers does not in any way take this control from them. It empowers them.

How to use this book

If you are already building a writing community in your classroom, you may want to browse through the writing process and content sections for additional ideas to enhance and supplement what you do now.

If you are just starting out, you first might want to read Chapter II, The Writing Process Classroom. I would recommend next reading Chapter IX, Writing Content, for help in planning your curriculum. The fold-out sheet tucked into the book at the back cover provides a scope and sequence model of writing development that details the continuum for emergent writers through developing writers in the elementary school grades.

In the Appendix is a sample year's plan for Grades 1-6. I also describe five consecutive writing workshop days at the start of the year and in midyear in grades one and two, and grades three through six. Having considered this material, you will be ready to use the models, procedures, and lessons in the chapters about the writing process.

Lessons

The lessons and demonstrations in this book follow a model based on requisite learning conditions set forth by Brian Cambourne, an Australian researcher,[1] who in the 1970s studied children who became successful literacy learners. Those conditions Cambourne related are

- Immersion
- Demonstration
- Expectation
- Responsibility
- Use
- Approximation
- Response.

Think of these conditions in connection with the way children learn to talk. We immerse children in language, talking to babies before they can speak. We demonstrate language, pointing to objects and repeating words. We fully expect that children will talk. They take responsibility for the words they say. We do not say to them, "Today you will use verbs only." Or, "Today you will talk only about the weather." They use language to communicate. We tolerate their approximations, accept their misspeaking, and continue to provide models. We respond to their language—handing them things, replying. We do not make children feel threatened and thus inhibited about their speech.

We must provide this same set of conditions for children as they learn to write. That is what creating a writing community in your classroom is all about.

Imitation And Need

The model for lessons and demonstrations in this book are based also on two of my firm beliefs: first, that need drives the acquisition of skills and secondly, that writing is a craft.

We learn a skill best when we need that skill and, therefore, have the incentive to learn it. We understand why we are learning and we fully engage

[1] Brian Cambourne, *The Whole Story: Natural Learning and the Acquisition of Literacy in the Classroom* (Ontario, Canada: Scholastic-TAB Publications, Ltd., 1988).

in the learning process. Consider, for example, how you learned to use a computer. Did you read the entire manual, memorizing how to do a mail merge when you were interested only in revising your memoirs? Did you take a class in spreadsheets when you only needed to know how to insert columns in a cooking recipe?

Apply the same principle to your writing workshop. The time to introduce dialogue form is when students start to use dialogue in their stories. The time to introduce paragraphing is when students write pieces that contain topics with sub-topics, or stories with changes of time, place, action. When you introduce each skill, do it by modeling.

We learn by copying — by imitating masters of the craft. Art students around the world take their easels to art museums and copy from the masters. Writers can do the same. We can examine the works of master writers and use their techniques.

What Works

The What Works sections of each chapter detail specific models, lessons, and procedures that have been tested in classrooms like yours. Each one works because it answers the needs of young writers. It contributes to the structure or maintenance of the classroom writing community or it provides the writing craft information young authors require.

The lessons, models, and procedures in this book are designed for developing writers. These are the writers who are able to read today what they wrote yesterday — which differentiates them from emerging writers who cannot.

The content and examples of the lessons are appropriate for different ages of developing writers. I have used grade levels to indicate the approximate age at which to introduce young writers to some concepts. In the United States, most first graders are 6-7 years old; second graders, 7-8; third, 8-9; fourth, 9-10; fifth, 10-11; sixth, 11-12. In multi-aged classes, lessons often serve as previews of coming attractions for early developing writers and reviews for more fluent writers.

You will not need or want to use all the techniques described in the book. Use the ones that support your year's plan and the styles and genres on which you will focus. Among them you will find those appropriate for your students, for your teaching style, and those that most support your efforts to build a community of writers in your classroom.

Time And Materials

Many models and lessons include a list of required materials and the estimated time for each activity. Some models and lessons are described in detail and even suggest a script for you to follow. You will find many instances of concrete materials or mechanisms in the models throughout this book. I am convinced that the key to successful teaching is finding concrete ways to illustrate concepts.

Let your students know when the lessons and models you present are new to you. Students need to see you as a learner, too. How can we develop life-long learners if we are not models for that goal?

I hope you will revise models, procedures, and lessons to suit your style and your class. Ask your young writers to help refine them.

Reproducibles

Record keeping devices, forms, supporting text, and examples for lessons and models are included at the end of the book. They have been perforated for your convenience. These 37 reproducibles are copyright protected and may be used only for student copies or overhead projection transparencies in your classroom. The remainder of the book, and the final foldout development chart, is copyright protected and may not be reproduced without the express written consent of the publisher.

The Writing Process Classroom

Visit a successful classroom writing community and you will be impressed by the level of involvement and the independence of its young writers. Talk to them and you will be amazed at their understanding of authorship, genre, and process. Read their work and you will be pleased to discover that writing is, after all, not a lost art. Study the wall postings and browse through student writing folders and notebooks. You will find a wealth of information about the writing process and the writing craft.

Teachers who create such writing communities value what children have to say. They believe that children can and will write. They are willing to relinquish control of topic choice, revision, and editing—allowing children ownership of their writing. They provide the time, structure, audience, tools, and resources for children to become independent writers. These teachers create a supportive and secure environment wherein young writers are willing to take risks.

Building a successful classroom writing community requires

- A philosophical and physical environment conducive to a sustained writing experience.
- A reliable, consistent, and sufficient block of time for daily writing.
- A set of rehearsed writing workshop procedures involving materials, movement, and writing process components.
- A continuing curriculum of content and skills—the tools of writing.
- Lessons in writing content, composing skills, and conventions through examples, demonstrations, and models.
- The use of writers' vocabulary. Self-evaluation procedures.
- Efficient record keeping.
- Parent education.
- Classroom management techniques.

The Environment

Philosophical Environment

The attitudes and behavior of the teacher and students in regard to the writing process create the philosophical environment of a classroom. Here is the environment that encourages developing writers.

Attitude

- Writing is important.
- Writing is an ongoing and creative process.
- Writing development occurs as a continuum.
- We share our knowledge of the writing craft with one another.
- Our writing belongs to us.
- We are all developing writers.

Behavior

- Teachers provide the resources and opportunities needed for young writers to progress in the writing craft.
- Teachers model the procedures and provide the structure that will help young writers productively pursue and practice their craft.
- Teachers do not take control of the content, revision, or editing of young writers' manuscripts.
- Writers conference with other writers and revise in response to their comments.
- Writers phrase their comments and questions in non-threatening ways.
- Writers keep their work in a personal folder and maintain a writer's notebook.
- Writers know the writing curriculum and take responsibility for skill acquisition.
- Writers evaluate their writing using criteria based on process and content.

Physical Environment

The arrangement of the room should support the goals of the writing community and the need for order. A consistent set of procedures governing both materials and movement will provide your young writers with the security they need to write. These procedures must be modeled for them.

Any room and furniture arrangement is suitable as long as it creates a sense of order and provides for the interactive nature of the prewriting and response-revision stages of the writing process, as well as for the quiet drafting stage. Most teachers with active writing communities divide the room into a student desk area and a working-gathering area. The latter is sometimes subdivided into centers. Try different configurations until you find the one that best suits your class.

What Works

1.   Side-by-side desks, a table, or two-chair nooks for peer partner work are necessary for developing writers. Like emerging writers who draw and talk about their pieces, they need to be able to talk to each other as they plan and

conference over their drafts.

2.   An Author's Chair makes the sharing of manuscripts a special thing for young developing writers. It is placed in a common gathering place, a cleared space before an easel or near a board. Some teachers provide an unusual chair or put a large label on a classroom chair.

3.   Large shelf areas make a good place for young writers to store their writer's notebooks. Folders and portfolios fit nicely into large, rectangular plastic tubs. The smaller the container, the messier the papers will become.

4.   Walls, ceilings, sides of filing cabinets, hangers, clothes drying racks, or chart frames can hold printed text and provide chart space. Attach papers and charts by magnets, tacky clay, clothes pins on wires, or Velcro.

5.   An overhead projector or a large easel with ample supply of both newsprint and lined chart paper is necessary for lessons and guided class drafting, revising and editing.

6.   Display space for published books and projects can be created using counter tops, a recycled cardboard display case from a retail store, a book-case, and paperback racks. Books can be clipped to vertical strings on a bulletin board or placed in labeled plastic tubs. Writers' published work should be displayed in a manner that invites their classmates to read it.

7.   A publishing center requires a supply of materials including all sorts of writing and illustrating tools, paper in a variety of types, sizes, and shapes, scissors, glue, a stapler, masking and duct tape, and a working area (See also Chapter VIII, Publishing).

Time for Daily Writing

Time fragmentation is built into the modern school schedule. No sooner do children become absorbed in one thing when we ring a bell, ask them to put things away, and move them on to something else. Is it any wonder that children are frustrated, lose their focus, and their engagement with their school work?

Time fragmentation is also a major creativity killer. For the successful functioning of a writing workshop we must provide consistent and uninterrupted blocks of time. If we can do that, and help children select their own topics — raising the chance for high level engagement with the subject — we will minimize disruptive behavior and enhance learning.

Finding this time represents the biggest challenge to all writing teachers. In classrooms where teachers have established a writing community, the challenge becomes one of finding more time for writing in response to the writers' demand. They can't get their kids to stop writing! If writing is high on your priority list, you will find time in each day. Here are a variety of ways to successfully employ a consistent writing time.

What Works

1.   **Use the same 25-50 minutes a day, five days a week.**
2.   **Use the same 25-50 minutes a day, four times a week**, in the same time

slot as a once-a-week special such as art, music, computer lab, chorus, or physical education.

3.   **Integrate writing**, reading, oral language, and listening skills in a whole language, literature, or theme based program. Dedicate a one-and-one-half to two-hour block of time, morning or afternoon.

4.   **Use concentrated blocks of time.** Conduct writing workshops in two-hour daily sessions for a two or three week period in each quarter. This is a less desirable means of fitting writing workshop into a schedule, but it may be a place to start.

5. **Implement a center-oriented approach** with daily independent work in centers for 45-60 minutes. This might consist of one writing group with the teacher for a lesson or conference, and the other groups working at writing, listening, illustrating and publishing, and reading centers. The writing groups with the teacher should rotate on a daily basis.

6. **Integrate writing with other subjects.** Writing and science are a good initial pairing. Skills of observation, description, classification and sorting, and re-cording information are basic to both.

Use folded paper booklets for students to journal class activities in a science study. In these journal booklets, students describe their activities, make glossaries related to the topic, compose questions, and tell what they think. The journals become a part of a student's collection of writing. They can be used for lessons about descriptive writing, for peer conferences, practicing revision techniques, practicing editing, discussion, and review of the science topic. Students who miss the activity can read other students' journals to catch up with the class or get needed information.

Janet Hammond's second and third graders, Gulf Gate Elementary, Sarasota, Florida, study meal worms in a life cycle project. Each day they make observations in a prepared folded paper journal. For each observation a writing target skill must be incorporated in the observation. It might be series commas—"My meal worms are yellow, brown, and white." It might be comparisons in description—"My meal worms are longer than an inch." It might be the use of question marks—"Is my meal worm molting?" In Hammond's class, science journaling is standard procedure.

7.   **Steal time from formal spelling work** by integrating spelling training with writing. For instance, students might take the time formerly set aside for writing spelling words in sentences to select several of the words that illustrate the spelling rule in the current lesson and incorporate them into their current manuscripts. Revise your spelling program to focus on teaching strategies for recognizing and correcting misspelled words. (See Chapter VII, Editing, Spelling.)

8.   **Replace handwriting practice time with writing and computer workshops.** For a really radical approach, drop cursive writing instruction entirely. The computerized future is based on typed print. Think how little environmental text is written in cursive. The only persons today who see and read cursive writing work for the US Postal service. For other than signature, perhaps it is an archaic skill.

Daily Writing

Writing daily means composing daily. Copying text from the board or books is no substitute. Writers must write to communicate ideas, convey meaning, and express feelings. They must write often to become proficient. Writing is a craft. We improve by practicing. We learn through our mistakes and by our successes.

What Works

1. **Writing Workshop.** Schedule daily ongoing workshop sessions for writing personal narratives and expository pieces, peer conferences, group and whole class lessons, teacher-writer conferences, and publishing. This schedule will provide the best opportunity for teaching both the process and the craft.

2. **The Morning Message.** *Nancy Erwin's first graders, Abel Elementary, Bradenton, Florida,* compose a morning message on a 2 x 3-foot white dry-marker board and present it to the class at 9:30 a.m. They work in pairs and are armed with a list of the specials for the day and the special teachers' names. Erwin uses the message for a brief lesson about phonics, numbers, editing, and anything else that arises from the content of the message.

In higher grades you can assign rotating pairs of students to write the message, having them compose it as an editing exercise. They should insert four to six writing convention mistakes in the message for the rest of the class to identify. This will increase their own awareness of conventions as they compose the message.

3. **Clinic Passes**. *Fran Reinel's second graders, Gulf Gate Elementary, Sarasota, Florida,* build a vocabulary chart of common illness symptoms. They write their own clinic passes including the reason to see the school nurse, or a peer does it for them. Reinel reads and signs their pass as they leave class.

4. **Entries in Class Logs and Charts**. *Marilyn Cafaro, Gulf Gate Elementary, Sarasota, Florida,* places a journal next to the classroom pet cage or tank. She invites her first and second graders to sit for five minutes during free time, observe the pet, date a page, and enter their observations. She reminds them to write neatly as others will be reading the log. Students read selections aloud from the log periodically. This is a composing activity that is useful at all grade levels, particularly in support of science skill development.

5. **Class Newsletter**. In classrooms that have a computer and printer, students enter brief items for a weekly newsletter. Besides their own class news they can cover school events. Assign several student reporters to each school assembly to write up a brief summary for the newsletter. They should take small coiled notebooks and pencils to the event. They can use this information to draft the news item, follow up with a peer conference for response, revise it, edit, and type the item into the newsletter document. The teacher, or older students themselves, can format and print out the document. (See Chapter VIII, Publishing, Kinds of Publishing, Newsletter.)

6. **School Post Offices**. Many schools, under the instruction and supervision of the U. S. Postal service, are establishing student operated, school-wide mail services. They are launched with great enthusiasm and an initial flurry of mail between students and between students and teachers. In order to sustain an interest, teachers look for practical and purposeful writing exchanges. Letters of invitation, book recommendations, thank you notes, traveling books, chess games by mail, student government political propaganda, and pen pals are ways to utilize the mail service. In schools where time is set aside to take part in these activities, the service flourishes. In schools where kids have to find or make their own time, the service flounders and fades.

7. **Homework Writing**. Writing as homework is one answer to daily composing. Students set up a notebook specifically for homework writing. Some teachers invite children to select a picture and focus on descriptive writing. Some assign a target skill for each notebook entry and send the information about that skill for parents to see.

Homework writing is a useful source of written material to use in peer conferences, class edits, and for revision practice. Start with short pieces with target skills. It's purely for practice. Check only that a student wrote something. Share occasionally.

Some schools ask parents and children to sign a contract that explains their responsibilities for the homework writing.

8. **Lyrics in Music**. A music teacher told me he asks students to write lyrics to a taped rap cadence. He shows them how to clap syllables to get the right number of beats in the lyrics. He models a rap narrative from a children's book.

This teacher also uses Venn Diagrams — a graphic schema, utilizing overlapping circles — to show students how to make comparisons between different styles of music. For example, rock and roll and country western. The students write comparison statements based on their Venn Diagrams (See Expository Writing in Chapter IX).

9. **Side by Side**. A common practice in Australia's primary schools, related to me by *Dr. Wendy Kasten, Associate Professor, Literacy Education, Kent State, Ohio*, is the side-by-side written dialogue. Conducted in silence, two participants communicate through writing only. They either use one paper, taking turns, or use two papers. This gives students a specific time to indulge in their natural inclination to pass notes back and forth.

10. **Journaling.** Journaling provides an excellent opportunity for daily writing. Encourage young writers to keep a personal journal for their own enjoyment and satisfaction. Start the youngest writers with half pages, either in small, folded paper journals or dividing a coiled notebook page in half with a colored line. A full page can be intimidating to new or very young writers. Some advantages of classroom journals:

- The writing is ungraded, which encourages risk taking.
- Writing progression can be noted since the journals are chronological records.

- Journals can be used for diagnosis of needed skills and lesson planning.
- The book is easy to maintain — no loose papers.
- The journal is a source of writing for lessons and practicing conferences, response, revision, and editing.

There are some disadvantages if journals are used as the mainstay for daily writing.

- Many elements of the writing process are missing. The student writes without planning, response, revising, publishing.
- If the journal establishes a dialogue between teachers and children, responding is very time consuming. One way to keep up in dialogue journaling is to establish a schedule for teacher responses. For example, you might respond to one out of every five entries. The students select the one for which they particularly want your response.
- You may find parental reservations about journal writing. Parents may equate it with diary keeping and resent intrusion into their family privacy. Some cultures are particularly offended by this intrusion. Modeling topic choice, choosing journal content to reflect school subjects and personal reading, assigning target skills per entry, using pictures to direct the content, and encouraging students to keep their own diaries at home may help allay parents' fears.

Here are some journal types that provide a variety of writing opportunities for young writers.

A. <u>Science, Math, Social Studies, Art, Music Learning Journals</u> — Students write questions, tell what they learned, describe activities, and create vocabulary lists. These journals should be kept on the desk during the subject period. Some sample journal entries may include the following.

- What I do not understand is...
- This relates to...
- This concept reminds me of...
- I wonder if...
- What really surprised me was...
- What if...
- In the experiment I didn't know...
- I am confused about...
- Why...
- I learned that...

(Model some of these journal entry starters and make this or a similar list available to your young writers.)

A teacher, reading over journal entries such as these, can see what the students missed and what concepts must be taught again.

B. <u>Literature Response Journals</u> — Young writers analyze or compare characters, comment on the author's style, identify fiction elements, summarize, note ideas that have special personal meaning, and make recommendations.

Literature Response Model.

Beth Severson, Grade Three/Four, Palmetto Elementary School, Palmetto, Florida, created the following Literature Response Journal Model. Her class uses it for short stories, chapter books from whole class reading, or independent reading.

Students choose from the following response prompts. They vary them depending on the chapter or book read.

- I learned that...
- I rate this story or chapter one, two, or three stars.
- I think that..
- I felt....when ...
- My question is...
- Construct a web for one of the main characters.
- Use a Venn diagram to compare two of the characters.
- This story or chapter made me think of...
- I like the way the author began or ended this story or chapter because...

A third grader's literature response.

You may want to add the following to Severson's model.

- Draw a scene from the story or chapter that reminds you of something in your life.
- Find your favorite line in the story or chapter and tell why you chose it.
- Locate examples in the text where you were able to say: That's just like me; That's just like I do; I've felt like that.
- Where and when does the story take place? Cite pages and write the words that tell you about the setting.
- Describe a character in the book in your own words. Cite pages and write the phrases and sentences the author used to reveal the character.
- Have you read another book that is similar to this one? How are they alike?
- Which of the six basic plots does this author use? (See Chapter IX for details about plot.) Is there a combination of two of them?

C. <u>Reading Journals</u> — Students inventory titles and write brief summaries and opinions.

D. <u>Trip Journals</u> — Students describe the trip, express feelings, and tell what they learned.

E. <u>TV Summary Journals</u> — These are similar to reading and response journals. Children respond to a specific task.

F. <u>Journal Responses to Pictures</u> — (See Chapter III, Prewriting)

11. **Integration.** Classroom projects that integrate math, writing, reading, science, and group work develop children's problem solving, critical thinking, and communicating skills.

Mary Compton, Gulf Gate Elementary, Sarasota, Florida, hit upon one such project when one of her second graders brought in a toy that did not perform as the package promised. The class thought he should complain to the company. From this grew a class consumer testing project.

The class of second and third graders brought in packaged and inexpensive toys. Compton contributed some to the pool. The children read the toy package texts and brainstormed a plan to study the toy and its packaging, the claims, and directions. They made recommendations about the toy for unsuspecting consumers. Working in groups, the students recorded data about the performance of the toy (measuring distances, observing performances, repeating performances, etc.). They considered the ease of unpacking the toy, the safety of the toy for little children, whether its difficulty level matched the recommended age, whether it was worth the price, and anything else they felt was significant.

They presented their findings orally with demonstrations. They wrote their summaries and recommendations and published them on their classroom computer. The students took a week to complete the project, working each morning for about 45 minutes.

Besides the obvious skills integrated — math, critical reading, problem solving, data organization, writing — the students learned something about advertising, making judgments and choices, and working cooperatively.

Police Pursuit

We looked at the Police Pursuit racing set. It is made by Marchon. It is a motorized track that runs on batteries. It is supposed to be easy to put together, but that is wrong. It took over an hour to put the track together.

The Slinky

We tested Slinky. We found that it only goes half way down the stair by our class. Our class stairs are too big. It works better on smaller stairs.

You can also play with it by making it go up and down in your hands. It is a good toy.

K'nex Helicopter

Our group put together the K'nex helicopter. We think it is a good product. It was fun putting the K'nex together.

K'nex does not have step by step directions. You just have to look at a picture. We think the people that work for K'nex need to make the little pieces bigger. We think K'nex needs a tool to connect the parts.

The spinner on the helicopter really works. It spun around for twelve seconds without stopping.

We liked K'nex a lot.

Dizzy Doodle Pen

The Dizzy Doodle pen makes big and small swirls. It has three colors, pink, purple, and blue. The pen wiggles your hand out and it feels like your hand is shivering in the cold.

Dizzy Doodle is fun for ages like five to ten. It costs 4 dollars.

Second and third graders' Consumer Report.

Other projects for integrating subjects often involve constructing, transporting, or packaging. During the project all students write daily in their journals about the activity, how the group works together, problems and solutions, calculations, data gathering, etc.

Some examples:

- Mail a snow ball to another school class.
- Package and drop a raw egg from a height without breaking it.
- Move a quantity of Ping-Pong balls across a distance without touching them with your hands.
- Present a plan for stocking an x gallon fish tank based on predetermined fish cost, volume requirement, and social behavior (predator vs. prey).
- Design a vehicle powered by kinetic energy (rubber band or spring)

- Construct and weight-test a structure built of fragile material—toothpicks, cards, paper.
- Design a timer for an eight-minute period for your writing conferences.

For more such projects, consult your district science coordinator, a science teacher, or The Olympics of the Mind chairperson in your region.

What Works

Workshop Materials and Procedures

Materials

1. **Writer's Notebook for Each Student.** A looseleaf book is the most useful writer's notebook for second graders and older. A set of these can be used repetitively for each incoming class. The writers empty and keep the contents of the notebook at the end of the year. Apply a new sticker to the binding each year and write the student's name on it in large print. Students can supply their own dividers, or you can provide for them in your budget. Each notebook should have at least two dividers with pockets. If the loose-leaf book itself has inside cover pockets, regular dividers will suffice.

Example of notebook sections:

- Narrative
- Expository
- Planners
- Names of Characters
- Editing Conventions
- Literary Devices
- Practice Writes
- First Liners
- Endings.

For younger students, a writer's notebook might be a coiled wire bound notebook. The papers they are asked to save for reference can be pasted into their book.

2. **Writer's Notebook for Teacher.** How many teachers consider themselves developing writers? Keep a writer's notebook and practice the same things you ask of the young writers in your class. Enter practice writes when the students do so. Make lists for topic choice. Use your writing to model conferences, conventions, revision, editing. Your doing so will have a major impact on your young writers.

3. **Writing Folder.** Students need a place to keep their manuscript-in-progress. The writing folder includes space on the cover for them to enter their current target skills, skills they have mastered and use, a record of past writing, and ideas for starting anew.

<u>Writing folder sample entries:</u>

Writing Skills I Use. (Back cover, top half).

    I have action in my stories.

    I use series commas.

    I plan using a web.

    I revise using a caret to add words.

    I use alliteration.

Writing Skills I'm Working on (Back cover, bottom half).

    Quotes around what was said

    Paragraphs when the time or place changes

    Similes

    Proper nouns instead of common nouns.

Published pieces, topics used (Back inside cover).

    My Cat - published

    Whales - finished

    The Cafeteria - discontinued

    Poem about cats - published

    My Best Friend - finished.

Ideas for new pieces (Front inside cover).

    Biking trip

    Letter to an author

    Lottery

    Game.

4.   **Journals.** Coiled bound notebooks or simple, folded and stapled paper booklets serve nicely as personal journals. Most professional writers keep journals. They are not simply diaries chronicling daily life but repositories of the writer's thoughts, wonderings, observations, imaginings, descriptions, and questions. A useful journal experience is for children to write about what they are learning, hope to learn, or did learn in a subject they study, or for a project they do. Some teachers ask students to share entries they would like to discuss, check that students are making entries, or even require a number of entries. Journal writing of this kind, however, is not evaluated or edited.

5.   **Greenbar Computer Paper.** The standard 8-1/2 x 11-inch, non-carbon variety computer paper is an excellent rough draft paper, inviting revision with its large alternating lines of green and white. The blank back can be used for planning and drawing. The paper is sturdy and withstands repeated erasures.

6.   **Laminated or Card Stock Copies of the Dolch Word List.** This list contains the most common sight words. An additional alphabetized list of the 240 most commonly used words is available from Heath Publishing Co. Both are helpful resources for developing writers during drafting and editing.

7.   **Hand-Publishing Materials.** (See Chapter VIII, Publishing, for a detailed list of materials)

8. **Illustrating Paper and a Variety of Writing Tools.** Appeal to the children's innate aesthetic sense and curiosity. Provide materials to use experimentally. Writing is great fun.

9. **Chart Paper, Lined and Unlined.** Permanent charts and charts under progress — built by the students themselves — provide environmental print for young writers.

10. **Audio Tape Cassette for Each Student.** Purchase audio cassettes in bulk, ask students to bring one in, or cover the write-protection slot on discarded audio cassettes. Students use these tapes to record and listen to their manuscript and to practice oral reading. They should place them in their reading and writing portfolios.

11. **Microphone/Cassette Player.** If you can arrange to have a microphone plugged into a cassette player or any other type of microphone and amplification system for Author's Chair, your students will profit. The microphone transforms them into performers. Their writing becomes more important to them when they can share it in this fashion. Also, faint-voiced children will not suffer by being barely audible.

12. **Clipboards.** Some writing work needs to be done away from desks and tables. Field trips, science recording, interviews, assemblies, and library work are a few examples. Clipboards come in handy for these instances. Some writers can use them to work on their writing during lunch and recess. Clipboards are usually available through your school supply system. Write your name or classroom number on them with permanent marker.

13. **Copies of the Curriculum for Each Student.** Students need to know what is expected of them. Give them a copy of the curriculum they can use to track their progress, set goals, and evaluate their work.

14. **All the Children's Literature You Can Amass, Display, and Store.** Good children's literature provides models for young writers. Read from all the genres — fiction, informational books, biographies, and poetry. Read to your students daily and use the books to show your students all the wonderful things authors do. When children read as writers, their comprehension of the text increases.

15. **Books About the Writing Craft.** There are numerous books written for children about the writing craft. Teachers should read these books for genre information and sources of lessons. A bibliography is provided at the end of this chapter.

Procedures

Invest time and effort in establishing writing workshop procedures. If your young writers have not come from similar classrooms, it may take most of the first half of the year to develop cooperative, independent, and engaged students. It is well worth it. When the class functions in this fashion you will be free to teach.

Workshop procedures include:

- How to move to Author's Chair.
- How to get help when the teacher is busy.
- What to do in a peer conference.

- Editing standards
- What to do when you are finished with your current task.
- Submitting manuscripts for a individual conference with the teacher.

Teachers at Palmetto Elementary Schools, Florida, in their third year of writing process school-based inservice with me, report that students now come into their classes at the start of the year ready to write. They are used to many of the workshop classroom procedures. They speak the language of a writing community and they expect to write — "When will we have Author's Chair?' "Where would you like me to put this rough draft?" "I'm using inventive spelling." "I need a peer conference."

What Works

1. **Getting to Author's Chair** (See Chapter V, Response, for more about Author's Chair). The term Author's Chair not only refers to the special chair itself but to the procedure used in the writing process workshop that involves sharing and modeling.

Whether the class gathers on the floor in front of Author's Chair or the students all remain in their desks to face a central Author's Chair, assembling should be a rehearsed procedure.

Not all children need attend every Author's Chair. If you are using Author's Chair for a lesson, call together those children who are working on the skill you plan to illustrate. If some children are absorbed in their work, do not interrupt them. Later, be sure to describe and practice how students can quietly join an ongoing Author's Chair.

Practice moving to Author's Chair. Stop and discuss the noise level, the time it took, seating arrangement and posture, and what to bring. Have your young writers compose a set of guidelines governing the maneuver.

Students can go to Author's Chair on their own or by row or table. They might assemble by some arbitrary order such as alphabetically, by student number, hair color, those wearing red, blue, green, etc.

Some teachers place pieces of masking tape on the floor to mark exact student seating. In some classes, children bring carpet squares to sit on and to function as space delineators. If students remain in their seats, they need to arrange their desks to minimize distractions. Moving chairs to an Author's Chair location is very difficult, noisy, and potentially dangerous. Keep the movement simple and efficient.

2. **How to Get Help When Teacher is Working With Another Writer.** To keep interruptions to a minimum, all your young writers must have acceptable means of getting help without interrupting other writers with whom you are in conference.

Teresa Matrisciano, a kindergarten teacher at Lincoln Elementary, Caldwell, New Jersey, wears a "magic scarf" when she is conferencing with writers. The others recognize this as a signal not to interrupt. They either go to another student or, if they absolutely need her, they sit on a rug in the center of the class and she gets to them between conferences.

A mechanism such as this works for older students as well.

Young writers become a source of help in lieu of the teacher. Through Commitment Statements, Author's Chair, and peer conferences, students learn which of their classmates are good at various writing skills. One of the young writers in my fourth/fifth grade class in Caldwell, New Jersey, had an uncanny ability to spot missing antecedents and recognize off-the-topic sentences. All the other children went to him for this editing ability.

Your class will include logical thinkers who can help others with organization problems, super spellers, illustrators, and writers who are sources of information and shared experiences. Everyone becomes a teacher in an effective writing workshop.

Practice the procedure a writer should follow to get help with the least disruption to the rest of the writing community.

3. **Peer Conferences.** Peer conference procedure must be modeled and practiced (See Chapter V, Response, for models and specific information about peer conferences). Before efficient conferencing can begin, you need to work out the issues of how to schedule a conference, where partners meet, how long a conference should last, what the focus of a conference will be, and how to keep records.

In younger grades, peers in conference read their manuscripts aloud to one another. Older writers, with bigger voices and clearer manuscripts, may read each other's writing silently. Peer conferencing requires an area in the classroom that allows for talking without disturbing other writers.

Assign peer groupings early in the writing workshop. They can be based on contrasting strengths and weakness of the writers, e.g., pair a detailer with a sparse writer, a speller with a nonspeller, or a writer and an illustrator. Or they can be based on commonalties in genre, topic, or interests. Further into the workshop writers can form their own partnerships as they discover others with whom they work well or who have a skill they need.

You should point out to writers that a peer conference with your best friend may not lead to the best revisions. A best friend is disposed by virtue of that friendship to respond, "It's great. I like it. That's good." Tell students they may want to get a first response from a friend. They might then move on to a writer who will help them critically examine their manuscript for loss of focus, sentences that hit the reader over the head with information, weak imagery, etc.

4. **About Editing.** Your class will need to establish an editing standard for published work. The standard must be based on what the young writers can do truly independently or with a minimum of help (Chapter VII, Editing, includes sample Editing Standards and Procedures).

Editing can be a class project at a prearranged time or it can be ongoing, whenever the need arises. Early in your workshop, models of editing should be conducted for the whole class. Later, editing may be done in peer or group settings.

Remind students to initial each other's manuscripts when they peer conference or edit. This will help them keep track of who was helpful.

5. **What To Do When You Finish a Task.** Since writing is an continuing process, young writers often finish a particular writing stage within a writing period. They need to know what options are open to them. Discuss the possibilities with them. Suggest that they could work on illustrations, read their manuscript over, arrange a peer conference, start a new piece, sign up for a teacher conference, meet with an editor, or read independently.

Conversely, when students finish other work during the day, they should have the opportunity to return to their writing. Writing folders should be readily accessible.

6. **Submitting a Manuscript to the Teacher For a Conference.** You will not have time to read every student's manuscript for a total critique. Nor should you take on the task of editing all the young writers' work. Your students should know what you are prepared to do for them and how to submit their work to you. Establish a set of guidelines including:

- Where to put a manuscript ready for you to read.
- What reason the writer has for your reading the manuscript — to evaluate? To check for specific ingredients? For a response to the piece? For a final proofreading after they fulfilled their editing responsibilities?
- Time between submitting a manuscript and having a conference.

Make a habit of reading two to five manuscripts each day after class, at lunch, or at home. Prepare comments for conferences. Compliment content, skill application, topic choice, and revisions. Diagnose the writing for students' skills needs. Record anecdotes about children's writing progress and style. In a month or two you will have a good sense of your writers' interests, strengths, and weaknesses. This will help you refine your writing instruction.

Content

While writing is dependent on our knowledge of the English language, it is not the study of language. Writing is about thinking and using language to express our thoughts, opinions, and feelings. It is about organizing and expressing our thoughts to communicate them to others.

What To Teach

There must be a concrete basis to a writing curriculum, consisting of styles, genres, composing skills, and conventions. Before you start your writing workshop, you will need to decide what you are going to teach.

Chapter IX, Writing Content, provides detailed lessons and models about:

- Descriptive, Narrative, and Expository Writing Styles
- Fiction and Poetry Genres
- Literary Devices

Chapters III, IV, V, and VI, about the writing process, provide detailed lessons and models about the composing skills of organization and conveying meaning through word choice and usage.

Chapter VII details lessons about editing for the writing conventions pertinent to developing elementary school writers.

This writing content information, and the "Scope and Sequence Chart of Writing Development," may help you construct a writing curriculum for your grade and school. Remember that they are only suggestions. Modify them to suit your needs.

Where to Start

A common plan for teachers committed to creating a classroom writing community is based on a progression of writing purposes or functions. The three basic functions are *personal, purposeful, and aesthetic.*

Young writers naturally start writing for purely personal reasons. They want to be heard and they are focused on themselves. Their writing, both expository and narrative is egocentric. As they mature, they begin to see other uses for writing. They experiment with purposeful writing, using the tools they have acquired. As they become fluent, they may begin to see the aesthetic potential and become poets, novelists, historians, or simply lovers of the written language.

An overall school strategy for writing focus should parallel this development. Developing writers need the skills to help them in their personal writing. Personal descriptive writing, both narrative and expository, is a good place to start. Developing writers need opportunities to use writing in a variety of practical ways and be introduced to the aesthetic uses of writing. The study of the various styles and genres and integrating writing with the rest of the curriculum, in addition to acquisition of composing and convention skills, is a good way to continue.

This strategy can be paralleled within a year's classroom work at any grade level. Start with personal narrative and personal expository based on existing background knowledge. Anyone who has struggled with an essay test question knows how difficult to it is to write a clear and comprehensive answer when you have limited understanding of the subject. The best writing from young authors will come when they write about the things they know best. When your writers gain competency and confidence, they can continue with a variety of purposeful or practical writing appropriate to their development level.

The early emphasis on personal writing greatly improves the chances of student engagement with their writing work. They will welcome the opportunity to express themselves and will come to view writing as a rewarding and positive activity. During this period your students can develop the skills and attitudes necessary for a functioning writing community.

Lesson Models

As discussed in Chapter I, the lessons and demonstrations detailed throughout this book are designed to satisfy the conditions for language learning set forth by Brian Cambourne. They include allocating time for young writers to approximate a skill, to practice it, to get a response, and to not be evaluated during the learning process.

During a lesson you may be learning the concept too. You may utilize the following model for all your lessons.

- Introduce a concept or skill through discussion, picture, by reading a selection, or noting the use or misuse in a writer's piece (Immersion).
- Provide many examples in literature (Demonstration).
- Analyze what it's all about (Demonstration).
- Try it out as a class group, to the point of ridiculous if you like (Expectation).
- Have everyone try it out independently (Approximation).
- Let writers share their attempts to apply the lesson skill (Response).
- Record information about the skill in writer's notebook.

After a lesson the young writers should:

- Hear or see the model material or skill again in charts.
- Try to use the skill in current manuscript (Use).
- Listen for usage in peer conferences.
- Help each other through compliments or questions to apply the skill to their writing.
- Self evaluate for the use of the skill (Responsibility).
- Record their own progress.

Inviting developing writers to try an idea, and to take the risk of getting it or not, is the important thing. Repeat the models and lessons, call for the skill in their stories, make it a target skill for conferences and self-evaluation. Developing writers are just that, developing. Their trials and errors should not be evaluated. Evaluate their accomplishments, not their failures.

What Works

1. **When to Give a Lesson.** The ideal time for a whole class lesson about a writing skill is when one third to a half of your class needs it. Diagnosis for need comes from reading or listening to your young writers' manuscripts. Some whole class lessons will be a preview for some of the children and a review for others.

The ideal lesson is a group lesson aimed specifically at the writers who can use the subject skill immediately because they have been trying it out and need some help. These lessons are usually short, no more than fifteen minutes.

The best place to give group lessons is in a central location where any writer who wants to can eavesdrop for preview or review.

> Do not be concerned that only four or five writers grasp the presented idea. The lesson introduces it to the writing community, and it will spread. When writers see others use the idea successfully they will follow. Children learn quite effectively from each other. For example, *Pat Veltz, Stewart Elementary, Bradenton, Florida*, relates that in Author's Chair a classmate said to a writer, " I could tell your character was running because his legs were bent." The next day a flock of writers had bent-legged characters in their picture stories.

2. **Lesson Length.** Whole class lessons generally take the longest, often running to 30 minutes including trial writing and sharing. But they also can be quite short, almost an aside or a reminder to all the young writers before they begin their work. Group lessons are generally shorter — 20 minutes maximum — often limited by how long the rest of your students can function independently. Vary the length of lessons so that writers have ample time for their ongoing writing work.

Here are some short lesson examples.

- I noticed when I was reading over some of your manuscripts last night that the pieces were about one thing and the next thing I knew they were about something else. Would you look at your planning sheet and read your manuscript? Write at the top of each sheet, "This is about ..." That might help you stay on the topic.

- I see several writers who described their pets by comparing them to people. I think one was, "My hamster reminds me of my aunt. They both have pointy faces." That was a great writer's ploy — description by comparison. I hope more of you can do that. Who was it? Jeannine and Toby! You might like to ask them how they do that.

- I see many of you were successful in adding lists to your stories. Don't forget the commas in between the items and just before the *and* (Write a model of series commas on the board.)

3. **Try Not To.** Some writing lessons can be taught by focusing on the "Don'ts" of writing and encouraging children to think up the most outrageous examples. Try not to, or avoid, is better language to use than *don't*. Some *Try not tos* and *avoids* include:

- Try not to end a sentence with a preposition, as in 'I don't want to, or, 'These are the things to start with.' Mark Twain once tweaked a critic with the advice, "A preposition is the worst thing to end a sentence with."
- Avoid using "not" if you can help it. Use a positive form.

   not honest = dishonest

   did not remember = forgot

not comfortable = uncomfortable

- Try not to forget (whoops!)—remember to establish antecedents. Children's writing abounds with shes, hes, its, and theys. Help young writers find them and ask, 'Who is this?'

4. **Kill Two Birds With one Stone**. Instructional time is limited. Whenever you have the chance to integrate curricula or skills, do so. one way to do this is using history and science material when you read to young writers to illustrate writing style and skills.

Go through your science text material and mark places that illustrate something you are working on in expository writing. Find children's literature that is historical fiction, biography, informational. "The Midnight Ride of Paul Revere" illustrates how poetry tells a story and adds to the students' knowledge of American history. A *Ranger Rick Magazine* article about manatees may illustrate development of ideas, or be used to illustrate webbing or organizing a topic. Your science book's text about the planetary system might illustrate the use of comparison as a basis for organizing expository writing.

The Vocabulary of Writers

All professions, branches of academics, the arts, crafts, and sports have their unique and specialized jargon that facilitates communication between members of the group. Children love the vocabulary associated with their work as writers. They love new and big words when they can immediately put them to use. They are surprisingly capable in this regard.

When children's author, Melissa Odom Fomey, visited a third grade classroom in Palmetto Elementary in Palmetto, Florida, she was astounded to hear a child ask her about the plot resolution in her book, A *Medal For Murphy*. She discussed it with the child, talking writer to writer, using the language of writers. She told me it was one of the highlights of her Author-in-Residence Day at Palmetto.

What Works

1. Make an ongoing chart for students to enter the vocabulary of writing. Publish it when it's full.

2. Ask writers to set up a glossary of writers' language in their notebooks. Compliment them on their use of writing vocabulary.

3. Use writers' language when you talk to students. Say *plot resolution* where you used to say *story ending, onomatopoeia* where you used to say *sound word, imagery* where you used to say *describing words,* and so on.

Writing process vocabulary shows up in a second grader's story.

> When the winter came Mary said, "I'm ƒ ƒ freezing." Mother made a response.

Self-Evaluation Procedures

Children need to develop self-evaluation skills. Self-evaluation, based on a reasonable set of criteria, will help them note the progress they are making as writers (See Chapter X, Evaluation and

Portfolio). They will develop a sense of authorship and a sense of accomplishment—a sense of accomplishment is the basis of healthy self-esteem.

What Works

1. **Criteria For Evaluation.** After several months of writing, lessons, conferencing, and sharing, the young writers in your class will begin to learn what constitutes good writing at their grade level.

A first grader evaluates his piece.

Call your young writers together with the goal of establishing some criteria for evaluating their own writing. Tell them they will be reading through their body of writing and making decisions about which ones to set aside in a portfolio of their best work.

Brainstorm with your class about what constitutes good writing in their class. Here are some criteria selected by students in several of the elementary schools I visit.

- It's long.
- It's got lots of action.
- It is funny—the other writers laughed when I read it.
- It has pictures.
- There is good imagery.
- The ending is a surprise.
- It has paragraphs.
- It's neat.
- It makes the reader keep reading.
- There is lots of detail.
- It sounds good.
- You feel like you are in the story.
- The writer stayed on the topic.
- You can tell the writer really knows what she is talking about.

Work with the class to come up with a reasonable number of criteria. Encourage them to consider content and style as well as the cosmetic aspects of writing. They might want different criteria for each genre or they might select criteria based on current skills. The criteria are not engraved in stone; they may change as the writers progress. Publish the criteria by chart or individual sheets to keep in their writer's notebook.

2. **Evaluation.** Devote a block of time for all writers to assess several pieces of their writing. Ask them to pick the best one and write why they selected it, referring back to criteria. Some writers like to spread their writing out in large areas such as the gymnasium, hall or on tables. Some writers might want to

ask others for their opinion. Provide space and opportunity for this.

Time spent in this fashion encourages the young writers to feel they are a part of a writing community. They support and help each other with comments and compliments.

Efficient Record Keeping

Good record keeping will save your sanity. In a well established writing process classroom young writers are working on many different genres, are in different stages of the process, and require different skills, materials, and resources. Keeping track of that diversity is challenging. Records, yours and the students', help in organization, lesson planning, and evaluation.

You will need to keep track of student participation in sharing their writing. You probably have a range of students, from non-writers to gifted writers, and all must have the opportunity to develop a feeling of authorship. Select volunteers on a rotational basis.

You will need to keep track of student involvement in chart production, notebook upkeep, peer conferencing, and editing.

You will need to keep track of and evaluate writers' progress through the writing process as reflected in successive manuscripts. You will record progress in writing craft skills, both for lesson planning and parent conferences/report cards.

In evaluation, the emphasis should be on earning a grade—the responsibility of the student. A wide base of evaluation criteria provides an opportunity for each student to do well.

What Works

1. **'Fair Share' of Sharing Time.** Keep a clipboard handy with a class list on it. Whenever you conduct an Author's Chair, model a peer conference, use student manuscripts in a lesson, or call for any manuscripts or practice writings, check off student names as they participate. Use the list to determine who needs an opportunity to share.

2. **Participation Records.** Participation, sharing, and cooperation are the mark of a successful classroom writing community. Students work together in peer conferences, group lessons, publishing, producing charts, keeping their notebooks up to date.

A. <u>Chart Production.</u> Though class generated charts will not look like yours or commercially produced charts, it is important that students make them themselves. Help them keep their entries legible by providing lined chart paper, large writing tools, and a flat surface for the chart when they make entries. Also, ask class members to read entries frequently. Children will be on notice to produce legible entries if other writers complain they can't read them or see them. Let consumer feedback affect the producers. Make chart entry participation part of the grading system.

B. <u>Process Participation.</u> All writers need to be peer editors, sounding boards, motivators, mentors, teachers, and readers for each other. Help the class determine how they will keep track of their participation in the writing process and explain that their participation will be reflected in the grade they earn. Examples: initialing manuscripts in peer conferences and editing sessions, initialing chart entries.

C. Writer's Notebook Upkeep. Every two weeks, set aside 20-30 minutes to conduct a notebook status report. Many writers will have pages they have created on their own or additional entries they have made to an established list or chart. Invite them to share these with the class (Check off their names on the class list share record). Establish procedures for writers who missed lessons or have incomplete entries to work with partners who can supply them with the missing information. Use class secretaries, appointed on a rotational basis. Post a list of required entries for the evaluation period. The responsibility for keeping their notebooks up to date rests with the children.

3.   **The Commitment Statement** (See Chapter V, Response, for a detailed description of the Commitment Statement as a kind of conference).

The Commitment Statement is a management technique used to keep track of where writers are in the process during each successive manuscript. It is not only a public announcement of topic and process stage but it is an announcement of intent. Writers tell where they are in the process and on what they will be working until the next Commitment Statement. This public announcement of intent helps keep students on task.

Most teachers using this technique keep a loose-leaf book with a commitment statement sheet for each writer (See **Reproducible # 1**). Students, particularly those who work on several manuscripts simultaneously, can set up their own commitment statements to keep track of their manuscripts and their progress.

Some teachers set up a magnetic board with the writing process stages in columns across it. Children's names and the title of their current piece are on a magnet. Young writers move them across the board, through the columns, to form a quick and highly visible record of their progress.

You should keep a record of successive topics or titles for each writer and his progress through the writing process. Peer conferences for revision and proofreading can be arranged as the writer needs them. Keep a record of participation in group lessons, teacher conferences, the time devoted to each manuscript, how far a manuscript was taken, target skills, and brief anecdotes about the writers and their work on the commitment statement sheet.

This sheet is invaluable at parent conferences to document the child's work, the lessons presented, skills worked on, and the time devoted to writing.

4.   **Writers' Progress.** Besides the Commitment Statement, the loose-leaf record book may contain anecdotes, your notes from individual conferences, and evaluation based on topic, composing, revision, editing progressions, skills application, or scoring rubrics (See Chapter X, Evaluation and Portfolio Assessment.)

Writing assessment should come only after young writers have had lots of opportunity for practice. No one should have to undergo assessment of a skill just introduced. That would be like giving a child his first two wheeler, running along side for the first ride, and saying, "OK, you're being graded now on how you ride."

While young writers are practicing, certainly for the first marking period, you might evaluate them on their use of the process, their upkeep of their writer's notebook, and their contribution to class charts. After they have created a body of writing and have evaluated it themselves, selecting their best papers, you should introduce them to the assessment mechanism determined by your school, district, or state. The students must know what criteria will be used to assess their writing. Show them how the scoring is accomplished. Model several for them. Let them practice scoring their own writing. Bring them into the evaluation process.

Parent Education

If you are newly establishing a writing program based on the writing process and are trying to create a writing community, you will need the understanding and cooperation of parents or guardians. They probably will not have been taught writing in this manner, if at all. You must communicate to them:

- the emphasis you are putting on writing,
- the ongoing nature of writing in your classroom,
- the emphasis on quantity to start and shifting to quality as students learn to revise and edit,
- their need to the focus on content and meaning,
- the class publishing and editing standards, and
- the procedures requiring their help and understanding.

What Works

1. **Letter at Start of Year.** Write a letter to parents at the beginning of the school year, including a brief description of the writing process and how writing instruction will proceed in your classroom. Explain how they can help students prepare to write. Invite them to come in and observe the writing workshop (See sample letter on next page).

2. **Parent Night.** Most schools schedule an evening for parents to meet teachers, visit their children's classrooms, and learn about curriculum and policies. Use part of your presentation time to explain your writing program. Use an overhead projector to show examples of student work, curriculum information, and assessment criteria. Display folders, notebooks, and hand published books to support your explanation.

3. **Homework Response.** Send an accompanying letter to explain the procedure when children use this response mechanism. (See Chapter V, Response, Homework Response.).

4. **Parent Conferences.** Be prepared to show parents writing progress through examples of their child's writing. Explain assessment procedures and

Dear Parents,

Your children will be engaged in the writing process this year. As authors they will plan, draft, revise, edit, and publish. The emphasis will be on the process and content of writing. The children will be working through the problems of organization, sequence, and presentation of ideas that all writers face. They will be practicing composing skills, different styles and genres, and writing conventions in their daily writing.

You can help your children by asking them each morning, "What will you write about today?" When you see their work you can help by talking to them about the content of their writing. Here are some comments and questions that help a young author.

I like the part about...

Can you tell me more about...?

What is the most important thing you are saying in this piece?

What else do you know about this?

Tell me what happened in detail.

Did you tell all about the picture? (k-1)

How does this piece compare to others you have written?

What will your next piece be about?

You, their audience and readers, need to bear with them as they learn their craft. Editing standards will be established and the children will practice editing independently. Still, their hand published books will not be perfect. But just as we can all enjoy a high school band's performance with the occasional squeaking of a clarinet or the misplaced toot of a trumpet, so can we enjoy these young authors' "performance" with the occasional invented spelling or misplaced period. Receive their writing in that same spirit and encourage them to become the best writers they can be.

Sincerely,

Your Name

expected progressions for young writers at this grade level (Progressions are detailed in Chapter X, Evaluation and Portfolio). Be sure to emphasize content, organization, focus, and composing skills. Assure parents that, yes, spelling counts, and tell them about class editing standards, spelling strategies and resources.

Have students audiotape their best piece. Set up a cassette player and give parents the tape of their child's work to hear while they are waiting for their conference.

Management Techniques

A variety of management techniques is needed to provide structure and order to a classroom writing community. Invest the time to model as many of them as you can.

What Works

1. **Group Work.** Several stages of the writing process, such as prewriting, response, editing, and publishing, bring students together in cooperative experiences. Students must understand that they need to assume different roles depending on the nature and goal of each group interaction.

   a) Model the division of labor and the roles individuals play when they work in groups. All groups need

   - A greeter, whose job it is to welcome students late to the group, perhaps coming in from a pull-out program or back from an errand. The greeter brings latecomers into the group and tells them what it is the group is doing.
   - An encourager, whose job it is to compliment and encourage the others in the group.
   - A gopher, whose job it is to bring materials to the meeting area or arrange the chairs for the group meeting.
   - An historian, whose job it is to summarize, report, or review the results of the group meeting.

   b) Create, and have the class simulate, class guidelines that will direct group behavior. These might include:

   - Forming groups quietly.
   - Staying in the group until task is completed or ended by time or the teacher.
   - Using soft voices.
   - Calling partners by name.
   - Knowing role and task.

Select a task for the first group meeting model. Provide directions and materials and tell the students this group task is a trial run. They can write questions and comments to be discussed after the model. Time the modeling session.

Sample model group tasks

   - Come up with a way to control the noise level during writing.
   - Create a response to literature based on a class reading.

2. **Coping With All the Writing.** Daily writing and the ongoing nature of the process results in large quantities of writing. Coping with that outpouring can be daunting to teachers. The most important thing is to remember that in order to write well, students must write often. The craft must be practiced. The following will help you cope.

- Do not feel that you must read and edit all writing.
- Do not read manuscripts to find errors. Read them to find use of skills, voice, topic choices, and to diagnose needs.
- Read selected pieces for specific reasons.
- Respond only to some of the writing.
- Train your young writers not to expect you to read and approve everything they do.
- Teach writers how to decide if something is good through self-evaluation procedures.
- Provide writers with the opportunity to read their piece to a peer.
- Encourage writers to read their pieces to themselves.
- Use Homework Response (See Chapter V, Response).
- Do not require that all manuscripts be taken through revision and editing.
- Train your young writers to revise and edit for specific target skills, leaving the rest as written.
- Set reasonable publishing goals such as the percentage of student work to be published and how much you will be involved
- Keep most of the writing in the classroom. When writing goes home, attach a note about what has been accomplished and what writing convention elements of the piece were edited by the student.
- Educate parents about your writing program so they do not expect every manuscript to be error free. Remind them of the school band concerts or Little League ball games they willingly attend. Emphasize the amount of practice writing your students do.

3. **Keeping Students on Task.** Free topic choice and continuity help keep young writers engaged with the writing process. Still, they may be distracted by other writers, noise, or movement. When they are, help them with the following techniques.

a) Take an abbreviated Commitment Statement at the start of some of the writing sessions. Students simply tell what they hope to accomplish in the allotted time.

> *Beth Severson, Palmetto Elementary, Palmetto, Florida,* uses this technique as well for a homework commitment as the children leave at the end of the day (Their leave taking involves 15 minutes of assorted bus calls and dismissal schedules). She asks them what homework task they selected and encourages them with comments such as: I'm glad you chose...That will be a challenge. I'll be interested to hear what you have to say about that book. Don't stay up too late with that. I'm glad you are working on...You certainly will surprise us on the next test.

b) When you see students in conference or group work who seem to be off task, ask them if the last thing they said was about writing.

c) Make sure students have the resources they need to perform their tasks.

d) Invite students to build and use their own timing devices for conferences, group meetings and timed activities of any sort. The construction of timers is an excellent project for the integration of science, math, research reading and writing.

4. **Model Everything.** Concrete models of both product and process enhance learning. Modeling procedures and samples of skills application, help your students learn how to operate in the writing community. Modeling writing for your students will help you become a better writer as well.

> *JoAnn Hughes' second graders, at Abel Elementary, Bradenton, Florida,* were working on pen pal letters when I visited their class. Hughes asked me to help her find a way to encourage independent revision and editing. I asked her young writers to make a list of a few things they thought their pen pals would like to hear about. Hughes printed it on the board.
>
> Next, we reviewed the conventions of personal letters that Hughes had modeled. That list was printed on the board. I asked the children to peer conference, help each other edit, and talk about their letters.
>
> They were invited to place their first names after any of the listed items they had included or accomplished in their editing. They were also invited to enter additional items they had used in their letters to the content list. Hughes and I roved about, conferencing and encouraging. There was a constant stream of writers to the board to enter their names.

The physical act of going to the board and entering their names provided the incentive to accomplish the task, to achieve the objectives. The class was drawn together as they peer conferenced and helped each other accomplish the objectives. JoAnn Hughes uses this technique frequently, and it is a successful step in building her writing community.

5. **Noise Level.** A functioning writing community generates noise from students in the prewriting stage talking about their ideas, students conferencing over their manuscripts, and students in group lessons. The class must determine a workable noise level and a schedule of quiet times.

One signal for lowering decibel levels is the light switch. Another method is for the teacher to start whispering to students near her and asking them to spread the whisper rumor. You might ring a small bell or speak directly to the noisy writers and remind them of others working around them.

The room can be divided into two zones — one for activities requiring talking and the other for quiet work. Students move between the areas depending on the writing tasks they are doing.

6. **Art Teacher Wisdom.** Art teachers are adept at handling project work under studio conditions. They often start sessions with a lesson, demonstration, or model. Their students may use several sessions to complete a project.

Meet with your art teacher and ask for help with classroom techniques that enable students to operate in a studio environment.

7. **Share.** It is important for young writers to share their successes, attempts, and even failures. When students try out a writing technique during a lesson or model, always call on a few volunteers to share early into their writing — as soon as you see some students have a few words or sentences. This will help the non-starters who may not know what to do, do not process oral direc-

tions, missed the directions, or need to know what is the "right way," what is "acceptable" before they will start. It also helps others who have started by validating what they have written.

Sharing should be modeled and its rules adhered to.

- Anyone who is in the middle of a thought and writing may continue. Be sure to let students know that capturing their thoughts takes priority over listening to a share. You might turn to the volunteer sharer in the model and ask, "Do you see that Jason is continuing to write? Is he disturbing you? Are you satisfied for half the class to listen while you share?"

- Anyone who is in between thoughts should listen to the volunteer who is sharing.

- No one may talk during a volunteer's recital. Remind the students who have continued to write during the model sharing that they may join in listening whenever they care to, but they may not talk to one another.

These rules promote and respect the most important aspect of a writing process workshop — continuity and the chance to become absorbed in work.

8. **Heterogeneous Classes.** The writing workshop is designed to accommodate the range of skills found in a heterogeneous class. Minilessons, group work, students teaching students through peer conferences and sharing, individual conferences, the nature of the writing process, and the individual nature of the product all support a diversity of talent and accomplishment. Some of the most successful writing communities are in multi-aged classrooms. The emphasis is on individual progress in skill acquisition.

9. **Peer Teaching.** As you learn more about your young writers, you can arrange peer partnerships to foster peer teaching. Matching peers by common interests and knowledge, spellers with non-spellers, and writers working on the same genre or topic increases the opportunity for them to help and support one another.

From memory, try to make a list of all your students and the things you know about them. If you can come up with the entire class and significant things about them — their interests, what they know — you are ready to guide the class toward symbiotic peer partnerships.

10. **Problem Solving.** When young writers come to you with a problem in their writing let them state the problem. Then ask them what they think they might do to solve it. Point out some resources they might use. Offer them all the help you can in finding a solution short of solving it yourself.

11. **Requests For the Spelling of a Word.** At the start of the year, ask the children to select a reasonable fixed number of words, per day per child, that you will help them spell. Tell them that during the first week of writing work shop you will only spell that number — and in the succeeding weeks one less each week. Help them try to sound out words and use inventive spelling during the next weeks until you wean them from your help. During that time, you must model strategies for spelling unknown words.

Also at the start of the year, set up a procedure for children to enter words they ask you to spell in a small personal dictionary or word bank. Tell them you will spell any word for them once, write it in their alphabetized book, and thereafter they are on their own. Again, in the interim, model strategies for spelling unknown words (See Chapter VII, Editing for more details about spelling).

12. **Is This Good?** When young writers try to hand me a piece of writing and ask, "Is this good?" I do not take it. I fold my hands and say, " It's not my job to tell you if it's good. What do you think of it? If you tell me what you think you did well, I'll be happy to listen to the piece, or part of it, and tell you the part I think you did well."

If a skill has been assigned, train young writers to ask, "What do you think of how I used skill x?" or "Listen to how I applied skill x." Then your answer is, "I hear how you used the skill and you did it correctly, very well, etc." Most children respond to adult approval and seek it. Let your writers know what it is that you are looking for in their writing work and praise that. You can be as specific as you like.

Encourage young writers to evaluate and satisfy themselves as well. This reinforces authorship and keeps them engaged in their writing.

13. **Choices and Parameters.** Independence is one of the primary objectives in the writing community. Independence comes from allowing students to control their writing. Topic, content, genre, presentation decisions, and graphic planner type and use are a few of the choices easily allowed young writers. When they can successfully handle these choices, you can begin establishing parameters such as themes, required portfolio inclusions, and assigned writing.

Please note that the independence of choice applies only to writing, not to how the children conduct themselves. It does not mean classroom anarchy. To be effective, the writing community must be built upon clearly established and practiced procedures that create a controlled environment. Commitment Statements require students to announce their work intentions. Writing instruction and conferences focus upon target skills. Standards are established for editing and publishing.

Sometimes, it will be difficult not to interfere with students' choices. Teachers are often afraid that students will make mistakes. Young writers may sometimes pick topics that will be impossible for them to handle. Or they may try a genre they know nothing about. Let them make mistakes. A large percent of learning comes from trial and error. Only when the writing process is ongoing and unassigned will students have the opportunity to experience trial and error in writing.

The following two anecdotes point out the difference between a teacher who overly controls learning and a teacher who encourages children to solve problems and take control of their learning.

A teacher, having invited me to her classroom, informed me her class was ready to write about topic x, her favorite project. They'd studied the topic, created the main character in art class, and were about to start a story about that character. When I asked how I could help, I offered to talk to her young writers about revealing character through dialogue. "Oh. No, no," she replied. "I'm not going to let them do dialogue. They don't know quotation marks yet."

Two girls, working on informational expository pieces, had decided to write their piece together, and it was to be about cats. They had developed an enormous web of the cat family and the many aspects of cat behavior, species distribution, care, etc., from their background knowledge and they had already started to do some research at the library. The teacher told me they had been working diligently for the past four days. She knew the topic was way too big but she didn't say anything.

In Commitment Statement on day five, she asked where they were in the writing process. The girls explained they were still webbing but hoped to finish it that day. During the writing period they came to her and one of them asked, "Can we divide this up and just each do one breed of cat? This is too much. There's too much to tell about cats. I'd like to concentrate on snow leopards and she wants to do lions. "

Many teachers would have considered the four days of cat webbing a waste of time. But this teacher told me, "I think they really did a great job figuring out that the scope of the topic was too big. The next time they start a new piece I think they will remember this, and if they don't, I will certainly remind them! Meanwhile they learned quite a bit about cats and did build a great organizational scheme."

14. **Deadlines.** Self-discipline comes from personal goal setting, expectations, organization, and the satisfaction of achievement. While writing is an ongoing process, students have the responsibility for meeting reasonable goals of productivity. These goals may include: X percent of manuscripts published, X percent of spelling corrected, writing element requirements, short writing assignments, and deadlines.

Deadlines are fine. Fine, as long as they are realistic, ample time is allotted for the task, students know what to do, are involved in setting the deadlines, and can meet the deadline with reasonable diligence.

> Note: I would not suggest deadlines for very young students.

15. **Starting Procedures, if Not Whole Class.** Some teachers of kindergarten, first, and second grades start their writing communities by working with a small group of writers. They teach the procedures, writing process, and minilessons to one group of writers who they feel can handle independent work. When that group is functioning, they start another group. They select children who are ready in terms of skills and interest. They use the first group for coaching and mentoring the new group. Finally, all the children are introduced to and included in the community. This might take half the year.

In a class where few of the students have had prior training in the procedures of a writing process workshop or who have had little writing in their school background, this can be an effective way to start.

16. **Student Access to Curriculum.** If our goal is to develop independent, life long learners, we must help students set goals and monitor their own progress and achievement. They should know what is expected of them in terms of skill acquisition.

Give your students a copy of the writing curriculum for developing writers. It should consist of the genre to be studied and tried, the organizational and composing skills appropriate to their writing level, and the writing conventions they will be learning. Let them highlight the areas on which your class will focus. Invite them to highlight some other areas in which they are personally interested or for which they think they are ready.

If they are building portfolios, they should have a list of the genre they are expected to demonstrate, a class generated list of the criteria for entering pieces, the log for their entries and justifications, and directions for maintaining the portfolio.

17. **Inventory Your Writing Skills.** In each marking period, ask young writers to make a list of what they know about writing. Be sure to remind them of the three content areas — style and genre information, composing skills, and conventions.

A sample list might look like this.

- how to use alliteration
- series commas
- fiction time transitions
- capitalize names
- paragraph when the time changes
- make a web
- skip lines
- circle words I don't know when I draft
- describe what's happening in a scene using verbs
- divide a topic up into chunks
- put setbacks in a story
- revise by adding a word
- find left field sentences
- find ands and thens and cross them out

Have students add to their list at the end of each marking period, and keep it in their portfolio.

Summary

Building a writing community takes courage, time, organization, knowledge, enthusiasm, and flexibility. Use the first half of the year to focus on establishing procedures in all stages of the process, on producing quantities of writing, and achieving some early publishing.

As you and your class become a functioning writing community, you will want to explore genre further, do author studies, focus on quality, add to composing skills, refine response and revision strategies and conferences, improve components of the process, integrate writing with other subjects, use writing workshop techniques in reading, science, math and social studies, work on evaluation techniques, celebrate authorship, and read more about writing.

The first year is guaranteed to be exciting, encouraging, and satisfying in spite of some chaotic, discouraging, and frustrating moments — in other words, all the characteristics of a learning experience. Do not give up! The second year things go more smoothly. You will have found what things went well, what needs improvement, and where you have attempted too much. You will have accumulated materials and books to support your writing workshop. You will have found colleagues who will exchange ideas, successes, and offer support. Best of all, you will have become a writer.

Children's Books About the Writing Craft

Asher, Sandy. *Where Do You Get Your Ideas*. New York, NY: Walker and Company, 1987.

Bauer, Marian Dane. *What's Your Story; A Young Person's Guide to Writing Fiction*. New York, NY: Clarion Books, 1992.

Benjamin, Carol Lee. *Writing for Kids*. New York: Thomas Y. Crowell, 1985.

Dubrovin, Vivian. *Write Your Own Story*. New York, NY: Franklin Watts, 1984.

Kinghorn, Harriet R., and Peltor, Mary Helen. *Every Child a Storyteller*. Englewood, CO: Teacher Ideas Press, 1991.

Greenfield, Howard. *Books: From Writer To Reader*. New York, NY: Crown Publishers, Inc., 1976, 1989.

Tchudi, Susan and Stephen. *The Young Writer's Handbook*. New York, NY: Aladdin Books, Macmillan Publishing Co., 1984.

Chapter III

Prewriting

Ready, get set, go. Your room is set up for writing workshop. Writing materials abound. Space for student and teacher generated text awaits. Writing folders, writer's notebooks, greenbar paper, journals, and a modest supply of blank hand-publishing books are on hand. A daily block of time is scheduled.

All you need now is to set the writing process in motion. To start, some children require only an expectation that they write. Others respond to a practical purpose. Most children write to be heard, to say to the world, "This is who I am; this is what I think; please accept me." (As the proliferation of computer on-line forums attests, many adults retain this basic need to be heard, to count.)

Before they start, all writers need time to gather their thoughts, talk, research, and plan. Nonetheless, teachers may become anxious as young writers go through this prewriting stage. It might seem as if little is happening or that the children are accomplishing nothing. This is not the case. Learning to develop and organize writing ideas is a writing skill even though it involves no writing. No one can achieve effective writing without going this stage of the writing process. Young writers often find it an uncomfortable time as well. You can help them by providing strategies to move successfully through the stage and by not communicating your anxiety.

The following conditions and lessons will allow young writers to successfully negotiate the prewriting stage of the writing process.

- Expectations
- Strategies For Choosing Topics
- Opportunity To Think And Talk About Their Ideas
- Planning Techniques.

Expectations

Learners are more secure when they know what is expected of them. There is nothing more unsettling to students than not knowing what they are supposed to do. Let them know you expect them to write daily. Let them know that what they write about is up to them. Tell them about writer's notebooks. Let them know that they will be expected to publish some of their work. Show them samples.

What Works

1. **Writing Every Day.** On the first day of school, tell the children they will be writing every day. Show them where writing materials are kept. Give them a writing folder or a journal. Let them know you will be writing, too. Start the first workshop with an invitation to write anything they choose while you write in your journal. Write about something that really interests you or about when you were a child. Invite children to share and share yours with them. Invite the children to respond to the content of all the shared writing. Remind them that they will write again tomorrow.

Repeat this invitation the next day. You and they will begin to know one another and discover the things that interest each other. Take note of which children are unable to write anything. Refer to this chapter's next sub-section, Strategies For Choosing Topics, to help them. On subsequent days, slowly introduce and model the practices and procedures that you will need to make your writing workshop work.

2. **Parental Notice.** Send a letter to parents or guardians telling them about writing workshop. Let them know their children will be writing daily. Suggest they ask each morning, "What will you write about today?" Later, in parent conferences and other communications with them, give further explanation about the writing process, editing standards, and publishing procedures in your classroom (See Chapter II, The Writing Process Classroom and Chapter VII, Editing, for a sample letter to parents).

3. **Books Waiting To Be Written.** Nothing better whets children's appetites for writing than blank, ready-to-publish books on display at the start of school. The initial batch should have attractive covers, be available in a variety of sizes, and include Title and About the Author pages. You should have enough for each student but display only ten to fifteen at first. If you put out one for each student, it looks like an assignment. If you put out ten or so, it looks like an invitation. Examples of previously hand-published books written by other students will show young writers the possibilities.

Directions for making these books inexpensively and simply, as well as directions for setting up a volunteer run publishing center in your class or school, are included in Chapter VIII, Publishing.

Strategies For Choosing Topics

In the early grades most children have no trouble choosing topics. At these ages children are egocentric. When they discover they have an audience, they write uninhibitedly and with great variety. Unfortunately, as they mature they tend to grow reticent about their private lives and lose the gay abandon with which they chose topics in kindergarten and first and second grades.

Teachers must have faith in these developing young writers and believe that they have something to say. We can best help them by showing them strategies for choosing topics. We will only hinder them by selecting topics for them before they have developed adequate writing skills and confidence in their writing ability. Only then will they be ready to write in response to prompts, i.e., topics not of their choosing. Happily, they will be able to do it well.

Writing Prompts

It is a certainty that young writers cannot write well in response to a prompt if they cannot write well at all. First things first. Extensive research [1] has demonstrated clearly that the high engagement gained by having children write about things dear to themselves facilitates their learning to write.

The early years, in elementary and middle school, are a time for children to become comfortable with organizing their ideas and expressing them in writing. They learn that language and convention are tools for expressing themselves and communicating with others. This is the time for them to develop a sense of authorship, a voice, and style. During this process young writers do not need the extra burden of having to organize and communicate ideas about subjects about which they know little or in which they have scant interest.

Writing to a prompt should come only after children begin to write fluently. The reason for prompted writing should be solely for the purpose of assessing children's writing skills. At that time you will have to model writing to a prompt. Young writers will require practice in determining the writing style expected from the prompt and the organizing their presentation (See Writing Assessment at the end of this chapter).

Prompted writing should not be the regular approach to topic choice when the focus is on developing and improving writing skills. It doesn't take very many, " Let's all write a leprechaun story for St. Patrick's Day," or "Everybody write a Little Snowflake story," to lose young writers. I've seen it happen.

You should have a non-writing objective when you require your students to all write on the same topic — typically, finding out what they know or have retained about a just completed unit (in science or social studies, for example, or for literature response).

Engagement

You reduce the chance that children will engage with their writing when you assign topics, give story starters, or try to involve them in your own pet projects. Engagement raises the probability that young writers will actively seek to acquire writing skills because they feel a personal need for them. Without this engagement they may feel that the sooner the writing task is over, the better. Loss of engagement breeds disruptive behavior.

A personal narrative about a fishing trip with a parent serves as well, if not better, than an assigned topic for a young writer to try out new writing skills. If a writer is deeply absorbed in his fishing story, he won't be disrupting a group lesson. You will find that, in all respects, it is well worth giving up assigned topics.

One of my favorite topic choice stories concerns a first grade teacher who

[1] Donald Graves, *Writing: Teachers and Children at Work* (NH: Heinemann, 1983).

politely invited me into her class after attending my workshops where she had sat with arms crossed and a general look of skepticism throughout. When I arrived in her class she said, "Let me watch you start the writing session. Show me what you mean about prewriting and topic choice at this grade level."

> It was a few days before national elections. The first graders were wearing red, white, and blue hats and had just returned from voting in the school election. Their writing assignment had been introduced. On their desks was a mimeographed copy of a view of the White House and the story starter — If I were the President of the United States I would...
>
> Two children were crying and several others were looking dazed. I gulped and gathered my thoughts, wondering how to be as diplomatic as possible. As I moved to the front of the children, I was wildly brainstorming to find a way to use the teacher's materials and objectives and still bail the kids out. A child provided the answer. He was drawing what looked like an animal on his paper, on the White House lawn essentially. I remembered Caroline Kennedy's pony, Fala, Her, Socks, et al.
>
> I sat down and began to talk conversationally to the first graders about presidents and pets — what pets the children had, and what pets they might have if they were the President. Before long most of the children had an idea and were ready to go. A few remaining ones wanted to talk and write about other things. I suggested they include some description in their pieces, giving them a target skill. I asked the teacher to join me in walking around to encourage all the writers and talk to them about their drawings and writing. Soon they were all writing — about their pets, a pet in the White House, and a number of topics having nothing to do with pets.

There is a nice postscript to this story. On that day, the teacher began to see that, in terms of writing development, nothing was being gained by having the children all working on the same topic — especially one to which many could not relate. As we continued to work together, she was greatly impressed by the writing success that resulted from her application of the practical techniques I shared with her over the year and by the accompanying reading achievement of her first graders. She has become one of the outstanding writing process teachers in the school and county. In two years, she has developed a set of practices and procedures to create a strong writing community in her classroom. By the way, it does not include story starters.

The high engagement with writing that results from personal topic choice is characteristic of a functioning classroom writing community. By helping children get into the flow and self absorption of the creative process, and by supporting them with ample time, resources, lessons, and materials, the teacher is rewarded with an involved and cooperative student body. Once this is achieved, and the children have had lots of practice writing, they can begin to branch out and use writing as a tool for learning and artistic expression.

Early in the year the focus should be on the *personal* function of writing. Personal narratives and expository writing about personal knowledge should predominate while the writing community is under construction. The level of engagement will be highest when young writers choose this focus. In addition, revision will be an easier task. Because of the writers' intimate knowledge of their topics, they are substantially more likely to find incongruities and to self-correct.

What Works

1. **What Do I Know?** Encourage all children to list, in picture, oral, or written form, things they know. For all listing activities, supply students with long strips of sturdy paper, four to five inches wide for younger children and three to four inches wide for older students—a list should look like a list. (A good source of list paper is a printing shop. They are happy to recycle trimmings.) Show students how to put the lower end inside their desk and pull it out as their list grows. Model a list of your own using the same paper.

A second grader's list of potential writing topics.

When your young writers have a few entries, ask volunteers to share their lists. Ask the students to star one or two of their listed items that they might like to write about. Give younger writers star stickers or colored labels to indicate their choices. Listing helps young writers think of the things they know and the things that interest them.

All ideas are acceptable. The object is not to see who can make the longest list. A list of three to four entries is fine. The children should tape their completed list into their writing folder or tuck it into the covers of their writer's notebook. Encourage writers to add to their list at anytime. Some teachers assign this list making for homework, bringing parents into the process.

2. **Anything I Know.** You can direct young writers to their personal knowledge through conferencing. In a fourth grade class in Bradenton, Florida, I talked to a writer who had started a story and abandoned it after one sentence. He had planned to write a story about a robber going to jail. He was particularly vociferous about not continuing. The teacher, in an aside, told me this was a problem student—uncooperative, wouldn't write, usually fighting with classmates.

I came back to him after a short cooling off period and said, "I understand you know a good bit about fighting. Why don't you write about a memorable fight? You see in it detective and adventure books. A mystery writer told me that describing a fight is really hard to do. The writer has to let the reader know where are the two fighters at different times, who's down, who hit when. Can you tell me about a fight you've seen or been in? Give it a try."

The student was so surprised that he did it. I had channeled his interest, given him the message that he had something worthwhile to say, and challenged him to do a difficult task.

You might want to keep a Dick Francis book (adult mystery, horse racing focus) handy for older students who might be interested in describing a fight. It is a very difficult description and Dick Francis does a particularly good job. (Step back from your role of playground peacemaker and remember, this is for fiction, and fiction is based on conflict. Describing a fight may be therapeutic for some—like taking out one's agression on a stuffed pillow.)

Another difficult writing task is moving your characters about in a scene. When you find good examples of this, read them to your young writers.

3. **List Everything.** Invite writers to make a list of anything. Emerging writers (K-2) pass naturally through an inventorying stage as they learn to write, making lists of letters they know, families of words, words they can spell.

I love my Mom.

I love my cat.

I love my dog.

I love my brother.

All learners retain that urge to inventory and should have the opportunity satisfy it by making lists, too.

- List making is classification — sorting things into groups based on common traits. This is a critical thinking skill and should be used in the writing workshop as well as in science and math. Listing all the words associated with a topic might lead to breaking the list up into three or four categories that will be the basis for different paragraphs within the piece.
- List making provides an impetus for research. Young writers may read books on the listed topics and gather new words for their lists. This might be a precursor activity before lessons about gathering information for report writing.
- List making leads to vocabulary expansion.
- List making is easy. When the task is simply to write single words, young writers who have a hard time writing sentences can excel.
- List making is an excellent prewriting activity. During the listing, usually confined to single words, a writer is gathering his thoughts on a subject. Each word of the list jogs his memory to connect other aspects of the topic.

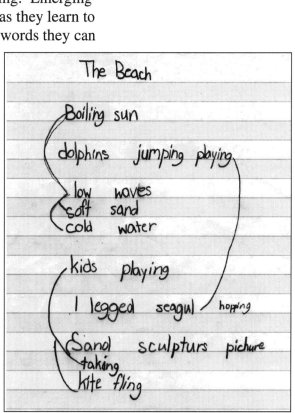

A second grader's grouping of words and ideas about a topic.

Topic related word list from a fifth grader.

I was invited into a fourth grade class comprised of an unusual number of nonwriters or reluctant writers. Their writing was limited, and the teacher was eager to find ways to help them say more in their pieces.

I introduced them to this writer's trick: I asked them to pick something they knew about or some topic they had been studying in science, social studies —something they really liked. I asked a few students what topic they had picked so everyone could hear the possibilities and wide variety. I gave them long strips of paper and asked them to write single words only about that topic. They thought that would be easy and started immediately.

After a few minutes, I asked a few students to share their lists. The lists were growing rapidly. After lO minutes, I asked them to stop and read their list to themselves. Now I asked, "Would you please pick one thing from the list and write a sentence about it?"

They did this easily. Some of them had already talked to another student about the words and subject on their list as they worked. How about selecting another word and writing about it. No problem. Another, no problem. And so on.

"This is easy," one writer announced. Others kept adding words to their lists. Many wanted to share their very long lists. I asked them to read their lists to their desk partners while others continued writing.

The reason they could write more than their usual two or three sentences was that they had really gathered their thoughts about their subject. And they had done it with an unintimidating task, listing single words.

List making can lead to early publishing of a "Book of Lists," with a list on each page. Younger writers might make a list and publish with an illustration, a word to a page. The class should find such listables as: toys, colors, girls' names, boys' names, states, flowers, songs, machines, tools, sports, birds, food, fruit, fish, vegetables, rivers, games, animals, jobs, streets, teachers, poems, clothes, teams, dinosaurs, ice cream flavors, endangered species.

4. **Ideas From Books.** Read fine children's literature to young writers daily. Picture books are great for all ages, not just for young children. Discuss themes, events, information, story, and characters, with an eye to finding similarities in their own lives.

Kill two birds with one stone and read non-fiction material on the history, science, art and geography topics under current class study.

Construct webs of some books, drawing attention to all the aspects of the book—people, places, information, and events. Invite students to share parallel aspects in their own lives. Suggest that they might have a story to tell, that they might want to write it.

Bibliographies of wonderful read-aloud literature are available from your school media specialists, Whole Language resource books, and professional journals and magazines.

5. **Personal Survey.** Create a personal survey to use in the first days of workshop. It should be easy to fill out (check-off boxes) and it should be appropriate to your grade level. Leave some blank lines in each category for later additions. A sample inventory is provided in **Reproducible #2.**

Suggested survey categories:

*   Places I have been: a park, a swamp, a beach, a mountain, a museum...

*   Things I can do: run a computer program, set the table, whistle, knit, fix a bike chain, roller skate, sew, recite a poem, collect baseball cards, saw wood, build a tree house, play cards, bait a fish hook...

*   Games I know how to play: Monopoly, Nintendo, Scrabble, Go Fish...

- My favorite kind of book: mystery, fairy tale, adventure, animal story, science fiction, poetry...

- People I know: a veterinarian, a nurse, a carpenter, a teacher, a police officer, a dentist, a farmer, a cousin, an uncle, a grand mother...

Complete the survey as a class project, inviting children to help one another. They will learn more about each other in the process. Fill out the survey for yourself as a model for your students.

Use these surveys with non-starters in group or individual conferences. Talk about what the children can do or places they have been in a friendly conversational manner. Encourage them to explain how they learned to do something or what they liked best about a place. Tell them a brief story about some place you have been or something you can do.

Invite them to write about some item in the survey. Students keep the surveys in their writing folders or writer's notebook.

6. **What Is Everyone Else Doing?** After the first writing session, ask those who have chosen a topic to share it with the class and tell how they decided to write on that topic. Many hesitant writers, who may not have had an opportunity to choose topics in the past, need to hear what other writers are doing.

7. **Broadcast of Topics.** Use the Commitment Statement (See Chapter V, Response) to broadcast topic choices throughout the year. Children learn the stages of the writing process and the kinds of topics other children choose when they hear writers declare their titles or topics, and ask for peer conferences or editing help.

8. **Everyday Stuff.** Model your own strategies for choosing what to write. Think aloud as you list some tentative ideas on chart paper or the board. Make them ordinary topics.

- I wonder why there are so few worms in my garden.
- My dog's trip to the veterinarian.
- How I am stuck on a writing assignment for an inservice course.
- My favorite aunt.
- Isn't it strange what makes some people laugh?

9. **Clipboard Trip.** Send the non-starters around the room with a class list on a clip board to find out what topics others have chosen and, if possible, why they chose them. When they finish, ask them to sort the topics into categories or construct a graph for the class. Use their survey results for your own records. Their interaction with each author counts as a conference for those authors. Record them as conferences on the Commitment Statement record sheet.

10. **The Story Behind a Picture.** Many children find writing ideas in visual sources. Utilize this learning style by providing a file of photographs, art prints, magazine pictures, and newspaper clippings for them to examine. Young writers might paste their choice of picture on a sheet of greenbar paper, unlined paper, colored stock, or a page in their notebook and tell something about the picture—react to it.

Do not require that young writers use this technique. You will find that many young writers have strong visions in their mind about what they choose to write about and they will not be interested in this. Offer it only as an invitation. Writers must always have choices. The following technique has been used successfully at all grade levels.

Marilyn Cafaro's first graders, Gulf Cate Elementary, Sarasota, Florida, select pictures from a class file. The pictures are gleaned from *Junior National Geographic, Ranger Rick,* and other science and geography oriented magazines. The young writers build collections of picture reactions. Cafaro reports that their vocabulary use is remarkable. They write words from their listening vocabulary, which is children's largest vocabulary in the primary grades (speaking, writing, and reading are the others).

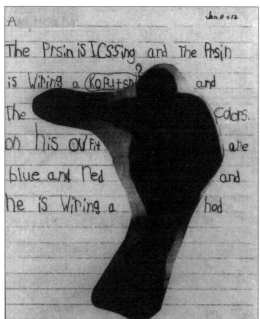

Picture response from a first grader.

A picture reaction can be used in conjunction with descriptive writing lessons. Young writers focus on one to several attributes and include them in their reaction to the picture. The attributes become the target application.

Picture reactions can be the manuscripts used for modeling peer conferences, revision, and editing. Picture topics can parallel themes, science and social studies topics, and math, encouraging the use of associated vocabulary.

What do you do when two young writers want the same picture? Share it. Paste the picture on a large sheet of greenbar unlined paper, divide the text area in two and invite each child to write on one half. Or, let them work together, to be co-authors of the picture response.

11. **Book Covers.** Encourage young writers to look at your supply of blank, ready-to-publish books. They will often get ideas from the cover pictures or the shape of the book

12. **Other Strategies For Non-Starters.**

• Call the non-starters into conference. Draw them out, getting them to talk about something that interests them.

• Give writers several days to come up with an idea. After they see you model types of writing and listen to what other students write about, they may be able to begin.

• Invite students to read a textless picture book and write a text for it to share with a younger student. This provides them with a pre-existing structure, a security they might need. Ask your school librarian for a list of such books or consult *Best Books for Children,* by John T. Gillespie and Corinne J. Naden, Editors, R.R. Bowker, NY, 1990.

• Invite students to draw the things they

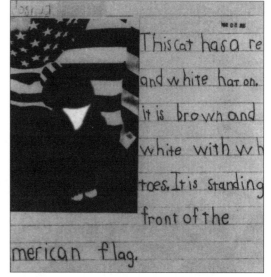

First grader's target attributes are color and action.

are planning to write.

• Invite writers to take an easy-reader text and expand the story with details and description (security of structure).

• Invite children to write their own version of a favorite story. This activity is called Innovation in Writing Process and Whole Language professional literature (security of structure).

• Suggest that the students write "Dear Mom" at the top of their page and see what they can come up with. Erase the heading later.

• Invite the children to listen to other writers' pieces. Direct them to make one nice comment and ask one question, and to write them on a piece of paper for the author.

• Help young writers by taking dictation or making a quick list outline of the events in their narrative (See description in Planning Techniques, this chapter).

• For advanced readers who are afraid their writing will fall far short of the literature they love, suggest a different genre for their first piece, e.g., an interview, an information piece, or poetry.

• Invite manually inept writers to dictate into a recorder or have a student scribe help them. Or invite them to write, in very large print, a short picture story for a younger audience. Large newsprint pages, folded once and stapled into a booklet, might appeal to them. (See also Chapter XI, Meeting Common Challenges.)

• Invite children to write about what they would like to be doing if they didn't have to be here in school. Many children can be quite passionate about this, and the resulting writing is often vivid due to their engagement with the topic.

• Invite children to learn a poem and recite it to the class. Then ask them if they could write one of their own. Some children are aural learners and love the sound of language. They may need to come to writing via the music and rhythm of poetry or song.

• Invite writers to interview a person in the school and present the results to the class orally or in written form.

• Reintroduce attribute, repetition, all about, example, and shape books to your older students. The books that charmed them in kindergarten will interest them in the upper grades. Suggest that students try one of the several fixed format book genres.

Repetition books are based on simple repetitive phrases such as: I love cats, I love Mom, I love school. Or, Apples are red. Fire engines are red. Stop signs are red.

Attribute books present an inventory of objects that share an attribute. An example is: Red — Red is for stop, Red is for apple, Red is for flag stripes.

All About books present lists of facts about a topic, usually one fact sentence per page and illustrated with drawings or pasted pictures. For example: Plants make oxygen. We can eat some plants. Plants make the world beautiful. We make things out of plants.

Example books present an array of examples of the topic. For example: Similes — as warm as a kitten, as tall as Shaq, as mean as Viola Swamp.

Shape books are a kind of All About book with the pages and cover taking the shape of the subject. For example, a cloud book, a whale book.

Ask the students to list topics for their Attribute and All About ... books. Some examples are: similes, alliteration, proper nouns, weather words, opposites, dogs, playing cards, etc.

• Last choice — Tell writers they will have to select from a list of topics you will offer on the following day. Give them the chance to come up with an idea overnight. Offer them a selection of genre and topics within the scope of their experience (I have never had to resort to this, but several teachers have told me it works and they feel comfortable using it to get a worst case non-starter going because there is still choice involved). It is a variation on the ploy, "Would you like to go to bed at 8:30 or 9:00 p.m.? Your choice."

Opportunity to Think and Talk

All writers need time to think and talk about their ideas. Young writers might have only a vague notion of their topic or may have selected a very broad one that overwhelms them as they contemplate the amount of writing will take. Talking helps writers focus their idea and discover how they want to present it. What looks like procrastination, frequently is problem solving.

We need to give young writers talk time. Students who request talk time in writing workshop need to know that they will be asked about their progress. Students must demonstrate oral or graphic work that will will use during Commitment Statement.

Rehearsing the things they will say in a piece helps students write in complete sentences. Chomsky's linguistics research[2] has confirmed that children learn the syntax of their native tongue intuitively. Children tend to speak in syntactically correct sentences and will write in that fashion if they have the opportunity to vocalize before they write.

What Works

1. **Draw It First.** The draw-first procedure, common to kindergarten classes, also works well in subsequent grades. Writers may want to draw the characters or settings they have in mind for a story. Some may want to use the filmmaker storyboard technique, drawing each scene of the story they envision. Encourage young writers in any grade to talk about their story while they draw. They will say sentences they will write later. Encourage students to write in a talking mode. They should be encouraged to speak their sentences as they write. If it sounds right, it probably is. A notable exception is 'Me and him... '(as subjects of a sentence). Keep correcting this. Don't give up.

2. **Think it Over Homework.** *Ginny Speicher, Gulf Gate Elementary, Sarasota, Florida,* assigns Think It Over Homework to her second graders

[2] N. Chomsky, *Syntactic Structures* (Mouton, 1957).

who are starting new pieces. They take their proposed topic home, written on a card. They think about it overnight, talk to anyone they like, and come back the next day prepared to start a graphic planner or draft.

3.   **Writer's Notebooks.** *Melissa Odom Forney, children's author and writing consultant, Palmetto, Florida,* advises young writers to keep a notebook to jot down items such as interesting names, funny things they have seen, or conversations they have overheard that caused them to stop and think.

Professional writers keep such notebooks as well. They record descriptions of people they want to use for characters in their stories, lists of writing ideas, first lines of fiction they have read, things they wonder about, excerpts from reading they especially liked, and examples of style and literary devices.

Some teachers ask young writers to make double entry pages in their notebooks by folding or lining pages vertically. In one column they write their observations and in the other they write what they think of it. They use these pages for science, field trips, school programs, film responses, etc.

Smaller handmade versions of writer's notebooks can be utilized in theme studies. Children can tell about activities they performed, observations and questions about films, videos, and reading, vocabulary associated with the theme, investigations they have made, etc.

Writer's notebook entries facilitate planning. They are the bits of information that lead a writer to focus and organize a piece.

4.   **Response Groups.** When your class is operating as a cooperative writing community, some young writers may form small groups (no more than four will keep the time spent in conference to reasonable limits). In these response groups writers tell each other about ideas for their next piece. You will need to model the activity, including the use of a class generated chart of guidelines for it. The guidelines should be short and specific, as these examples.

- •   Who is your intended audience?
- •   What genre do you intend to use?
- •   What pieces of information have you collected?

Beverly Eisele, whole language consultant, suggests that when children meet in small task groups they must fulfill the requirement of the task. Whether or not they do is determined by the other members of the group. She calls that determination a Check Mate. A student who declares, "I'm done," must obtain the confirming initials of the other group members before leaving the activity.

Young writers might fill out a Prewriting Response Group form such as this.

Prewriting Group Conference

Topic: _____

Ideas: _____

Check Mate: _____

Procedures such as this and Commitment Statement are designed to encourage cooperative and responsible behavior in the writing workshop. Modeling these procedures, expecting the children to comply, and establishing and enforcing consequences will result in a secure environment conducive to risk-taking, investigation, and accomplishment.

5.   **Themes.** Many teachers ask children to write in a topic area following total immersion — extensive study of a theme or class topic that includes multimedia presentations and hands on projects. Writing about the topic is one way for children to demonstrate what they do and do not understand. Preparation for this writing should include talk time, research time, and choice of genre. (See Chapter IX, Expository, Writing Content, Informational Writing.) For writers in the developing stage, the focus of this activity should be on the content of the writing, not on the assessment of writing skills.

Planning Techniques

Writing takes organized thought. The organization might be

- chronological
- in order of importance of the ideas
- alphabetical
- by comparison
- by viewpoint, or
- by sorting and grouping.

Graphic organizers are helpful tools for both developing and fluent writers, but they require abstract thinking. Children who have not made the transition from the concrete to the abstract may find graphic planners confusing. For example, picture planning and lists are appropriate to first, second, and some third graders. Independent webbing, constructing timelines, and building complex fiction planners are not. The latter can be modeled and used for teacher guided class writing and teacher assisted planning in the primary grades, but do not expect children below late third and early fourth grade to generate them independently.

Model all the planning techniques and encourage young writers to use all their own hybrid versions (See also Chapter IX, Writing Content).

What Works

1.   **List Outline.** A list outline is useful for young writers who have a story idea but lose it if the writing occurs over several days or becomes lengthy. Make a list outline for these children from their telling you the story. This can be done in a brief conference or with the help of a peer scribe. The young writer keeps the list outline taped to his desk or in his folder as a constant reference.

Here is an example of a list outline for a narrative as told to a scribe.

My trip to Aunt Lissa's

- In the car
- Aunt Lissa's dog
- To the llama farm
- A llama liked me.
- I fed a llama dog biscuits.
- Llamas were brown and white.
- Picnic at Aunt Lissa's
- Swimming
- Home and I forgot my llama picture.

2. **Picture and Message Transitional Plan.** Young developing writers in kindergarten and first grade, in transition from story writing based on their large drawings, may find this graphic planner helpful. They can start to consider the elements of fiction.

3. **Story Map or Storyboard.** Sequencing is the underlying objective for using a storyboard in narrative planning. It is a picture version of a list outline. The young writer draws the sequence of events in his narrative. He writes key words and phrases about the details under each picture. A sample is provided in **Reproducible #3.**

Young writers often write short sentences under their pictures as they work. When they subsequently write a draft using the storyboard, they often restrict their writing to those short sentences. Therefore, it is important to model this graphic planner with single reminder words under the pictures. Follow the model with a draft that enlarges on each picture with multiple sentences. (See student example on following page.)

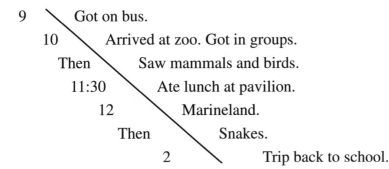

4. **Narrative Timeline.** A timeline is another way to organize narrative writing since narration is characterized by the passage of time. A diagonal orientation of the timeline, as in the following example, allows children to write horizontally.

Transitional Story Planning sheet.

Our Field Trip to the Zoo

```
9  \       Got on bus.
  10  \        Arrived at zoo. Got in groups.
   Then  \        Saw mammals and birds.
     11:30  \        Ate lunch at pavilion.
        12  \        Marineland.
       Then  \        Snakes.
           2  \        Trip back to school.
```

In narratives that detail a sequence such as trips, training programs, and vacations, timelines may be more useful than storyboards (See **Reproducible #4**).

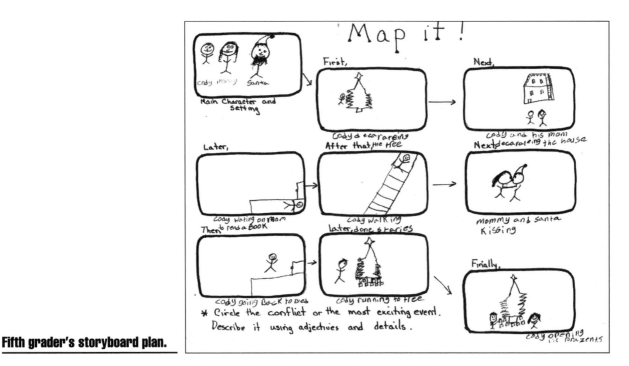

Fifth grader's storyboard plan.

5. **Webbing After Gathering Data or Brainstorming.** Webbing can be introduced to young writers after they have sorted the information they have already collected about a subject. This is a concrete approach that will pave the way for the more abstract task of creating a web by mentally sorting information. Here is a demonstration of webbing from a random ordered list of information (30 minutes).

Requirements:

- copies of list of information generated by class or an overhead
- transparency masters (See **Reproducibles #5 and #6**)
- students in working groups
- copies of a web structure on board, overhead, or paper
- scissors
- colored markers.

Sample information list for subject of water.

> All living things need water.
> People cannot drink sea water.
> Water is a liquid which takes the shape of its container.
> Water is a compound made of hydrogen and oxygen.
> Animals obtain water by drinking and from their food.
> Water is colorless.
> Water occurs in three forms: gas, liquid and solid.
> A person should drink several glasses of water each day.
> A fish gets its oxygen from water through its gills.
> Plants obtain water from the soil through their roots.
> Seeds need water to sprout and grow.
> Water turns into ice at 32 degrees Fahrenheit.

Give each student a copy of the appropriate list (the material in the two reproducible samples are for different age levels) prior to this demonstration; or have them list, in random order, all the information they know about a science or social studies topic the class studied together.

a)   Ask the students to form their assigned groups. Weekly or monthly schedules of group formations also contain a definition their roles and provide directions in case of missing members.

b)   Ask a volunteer to read the list with the class in unison or ask students to read the list in their group.

c)   Next have them look for any groups of information, sentences that seem to be about the same aspect of the topic. Examples: Water; physical description, living things need of water, how they take water in. Rabbits; as mammals, physical description, where they live.

d)   Then ask the young writers how they would like to divide the list into groups of information. These might include color or number coding them on the sheet, or cutting the list up and putting the strips in piles. Each group of information represents a subtopic of the overall topic.

e)   Have writers try all of the sorting methods. Share the results.

f)   Show your students how to construct a web from the groups of information. Have them tell you, as you model the webbing, where to add the pieces of information.

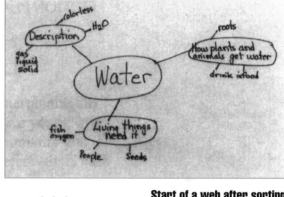

Start of a web after sorting water facts.

Invite young writers to use this technique when they write informational pieces. Meet with writers whose current piece is informational and help them repeat the activity using the data they have gathered about their topic.

6.   **Webbing.** Webbing requires abstract thinking. It requires a child to recall or think about an event or topic and mentally divide it into discrete sections. It requires an ability to classify ideas and bits of information and relate them to central topic. As such, it is an advanced skill that most children cannot do independently until they are ten or older.

Webbing is useful for expository writing, not chronologically organized narrative. Model webbing for your students.

Thoughts rarely occur to us in a linear or logical sequence. A web captures and tentatively organizes our thoughts as we contemplate a subject and the thoughts buzz around and zing into our consciousness from all directions. A web allows us to fit them into a pattern that will help guide us in writing about the topic. A web remains open to additions and deletions during the planning, drafting, and revision of the piece. A sample web to copy for your students is provided in **Reproducible #7.**

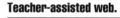

Teacher-assisted web.

7. **Fiction Planners.** Young writers who are avid readers of fiction, or have been read to consistently, are at an advantage when it comes to writing fiction. Children should be introduced to characters, setting, and plots as early as possible. Kindergarten children can tell you the characters, setting, and plot of *The Three Little Pigs, Little Red Riding Hood,* and any other stories in which you draw their attention to the components of fiction. Familiarity with these components help young writers plan their stories.

Graphic planners for fiction focus on the elements and the form of a story. While webbing is useful in developing the characters and setting, it does not graphically represent the form of a story. Use this plan as a model for a class generated story. A sample fiction planner is provided in **Reproducible #8.**

FICTION PLANNER

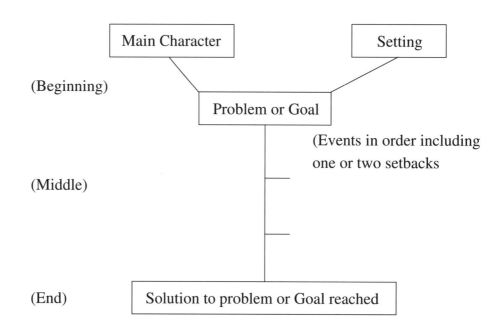

The terms *beginning, middle,* and *end* appear in many language arts curriculum guidelines. Because of their common meanings, they are frequently misunderstood. Young writers often equate them with the physical aspects of their papers and are thus confused, for example, when teachers ask them, "Where is the end of your story?" Students point to the bottom of the page and answer, "It is right here, The End."

If, rather, we would talk about the resolution of the plot or the solving of the problem, the children would come to understand the literary meaning of "the end" as an important concept (See Chapter IX, Writing Content, Fiction for details about characters, setting, and plot, creating tension, point of view, etc.).

8. **Persuasive Planner.** A planning technique for a persuasive piece is based on allotments of content and space by percents. A good allocation is

20%	State your proposition, proposal, or opinion.
	Acknowledge the likely opposition.
70 %	Present your case, your arguments.

10%   Conclusion — This might be a personal statement, a
             prediction or a summary.

A concrete way to demonstrate this space allocation is to have students
fold their papers to reflect the three sections and percents, as in the following
diagram.

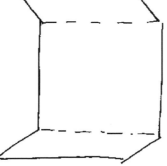

(See Chapter IX, Writing Content, Persuasion.)

Some Words of Encouragement

Do not be discouraged if the children do not immediately start to use the
minilessons and models you are providing. Usually three or four young writers will try them out. The ideas are now out in the writing community you
have created in your classroom. As the need arises, you can refer writers back
to the techniques and to writers in the class who have used them.

Assignments and Assessment Tests

Writing Assignments

Before students know how to write well, asking them to write reports
about subjects of which they have meager knowledge and experience is asking them to do a job without the prerequisite tools. Once young writers have
learned to take control of and have confidence in their writing, they can make
an effective transition from free topic choice to assigned writing —from
learning to write to writing to learn.

Make a gradual transition to assigned writing by setting topic parameters
that offer a large choice within those parameters. For example, a sixth grade
class assignment is writing on a theme such as exploration or settlement.
Students are to illustrate that they understand the underlying concepts of the
unit. The assignment should have choices of form (fiction, report, journal of a
person living through that experience, etc.). A vocabulary list of related words
(content words) might accompany the assignment, and some percentage of
the list can be required in the piece.

Evaluation should be based on meeting the predetermined criteria of required
information and several predetermined organizational and composing skills, and
specific conventions. Some teachers allot points for each of the required elements and the grade is determined by the number of requirements satisfied.

Writing Assessment Tests

If statewide writing assessments are in place, we need to prepare children for the prompted tests. Teaching the vocabulary of the test directions is an important part of that preparation. If a writing assessment uses the word *narrative* to describe a personal experience or fictional account, we must use that word in our writing workshop. If the assessment uses the word *explain* to indicate expository writing, we must use that term in the writing workshop. We can help our children prepare by researching the testing vocabulary used and making it part of the regular classroom writing vocabulary.

Recognizing the difference between a narrative and expository prompt is another important aspect in the preparation for a writing assessment.

Brainstorm a list of prompts with your class of young writers. See where the prompts lead. What are the elements of the prompt that cause a writer to tell a story that relates events and the passage of time, to explain or discuss a topic, or to try and convince the reader of some point? Here are some examples of prompt vocabulary.

Narrative prompt cues: when, story, happened, time, event, occasion, verbs usually in the past tense.

- Tell about the best trip you ever *took*.
- Your teacher left a bag on the floor of the classroom and left. It *began* to rattle and move. Tell what you think *happened*.
- Weather affects us all. Describe one *time* when weather *affected* your life.
- Describe how you *became* friends with your friend.

Expository prompt cues: select or choose and tell why, directions, explain, plan, verbs usually in present tense.

- Weather affects us all. *Select* some weather conditions and tell how they *affect* people.
- Your class is choosing a pet. What animal do you think the class should choose and *why?*
- Most of us have chores we have to do. *Explain* about the chores you *do*.
- Friendship is important to us all. Tell what you *look* for in a friend.

Writing assessment should be an opportunity for children to show off their writing craft. We should encourage our students to view it in this fashion.

Chapter IV

Drafting

A blank piece of paper. Think of the freedom this offers. Scary though, isn't it? All writers, young and old, are faced with the challenges of how to start and what to say. The very young jump right in, eager to tell about their picture and themselves, concerned only with what they will say next. Developing writers think about sequence, but their concerns also include audience, purpose, exciting beginnings, satisfying endings, vivid details, colorful description, tone, dialogue, and conventions. Fluent writers have additional concerns about point of view, literary devices, clarity, unity, cohesion, and style.

The only way to get started is to start writing. You cannot address any of the concerns about style, audience, tone, etc until you have something to work with. The focus in the drafting stage should be on getting thoughts down as quickly as possible. Here are some practices and lessons that help young writers create the rough drafts they will develop through the writing process.

- From Graphic Planner to Draft
- Skipping Lines
- First Draft Practices
- Great Beginnings
- Expanding and Developing Ideas
- No Copying Drafts.

From Graphic Planner to Drafts

A plan of any kind helps young writers get going on their drafts. During the planning stage they are rehearsing the things they will say in their piece. The plan reminds them of the thoughts they gathered about the topic and helps them determine the order in which they want to present them.

What Works

1. **Narrative Plans to Drafts.** In successive sessions, model a class narrative using each kind of narrative graphic planner: timeline, storyboard, list outline, and fiction plan. (See Chapter III, Prewriting, Planning Techniques.)

Ask young writers to develop a class story using one of the graphic planners provided in **Reproducibles #3, #4, #8**. Draft the story on chart paper or on an overhead transparency. Better still, use a story plan devised by a student. Make a transparency of the student's planner or copy it on chart paper. Emphasize that the brief notes used in a planner, the writer's first thoughts, are a guide to the draft. Have the students add details about who, what, when, where, how, and why, feelings, and dialogue to develop the ideas in the planner. Leave the planner and story on view for a few days following this model.

Show how new ideas can be added to the planner as the story develops. Writers often find that new ideas about later parts of the story might come to mind when they are writing the beginning. Often the original idea for the ending completely changes. Characters sometimes come to life and take over, sending the story in a whole new direction. Writing changes and develops our thoughts and ideas. Writing is thinking and creating.

A writer often knows he wants to say something, but he does not know what it is until he states it. Graham Wallas, in *The Art of Thought,* puts it this way. "The little girl had the making of a poet in her who, being told to be sure of her meaning before she spoke, said, 'How can I know what I think until I see what I say?' "

2. **First, Second, Third.** When young writers use a web as a graphic planner, they are beginning to sort information. Show them how to number the different areas (sub-topics) of the web before they begin their draft. They will have to make decisions as to which clump of information will come first, second, third, and so on in their draft. Ask them to put the numbers on the graphic planner and next to the corresponding information in their draft.

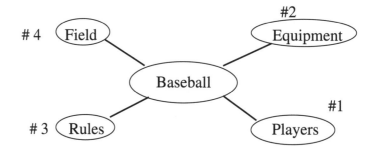

Later, in peer conference or any other response situation, they may find information from web section #3 in their draft mixed in with section #4 information. They can move the out-of-place sentence to the draft section containing the other #4 information. (Do not expect smooth transitions from one piece of information to another if a writer moves a sentence. This is a very difficult skill.)

3. **Paper Halves For Paragraphs.** Commonly, young writers draft expository pieces from a web planner, writing just one sentence for each sub-topic. The web plan looks like the spider rather than the web. This is appropriate for writers new to webbing; second or third graders. The resultant writing is undeveloped, lacking in detail and interest.

To help young writers develop paragraphs, direct them to divide blank papers in half horizontally. They will use each separate half sheet for drafting one sub-topic or branch of their web. Allow them sufficient time to think and talk further about the topic and to add new information to the appropriate half sheet (paragraph). They can staple or tape the sections together after they have added as much information as they want.

Again, do not expect smooth transitions between sentences or paragraphs in young students (grades one-three). Older students may be ready for lessons about placing related sentences close to each other and lessons about transitions between paragraphs. In appropriate grades, save the rough draft for later lessons on transitions and summaries in expository writing.

4.   **Indenting.** Indenting is a difficult convention for most developing writers. It requires that they leave space, that they delay writing, and that they change their focus from writing to space management. The best way to get young writers to indent is to ask them to put something concrete at the start of a paragraph—a star sticker, a colored rectangle or a numbered rectangle to match the color or number code on their webs.

Concrete indent holder used by a third grader.

Skipping Lines

Train young writers to use every other line and one side of their paper. This will encourage revision. Show them examples of students' rough drafts that have revisions in the skipped line.

What Works

1.   **Greenbar Paper.** Start the writing workshop with a supply of 8-1/2 x 11-inch greenbar computer paper (the carbonless variety). It is available in office supply stores. Ask your principal to include it in the school's paper budget. Students write on the white lines and revise using the green, or visa versa. There is a slightly larger first line that is perfect for titles. The back of the sheet is unlined, handy for planning and drawing.

2.   **Highlight Every other Line.** Hightlight, in pink or yellow, every other line of a sheet of regular loose-leaf paper. Using this as a master, make enough copies for your writers' first two pieces. The highlighted lines will come out a faint gray on a copier. Ask young writers to write their rough drafts using every other line and just one side of the page. Tell them this will give them space to add information later.

A fourth grader skipping lines on greenbar paper to leave room for revision.

3.   **X Every other Line in Journals.** To remind young writers to skip lines, ask them to put an X at the start of every other line of the next few papers they will be using in workshop or in their journals and writers' notebooks.

First Draft Practices

In order for young writers to write quickly enough to get their ideas down, they must be shown some helpful techniques. The brain works so much faster than a pencil that it is important for writers not to spend time during initial drafting worrying about conventions and mechanics. They should be concentrating on writing down their thoughts quickly before they lose them.

Besides the speed differential, another reason drafting and editing don't mix is that the two processes employ different hemispheres of the brain. Drafting is a creative activity requiring us to 'get lost' in the right side of our brain. Editing is an analytical, left brain activity. It is difficult to switch back and forth effectively.

By modeling drafting practices for your students, you will show them ways to capture their thoughts before they get away. Think aloud as you write. Use the blackboard, chart paper, or an overhead transparency.

What Works

1. **Leaving Blanks.** Ask young writers to leave blanks for words they can't think of during drafting. Model an example for them on the board or on an overhead transparency. We went to the bowling _____ and I won. (tournament, rink, alley?)

2. **Inventive Spelling.** Encourage young writers to use inventive or temporary spelling instead of stopping to find correct spelling. Encourage them to circle words they have sounded out and they think are misspelled. Example, I had lunch in the cafiteria.

3. **Vocabulary of Drafting.** Change your writing workshop vocabulary about drafting to "How do you write the word _____?" instead of "How do you spell the word_____?" Ask your students to do the same. This will encourage the use of inventive spelling.

4. **Write, Read, Write, Read.** Encourage young writers to write a sentence or two and read it back to themselves. They should then add a sentence or two more and read them back. Doing this through the whole draft will help them keep the thread of their story or piece.

5. **Label Each Page with Topic.** Ask writers to write their topic on the top of each sheet as they draft —e.g., "This is about my gymnastics class." If your students are working in journals, have them write that statement at the top and at the bottom of the sheet. In fiction, they may write a statement of the plot or what part of the story they are working on at the top of the page. This practice will help them stay focused on the topic and main idea of the piece.

Great Beginnings and Great Endings

Did you know that fine art students at Pratt Institute in New York set up their easels at the Metropolitan Museum of Art and try to capture the essence of painting lace in oils by copying a Van Dyke? Piano students listen to recordings by virtuosos to hear the different interpretations of the piece they are learning.

Young writers need such models, too. They can imitate the style of the masters of their craft just as art students do. They need to see how the professionals start personal narratives, fiction, descriptive, biographical, and expository pieces.

What Works

1. **Copy the Pros.** Use this procedure with your class when some of the young writers voice concern about good beginnings or endings and are unhappy with their piece in these regards — i.e., when they need the resource. Repeat the demonstration for the beginnings and endings of each genre as it is studied. (About 30 minutes, in a needs group or with the whole class)

When young writers have had a chance to see models of beginnings and endings and see the kinds there are, they can decide for themselves which works best for them and which works best for their piece.

Requirements

- A large variety of library books or magazines of the genre for which students need beginnings. Give each student time and opportunity to collect five or six examples.
- Writer's notebooks.
- Chart paper or overhead transparency.

Beginnings

a) Introduce the young writers to the idea of mimicking the pros. Discuss sports, art, carpentry, TV programs ("This Old House" or "Home Improvement").

b) Tell your students they can mimic professional writers. Talk about the need for writers to hook their reader with the opening sentence. Read them some examples of poor beginnings like these.

- Hi! I'm Marc and I am going to tell you about whales.
- There was a house and a boy.
- This is Paula and Trina. They are sisters.

c) Invite them to examine the books they have collected. In a group lesson, students should read the starting sentence of each of their examples. You should write them on a chart, the board, or an overhead transparency. Older students can copy these sentences into their notebooks. In a whole class lesson, write as many examples as you can in the time available.

d) Next have the young writers look at the list and look for similarities among them. They will notice that beginnings fall into categories. This is particularly noticeable in fiction. See list provided in **Reproducible #9**. Here are some sample categories of beginnings.

Fiction

- The main characters are talking.
- The time and place setting are described.
- The main character is introduced by description.
- The main characters are doing something.
- Some action is taking place.

Expository and Personal Narratives

- Author asks a question.
- Author defines the topic word.
- Author tells of personal involvement with the subject.
- Author describes a situation or event.
- Author describes the time and place.

Biographies

- Author establishes the time of the first event or start of life of person.
- Author describes the person.
- Author introduces the subject with which the person of the biography is closely associated (Baseball-Babe Ruth, Radium-Marie Curie, Basketball-Michael Jordan).

e) Leave the chart out and ask students to add to it as they find other types of story starts. Make copies of the samples provided and have students add examples and other kinds of opening sentences they find on their own. Keep these in writing folders or notebooks.

f) Some teachers have their classes go through this search, genre by genre. Others encourage writers to conduct independent searches and combine their finding into a class document. If students needs help finding a good expository start, they go to students who researched that style or specific genre.

g) Encourage students who are unhappy with their story starts to select the same kind as a professional used. Imitate the masters.

Endings

For help with all kinds of endings:

- Help your students search through endings in the various genres.
- Ask them to list final sentences by genre.
- Help them sort and classify them by ending category.

Make copies of the research results for all students to place in their writers' notebooks.

Fiction: Resolutions are controlled by the initial plot problem or conflict. At the end of the story, the character has resolved his problem or has reached a goal. If writers have not used a graphic planner and are wrestling with an ending, they can construct after-the-fact fiction planners and use them to develop a satisfactory ending. (See Chapter IX, Writing Content, Fiction.)

Personal narratives: Children often end their narratives with bed or going home — not the most satisfying ending. Call a group lesson for children who have endings of this nature. Suggest that they try to summarize their narratives by telling how they felt about the event or how it compared to another similar event. Use the vocabulary list associated with feelings provided (See **Reproducible #10**).

Some personal narrative ending categories:

- Feelings about the event or occasion
- Questions
- Finalities.

Expository: Endings of informational, persuasive, opinion, reviews and such summarize the material or lead the reader to investigate the topic further. Researching informational and expository writing will lead to the following categories of endings professional writers use. This list is provided in **Reproducible #11**.

Some expository and non-fiction narrative endings:

- Reminders

    Be sure to ...
    Remember that...
    So, if you...
    The next time you...
    Finally, eventually:
    The last thing you need to know...
    The last thing to do is...

- A quotation concerning the whole topic — expert or object of article

    "Let us all join in preserving the ..."
    "I owe my success to ..."
    "I hope..."

- Feelings about the event:

    The best part about...
    I knew then...
    The most important thing I learned...

- Predictions:

    The next time you will know...
    In no time you will be able...

One Day at 2:00 My Mom and I were in publx for one hour and and ran bown a aisl my sister erica pushed me and a litter gril with long hair. And she ran in frunt of me, and I thouth she was my sister and I pulled her hair. and she stared crring and told her mom that I pulld her hair and I ran away so her mom coulded see me. I was so embarassed

A fourth grader ending a narrative by expressing feelings.

- Summary statements:

  To survive, they must..., ..., and...

  And they all...

  No matter how you look at it...

  For more details about...

As a result of analyzing examples from published text, young writers

- become aware of different kinds of beginnings and endings.

- have a resource list of beginning sentences and endings and can substitute their own information, names, places and times.

- are encouraged to read as writers, studying the form and style of professional writers.

Expanding and Developing ideas

The following lessons and techniques will help young writers expand and develop their ideas. Lessons should be short—fifteen minutes or less. They should be responsive to writers' needs and include models and the invitation to try the topic skill. They should be repeated several times.

What Works

1. **Prove It!** Prove It! is a technique to help young writers expand ideas. It is particularly useful in expository writing. Begin by writing a few simple declarative sentences on the board or chart paper. Sentences contributed by the class are best.

    I am good at art.

    The cafeteria food is not good.

    Whales are mammals.

    Read them to the class and after each one say, "Prove It!" (Take a hands on hips, playground challenge stance.) Ask the writers to come up with proof of the statement.

    I am good at art. (Prove It!)

    Add: I can draw people running and animals too. Kids ask me to illustrate their books.

    Whales are mammals. (Prove It!)

    Add: They have live young and nurse them. They breathe with lungs.

    After several examples, have the writers search for a simple statement in one of their own expository pieces. Ask them if they can add something that will prove it. Invite several writers to read theirs and share their proofs.

    In the next Author's Chair, ask the audience to listen for the proofs and acknowledge them by compliment. Young writers can begin to listen for sentences that cry out for Prove Its and give stickers to authors reminding them where they need one (See also Chapter VI, Revision.)

2. **Don't Hit Your Reader over the Head.** One of the joys of reading is figuring things out for yourself, using the author's clues. One of the joys of writing is providing those clues. Show young writers how to do this. Share with them the concept of not hitting your reader over the head with information.

    a) Write the following on the board or overhead projector. I went to a party. It was fun.

Read it with the students. Orally and physically punctuate the second sentence with a BOING!, tapping yourself on the top of your head. Invite them to mimic the gesture. Ask them if the sentence 'It was fun' is challenging or exciting. This is hitting your reader over the head. The reader has no fun figuring out if, or why, the party was fun.

    b) Erase or cross out 'It was fun.' Ask the students to provide information about a party that was fun. Write them after the first sentence. Example:

> I went to a party. We played games in the pool, ate cake, and everyone got a present. Cathy let us all ride her pony and no one fell off.

    c) Invite the students to try this technique with the sentences: 'I have a dog. He is mean.' Ask the students to say, BOING! and tap themselves on the head when they read, 'He is mean.' Revisions might look like this (See student sample).

A third grader trying out Don't Hit Reader Over the Head; a practice write.

Invite students to share new sentences that give their readers the joy and satisfaction of figuring things out for themselves.

    d) Ask young writers to look for adjectives such as *nice, fun, mean, pretty, cold,* etc. in their own work. Ask them to listen in peer conferences for places one of their peer authors might have hit his reader over the head.

3. **Just Like Me.** Another joy of reading includes the feeling of recognition and familiarity that writers generate. "This character is just like me! I feel that way too." "That's what I do! I eat Cheerios, too." Young authors need to consider their audience and describe characters, events, or set forth opinions that will cause a 'Just like me!' reaction in their readers. That means they must be specific in their descriptions.

> Note - The advice 'Show, Don't Tell,' frequently used to address this same issue, often leads young writers to illustrate. They interpret it literally. To them, 'show' means draw a picture and 'tell' means write.

Specific nouns are one way to achieve this. Read children's literature that demonstrates this technique and point it out to young writers. Have them respond to a book, focusing on finding the instances where they could say, 'That's just like me.'

At Author's Chair or in peer conferences they might ask, "What did the character wear, jeans or shorts?" "Which rides did they go on at Disneyland?"

The addition of specific nouns helps a reader identify with the writer.

No Copying Drafts

The single best way to turn kids off to writing is to ask them to copy over multiple drafts of their manuscripts. No, I take that back. The very best way to turn kids off to writing is assigning it for punishment. Copying multiple drafts is the second best way.

If young writers skip lines and use one side of their papers, they will have plenty of space to revise and edit their original draft. In an active writing process classroom, young writers will usually write with a semblance of neatness because they want other writers to read their manuscripts. Only a small percentage of rough drafts need be published, and thus recopied. Keep copying to a minimum — divorced from publishing, it is non-productive.

The rough draft, clipped together with the planning sheet, is an excellent record of a writer's passage through the writing process. It can be used in parent conferences and should be saved in the student's writing portfolio with a Xerox copy of the published version.

When young writers generate their work on a computer, they should print out the first draft and some subsequent revisions. They might need these to demonstrate their use of the entire writing process— responders comments, revisions addressed to those comments, reorganization, and so on (See also Chapter VIII, Publishing).

Summary

Young writers need to know that their drafts are just one step in the process of gathering and presenting their thoughts about a given topic. A rough draft represents a starting place. If it is constructed as a document with lots of room to add and move text, then the successive stages of response, revision, editing, and publishing will be much easier.

Chapter V

Response

Response to a first draft is the most important part of the writing process for young and developing writers. Through feedback from potential readers, young writers discover how well they have communicated their ideas and whether their readers seek more information or clarification. Response engenders revision and a sense of authorship.

Besides generating the impetus for revision, response mechanisms provide an opportunity to integrate the four language arts: reading, writing, talking, and listening. Children need such opportunities both inside and outside the classroom.

Do not be concerned with the amount of revision generated by students' comments and questions. The objective of this writing process stage is for young writers to understand that a piece of writing is not finished at the end of drafting and that all good writing takes revision and reworking. This realization and the willingness of writers to consider their audience in written communication are two of the primary goals of a developing writers' program.

The response mechanisms and practices described in this chapter will help you achieve these goals. This chapter covers

- Author's Chair
- Peer Conferences
- Homework Response
- Self Response
- Individual Student-teacher Conferences.

After experimenting with the array presented, decide which ones work best for your class. Create others.

Author's Chair

Author's Chair is an excellent writing workshop response mechanism. Although it may be used to share an entire manuscript, it is best utilized to share a portion that is particularly well written or has a problem. If modeled and conducted correctly, it will foster a sense of ownership and authorship in writers and a sense of a community in the classroom.

If, however, you do not take the time to model the procedure — especially the language of compliments, comments, and questions — or, if you fail to keep adequate records and ensure all children's involvement, Author's Chair can be a waste of time and may cause more harm than good.

Audience response largely determines the effectiveness of Author's Chair. Proper responses will spur writers to revise in response to classmates' concerns. Improper responses will cause writers to cease writing and sharing.

What Works

The following are two models for conducting a positive and efficient Author's Chair. Both require the following:

- A comfortable chair labeled "Author's Chair."
- Two volunteer writers, each with a rough draft they have practiced reading.
- A clipboard with a class list, Commitment Statement **(Reproducible #1)**, or a blank paper for your record keeping.
- Designated class seating in front of the chair. Some elementary school teachers mark off seating arcs with masking tape or place stickers on the floor for each child's place. In older groups, the Author's Chair is placed so that all students at their desks can hear the writer.
- A microphone and amplication system is optional, but desirable. Portable cassette tape players often have a microphone input.
- Estimated time for each of the following models is 30 minutes. Repeat several times in the first half of the year.

1. **Compliments.**

   a) Introduce Author's Chair to your writers by explaining that authors need to learn what potential readers think of their writing, what they might not understand, and what comments and questions they may have about the piece. Tell how you ask a colleague to respond to your rough drafts of letters to parents, presentations you may make at meetings, or reports to the principal.

   b) Explain how Author's Chair will work in this class. Start with the students practicing how to take their places. Help the class work out a quick and quiet procedure to form the audience for Author's Chair. Model acceptable noise levels, order of seating, seating posture, what they will bring. Ask two students to list and chart the steps for the assembling procedure.

   c) Ask the first volunteer to sit in the special chair. Sit off to the side, slightly behind the writer.

   d) Explain to the audience that the writer will read x amount of his manuscript.

   - A manuscript of less than two pages of skipped lines — Read entire manuscript.
   - A manuscript of more than two pages of skipped lines — Read two pages of the writer's choice.

- A selected portion, not more than two pages of skipped lines, for which the writer seeks readers' responses or help.

Explain that the audience will listen to the piece and prepare to tell what is was about, to react to the content, or to give a compliment about a specific part of the piece.

e) Direct the writer to read his piece slowly and in a loud voice. Encourage soft-voiced writers to 'Use your playground voice, please.' If students cannot hear the writer, Author's Chair is useless. Some teachers use a microphone system, which the children love. Others conduct a limited Author's Chair for one half the class while the rest of the class writes.

f) Do not read the piece for the writer. If a writer is not ready to read in front of his classmates, do not call on him to volunteer. Some writers may take several months before they feel confident enough to share. Once they see that Author's Chair is non-threatening, most writers will readily volunteer.

g) When the writer has finished reading his piece and, perhaps, showing its pictures, ask the students to raise their hand for the author to call on them to react to the piece. Remind them they can tell what they heard it was about or give a compliment about the part they liked the best.

h) Typical first reactions are general and do not reflect any listener engagement with the piece. Such comments are not useful to the writer.

- I liked it.
- It was good.
- That was good writing.
- It's about your dog.

Invite the responders to pick out exactly what they liked. Give an example yourself.

- I liked it when you said crashed and smashed. They were great action words.
- You made it seem really scary.
- I liked it when you said the dog was as big as a pony.
- I like the part where you said pounced.
- I have a cat, too. And he looks like yours!
- I could really picture it when you told all about the touchdown.

Compliments validate a student's work and himself. The ability of students to compliment each other's work and to celebrate each other's accomplishments are very important aspects of a writing community.

i) When a young student gives a specific compliment, write it on your clipboard along with the responder's name. Tell the class what you are doing, thereby letting them know that you think their response is important.

j) Thank the writer and call for the second volunteer.

k) Repeat the directions and the procedure. Help the students with reactions and compliments by modeling more yourself.

l) Ask the two volunteer writers how they felt in Author's Chair.

m) Read back the effective compliments you entered on your clipboard. Tell the class they will be building a bank of these compliments to post in the room for all to see. They can copy the ones they like on a card and bring them to the next Author's Chair.

n) Keep the first model of Author's Chair simple and limited to compliments only. The main goal of this model it to achieve specificity of compliments. If the student writers have had prior experience with Author's Chair, direct their compliments to specific skills that they have been studying. For example, "I like the way you used a simile to compare the boat to a sofa."

2. **Comments and Questions.**

a) Call the class together for another modeling of Author's Chair. Follow the assembling procedure. Explain to the class that in this session they are going to work on a Compliment Sandwich. They will not only give the author a compliment, but they will have the opportunity to make a comment or a suggestion or to ask a question about the author's writing. When they have done so, you or another student will give a final compliment, usually skill based, to complete the "sandwich."

Pam Willingham's fourth graders at Palmetto Elementary, Palmetto, Florida painted slices of bread and bologna on oak tag cards and laminated them. They raised these during Author's Chair when they had either a compliment (bread) or a comment or question (bologna).

> This is another example of a using concrete items in a writing process activity. Use of such materials and examples is a very important principle governing the instruction of elementary children. Look for ways to use this principle.

b) During Author's Chair coach the class in the language of comments and questions. Introduce comments and questions with:

- I wondered if...
- I understand the part about... but I can't figure out...
- Could you tell me more about...?
- It seems there are a lot of...
- Did you mean to...?
- I can't picture the part...

Avoid such comments as:

- You should...
- You didn't...
- You forgot...

After the model, post a chart of this language for the students to make cue cards. They will utilize them in peer conferences as well (See Peer Conferences in this chapter).

c) Do not allow a verbal attack on the writer in Author's Chair. If the writer becomes defensive, stop the comments and questions. At the conclusion of Author's Chair, remind students that the writer is the boss of his writing and may respond by revising or ignoring the other writers' comments and questions.

d) Record useful compliments, comments, and questions with the responders' names.

e) Ask older students to write questions they would like their audience to ask them when they present a manuscript. With younger writers, do this in a group discussion. Make a copy of the comments and questions for each student to keep in his writer's notebook.

An effective Author's Chair yields many positive results.

- Young writers know that you value what they have to say.
- Writers have an opportunity to hear their own work.
- Writers find mistakes on their own when they hear themselves read their manuscripts.
- The class knows what everyone else is writing.
- Students practice attentive listening.
- Students have an opportunity to frame and ask questions.
- The student audience hears compliments and comments and might see how they apply to their own writing.
- You have the opportunity to give brief, on-the-spot lessons.
- You hear the application of skills you have been teaching. Record instances of writer's achievements in your anecdotal notes for grading and conferencing.

Peer Conferences

In kindergarten and first grade you can use Author's Chair frequently for sharing and responses. In subsequent grades, as the length of children's manuscripts grows, Author's Chair becomes an inefficient means for sharing and response. It takes too long to cycle all your writers through Author's Chair, and the attention span of your class may not allow children to read their entire piece. For second grade through college, Author's Chair is used primarily for modeling specific skills, problem solving, and special sharing.

Peer conferencing replaces Author's Chair as the primary response mechanism for developing writers. As with Author's chair, you must model peer conferences if you want them to work. Peer partners must know exactly what their jobs are and exactly what the purpose of the conference is. The most efficient peer conferences involve a narrow focus or a single, specific task.

The first peer conferences for young writers who have no prior training in writing process classroom procedures should be limited to identifying the application of a target skill and complimenting the author on its use. As students become adept at this form of response, develop this response mechanism to include questions and comments that cover a larger range of writing considerations.

Do not expect young writers to critique and correct their peers' manuscripts for all the composing, organization, and mechanical components of good writing. Do, however, show them how to help each other expand, clarify, and refine their peers' manuscripts through compliments, comments, and questions.

As with all writing workshop procedures, use these models early in the year. Although they take time, they will pave the way for more productive writing sessions in the rest of the year.

What Works

1. **Listen To This.** Encourage young writers to stop periodically and read what they have written to their partners. In first and second grade classes, reserve the last five minutes of the writing workshop session for writers to read their piece to a partner before putting it away.

2. **Knee to Knee.** Developing writers should be introduced to peer conferencing, called Knee to Knee, as early as first grade. *Carol Collins, Palmetto Elementary, Palmetto, Florida,* developed Knee to Knee for her first graders as a variation on a model for older students that I presented in a staff development inservice workshop. She introduces the activity to her first graders when most of them can read back what they wrote the day before. Her students regularly write in spiral bound journal notebooks. In a week of writing workshop, the class will do one or two Knee to Knee peer conferences.

In Knee to Knee, two students move their chairs to face each other and sit with knees almost touching. They take turns reading their journal entries to each other. The listener watches the reader's mouth and, when he finishes, tells him, "I heard your piece was about ..." Collins models this with two students in front of the class. To start, peer pairs are students sitting in adjacent desks. As they become proficient with Knee to Knee, the children begin to select particular partners and may sit together anywhere in the room.

The class adds to this model throughout the year. Collins models every new step in the progression. When the students have mastered the first response, she introduces the next one. Here are the steps.

a) First response: Responder says, "I heard your piece was about..."

b) Add to the first response: Responder reacts to the content, "I have a dog too!" "That sounds like my mom." "That's funny!"

c) Add to the two responses: Responder gives a compliment—These become more sophisticated and specific as the children's knowledge progresses.

Early compliments you may hear:

I like your drawing.

I liked the funny part.

I like it.

I like your words.

Later compliments:

> I like the way you had action in your story.
>
> You have good finger spaces.
>
> I like the way you told about your dog's fur.
>
> I like how you put number words in your story.

    d) Add to the three responses: Responder asks for more information. The writer can ask his peer partner, "What else would you like to know?" or, "Can you picture this?"

The children in Carol Collins' class brainstorm lists of specific compliments and useful questions. These are placed on charts accessible to the students during writing.

> Model hint — Invite your young writers to chorus each of the responses and authors' questions during the modeling.

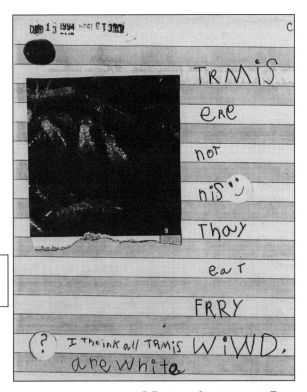

A first grader was complimented on the word *nice* and asked for more information.

3. **Peer Conference Simulation For Target Skills.**
Recognizing and identifying a single and specific writing element in another writer's work is a good starting place to model peer conferencing. It is a well defined task at which young writers can succeed. In later models, more complex elements, such as organization, clarity, development of ideas, and maintaining focus, can be considered. (See Chapter VI, Revision, Remembering Responses.)

When establishing partnerships for peer conferences, set the stage for the children to accept any fellow writer as a partner. Point out that while a best friend might give you a great response, telling you how much he likes your story (That's what best friends are for!), another writer may give you useful responses that will help you improve your story. As young writers conference with different partners, they will find the classmates who are the best responders for them. They will find other writers who excel in different aspects of the writing craft and who make excellent comments and ask productive questions.

Side by side conferences work best at the start of the year, requiring a minimum of movement and causing a minimum of interruption to surrounding writers. Later you may find, as *Beth Severson, grade 3, Palmetto Elementary, Palmetto, Florida,* did, that when writers conference for clarity and sense, they tend to sit facing each other and, if they are looking for specifics or editing, they tend to sit side-by-side. Severson says she can tell what kind of a conference two students are having by their seating arrangement and where they are in her room — on the rug or at a table.

The following simulation demonstrates effective peer conferencing. It requires approximately 30 minutes.

Requirements:

-     Two students with rough drafts you have read that exhibit the application of a skill currently under study or a need for that skill. These might include descriptive words, cohesive paragraphs, use of a literary device, variation in sentence length, development in terms of who, what, where, how, and why. Write these skills down to help you guide the volunteer writers through the peer conference.

- Sets of 3/4-inch round white labels or small Post-it notes.
- Two chairs or desks arranged for the students to face each other.
- A charted list of skills under study or personal lists from writers' notebooks or folders.

Procedure:

a) Advise the class that this model will be a peer conference simulation (an acting out of a peer conference). After the conference, each writer will have a specific response to consider for improving his piece. Remind the class of a composing skill they have been studying. Write it on the board. Tell them the conference will focus on this skill. Remind them that, as in Author's Chair, reacting to the content and giving compliments comes before comment or question. The conference simulation will be open to coaching from the teacher and to comments or questions from all writers in the class.

b) Position the two volunteer writers so that the entire class can see the demonstration. If your class is large, do this demonstration for half the class and repeat it the next day using a different peer partnership.

c) Tell the first writer to read his manuscript slowly and with feeling. The writer must stop after one page and ask, "How does it sound so far?" or, "Do you understand it?" The responder must react with a compliment or say that he understands the piece to be about such and such. It is important that the responder be able to summarize what he has heard so far. The writer then finishes the piece or the two pages allotted and asks, "What part do you like?" and "Do you think I have used the target skill?" The responder must react to the piece, give a compliment, make a comment, or ask a question.

d) Have them begin. Remind the audience that they may help out by thinking of specific compliments or questions relating to the use of the target skill.

e) Remind the writer to ask the responder, "Do you have a comment or question? Do you think I used the target skill?" Ask the responder for a comment or question. Direct him to write a key word on the sticker and give it to the writer to place on the manuscript at the relevant word or sentence. Here's an example.

Writer: "The dog was loud. He barked all night. The neighbors were mad."

Responder: "In the part about the dog barking, all the sentences were short and sounded the same. Do you think you could make one of them longer?' (Responder gives writer a sticker with the words *"longer sent"* on it.)

f) Have the writer ask the audience if they have a comment or question. Hear one or two. Ask anyone else who has a comment or question to write it on a sticker and give it to the author after the conference. Refer to your notes about the piece and make a comment or ask a question yourself. Give the author a sticker with a key word on it.

g) Remind the writer that he is to consider the comments and questions and make a decision whether to address them, adding or changing the writing, or to ignore them. He is in control of his writing. Remind him that potential readers of his work might have similar questions.

h) Repeat the procedure with the pair exchanging roles.

i) Ask the two volunteers to put their initials and PC (for peer conference) at the top of each other's manuscript. Ask the volunteers how they felt about the conference. Remind the class that their conferences should always proceed from noting the parts well done to considering a target skill.

Results of peer conferences that focus on a target skill:

- Conferences are short, to the point, and productive.
- Writers are encouraged to make specific revisions in response to the sticker comments and question.

4. **Peer Conference For Clarity and Information.** Conduct a class brainstorming session to generate a list of purposes for a conference.

Example of a list from a third grade class in a Florida elementary school.

- To see if it makes sense
- To know if I gave enough information
- To see if the reader can picture it
- To see if I told enough about the main thing
- To see if I use a simile
- To see if I wandered off the topic
- To see if I have any left field sentences.

Some of the reasons for a conference have to do with clarity and interest.

a) Model a peer conference similar to the Target Skill conference. In this model instruct the authors to ask:

- Does it make sense?
- Is there anything you don't understand?
- Is the sequence clear?
- Can you follow it?
- Is there anything else you would like me to tell about...?
- Can you picture this?

b) Help them by aiming your comments and questions at the development of ideas. "What exactly was happening when...?" or, "I can't quite follow how such and such happened. Where was all this?"

c) Following the model, invite the whole class to meet in prearranged partnerships for a similar conference. Ask them to note any good questions and comments they received.

d) In 15 minutes reassemble and share some of the useful or interesting comments and questions writers received. Make a list of them to give writers for their notebooks. They can use these as cue cards in their next conferences.

Some results of modeling a peer conference.

- Writers understand what they are suppose to do in a peer conference and that they do not have to critique and correct each other's paper.

- Students acquire a supply of basic compliments, comments, and questions to use in their first conferences.

5. **Peer Recording Partners.**

Camilla Nicholas, Miller Elementary, Bradenton, Florida, encourages her second grade writers to help each other read their stories into a tape recorder. Working in pairs, one acts as a technical advisor, working the recorder and providing sound effects, while the other reads. The team works this out beforehand, the advisor and writer deciding what effects to use and when. They revise as they play back what they have recorded, deleting and redoing portions as they work. The finished tape is moved to a class listening center for children to use independently.

This activity approximates what is happening when writers compose, read back what they have written, and revise as they go.

6. **Response Requirement.** Require a minimum of one or two responses for each piece a writer takes through the process to publication (presentation). One of the responses may be a Homework Response (see details later in this chapter). Responders may be a classmate, a group of peers, an adult, or a younger listener. A responder must initial the manuscript and write a comment or question on a sticker, in the margin, on the back, or on an accompanying response form.

A second grader received questions in Author's Chair.

7. **Peer Response Form.** Some young writers clip a peer response form to their manuscripts and pass them to several peer partners. Each peer responder enters his name and comments or questions on the sheet. The comments and questions must be specific. The writer considers all the responses and revises as he sees fit. Before he meets with the teacher for a conference, he indicates on his manuscript where he has addressed the responders' concerns.

8. **Peer Recommendations.**

After *Miriam Pante's third grade writers at Abel Elementary, Bradenton, Florida,* peer conference, they often recommend to her that the class listen to a piece they heard. They tell who the author is and what they think that author did especially well. She invites the author to read the piece, or the referenced part of it, to the class.

This not only serves to compliment and encourage an author, but it reviews a skill for the class and gives them a model of its application. This is the writing community at work.

Homework Response

Homework Response is another way of providing a response mechanism for young writers. In a community of prolific writers, it frees classroom time for minilessons, drafting, research, conferencing, editing, and publishing. Homework response should be modeled before it is utilized.

In Homework Response, the writer takes his rough draft home and uses an adult responder. Homework Response is not for the purpose of editing a child's work.

Beth Severson, Palmetto Elementary, Palmetto, Florida, designed Homework Response to give her third and fourth graders an additional constructive response mechanism. At the start of the year, and several times during the year, she reminds parents by letter of the intent of the activity as well as the role they play in their child's writing development.

The Homework Response model takes an estimated 15 minutes.

Requirements:

- A volunteer writer with a rough draft.
- A volunteer to play the role of parent, brother, grandmother or baby-sitter, etc.
- A Homework Response format and the form to attach to manuscript is provided in **Reproducible #12**.

a) The writer asks the student acting as responder to please listen to his manuscript. He tells the responder that he, the writer, must hold the paper and read it to the responder. He gives the responder the Homework Response form. He advises the responder to listen for what he has done well and what he has done in regard to one or two target skills. The writer explains the target skills. He reads the manuscript.

b) The responder gives compliments, makes comments, and asks questions. The class can help out in this model as they do in a peer conferencing simulation. The writers should anticipate that their grownup responders may not know how to compliment, comment, or question effectively. They may have to coach them.

c) The writer enters the compliments on the form, the back of his paper or, in case a writer forgets to take home a form, even on a paper bag.

d) The responder initials it. The writer thanks the responder.

Some results of homework response

- Young writers reinforce their understanding of the target skills by explaining them to their home responders.
- Responders at home learn about writing and the writing process.
- Responders are encouraged to focus on the organizational and composing skills under study and help the young writers apply them.

Self Response

It is very difficult to find inconsistencies, disorganization, or lapses in logic in our own writing. We know what we want to say and can't always see when we have failed to communicate our ideas clearly. The more times we read our piece over, and the longer we wait between readings, the more chance we have of recognizing our mistakes. The best way to help young writers develop the ability to read their pieces critically and to self-correct is to ensure that they read or hear their manuscripts frequently.

What Works

1. **What Did I Say.** Encourage writers to stop periodically during composing and quietly read aloud to themselves what they have written so far. Model this in your own writing. Write, read over, write, read over, modify, write, read over. Every time a writer hears what he has said he has the opportunity to clarify or enlarge upon it.

2. **Recordings.** Provide each student with a blank tape at the start of the year. Show the students how to use the class tape recorder. Have them select their best piece and practice reading it to a peer. Schedule time for them to record the piece on their own tape. Require a number of entries for the year. Place them in the student's portfolio.

Make these tapes available for parent conferences, perhaps setting up a listening station in the hall where parents waiting for conferences can listen to their child's tape.

3. **Give Yourself a Sticker.** After some successful peer conferences, young writers should be encouraged to give themselves stickers both for compliments and to reward the ability to anticipate a reader's question. In a group setting or an individual conference, show young writers how to ask themselves questions about information, organization, and details. Have them pretend they are the reader and listen while you read their piece. This is the first step in the direction of independent revision.

Individual Student-teacher Conferences

Young writers seek conferences with their teacher in the writing process. Class size and time constraints discourage many teachers as they contemplate using this response mechanism. Though it may not be possible to conference for ten minutes with each of your young writers on each of their manuscripts, it is possible, and important, to respond to all your writers and to provide continual encouragement and guidance. A number of considerations and techniques are available to help you accomplish this.

What constitutes a writer-teacher conference? Think of a writer-teacher conference as any one-on-one exchange between a writer and the teacher. Consider the following as conference opportunities for your class of writers.

- Taking Commitment Statements or the Class Status.

- Author's Chair.

- Roving conferences.

- Group lessons and conferences.

- Short prepared conferences with individual writers.

- Comments made to a writer on the playground, in the hall, or in passing.

What is the primary objective of a Writer-Teacher Conference? Think of a writing conference as a time to leam what the student is writing about, to react to his content, and to encourage him with a compliment, comment, question, or guidance. With practice, this can take very little time.

You should not anticipate a conference as an opportunity to locate and correct all the mistakes a writer has made. Most children's writing should be viewed as practice, not as a finished product. As is true for any skill or craft, writers have to write badly before they write well. By focusing on the things a writer has done well, you encourage him to write again.

What Works

1. **Some Positive Things to Do or Say.** Receive the content, tell it back, enjoy it, relate to it. These phrases and sentences help.

I like the way you have...

I can really picture ....

How did you learn that?

I do the same thing...

What happened? Did you put it down that way?

What do you want your reader to know?

How did you select this topic?

I see you have included the content words of this topic.

I wish you would explain this further.

2. **Some Things Not to Do or Say.**

- Try not to get more information by asking leading questions. (This may be the most difficult challenge you face in conferencing with young writers.)

- Don't take control of the piece by interjecting your ideas or by soliciting information that takes the piece in a direction you think it should go.

- Avoid: "I think you should"... "Don't you want to tell..?" "Here's a place you could..."

3. **Cue Cards.** Prepare a set of cue cards for your first conferences. On them, write the comments and questions you intend to ask writers. Some comments and questions may be suitable for a specific genre, others may be general. As you become facile with conferences, you will dispense with the cue card and

rely on your knowledge of your students and their writing to guide the conference. (See sample cue card, **Reproducible #13.**)

4. **The Commitment Statement.** The Commitment Statement is a classroom management practice that helps keep students on task, allows all writers to know the status of the writing community in terms of topics, titles, genre, and writing process stage, and acts as a brief individual conference. It is a record keeping device as well.

Commitment Statements are taken at the start of a writing session or during any part of the day when all the students are present. The first two or three Commitment Statements need to be modeled. The first one will take up to 30 minutes. With practice, you and your students should be able to do it in 15 minutes.

Commitment Statement Model—Estimated time for first model, 20 minutes. You might want to do just half the class one day and finish the next day. Repeat the model after a week.

Procedure:

a) Explain to the class that Commitment Statement is used to keep track of where writers are in the writing process. In addition, writers seeking help through peer conferences can be paired. Commitment Statement helps everyone learn what topics writers are using. Other writers may be able to supply information, make suggestions, or want to hear the piece.

At the start of Commitment Statement, everyone should be working independently. If writers are waiting for a peer conference, they can read over their manuscript in preparation for the conference and to determine the areas in which they are seeking help.

b) Tell the students when their name is called they must be prepared to tell you:

- the name or topic of their piece.
- its genre.
- what stage they are in.
- if they need a conference.

They will need to be ready to answer questions concerning:

- the target skill(s) they have selected for that piece
- what they plan to accomplish that day.

c) Call the name of a student. Other writers may listen to the Commitment Statement or commence writing tasks that do not require interaction with another student. For example, they might read their manuscripts, continue a draft, look up information in a book, illustrate, or work on revisions,

d) The student called announces the topic, title (if available) of his work in progress, and where he is in the stage of the writing process. Ask him about the target skills for the piece, and what he intends to accomplish today. This is the public announcement of commitment. It acts to keep many children on task.

e) The student may request a peer or teacher-writer conference. Instruct the writer to join up with the next person to announce need of a peer conference. Tell the two writers that they may move to the place of their conference but may not begin to talk until the Commitment Statement is over. They should use the quiet time to read their own and their partner's manuscript in preparation for the conference.

f) Ask if the student called needs help. If help is required, arrange or schedule it. The help might come from a peer, by invitation to a group lesson, or by the promise of a quick conference with you after the Commitment Statement.

g) Instruct writers to resume the work to which they committed after they give their statement.

Once young writers know the procedure, taking Commitment Statements for a class of 25-30 writers should take about 15-20 minutes.

A useful record keeping device is a loose leaf notebook with a Commitment Statement sheet for each student. Records of time spent per piece, topics chosen, skills under study, and the level of understanding of the writing process help you in evaluating progress of writers and in parent conferences. A sample Commitment Statement Record Sheet is provided in **Reproducible #1.**

Some teachers have students keep a Commitment Statement of their own. They are simplified versions of the teacher's records. They list the titles of pieces, the date, and what the young writer plans to do that day. They are displayed on the student's desk during writing workshop and are stored in the writer's notebook.

On the days you do not take a Commitment Statement, young writers fill their own out. As you move about the room, you can see what each student has planned, where they are in the process, and remind them of their tasks if necessary.

5. **Roving Conferences.** Roving conferences are short exchanges in which the young writer may ask for immediate help or discuss something with the teacher. Like all other conferences, they need to be modeled and practiced so that students and teachers know how to use them efficiently. The first ones may be awkward for both teacher and writer. Ultimately they will be useful for quick lessons and problem solving. Take the risk; that's what learning is all about.

Roving Conference Model — Estimated time, 20 minutes. Repeat model one or two times in first half of the year.

Requirements:
- Class list
- Cue Card for the conference (**Reproducible #13**).
- Writers working on manuscripts with their writers' notebooks on hand.

Procedure:
a) Explain to the class that you are going to be conferencing with as many writers as possible on some days of writing workshop. In the roving conferences, you will be finding out how they are doing and if they

need help. It will not be a time for them to ask you to hear their entire manuscript. Tell them they must know what to say when you get to their desk to speed the process.

b) Explain that you will demonstrate a roving conference.

Here are the things they must be prepared to say.

- "I'm writing about..." (name the topic)
- "It's narrative, expository, poetry, fiction, a report, a play," i.e., name the style or genre.
- "I'm in the (   ) stage." (Planning, drafting, revising, editing, publishing)
- "I need help here." Name the specific place.

Here are the things you will say and do.

- React to the text and author's knowledge.
- Compliment: "I like the way..." "I noticed you..."
- Ask: "What are you trying to do in this piece?"

   "What do you want your reader to learn?"

   "What writing skill are you working on in this piece?"
- Help: "Do you need any?" Provide a resource if needed: another writer, a book, a library pass, information in their writers' note book, charts in room.

c) Ask for a volunteer for the first model roving conference. Tell the class that you will keep track of the writers to whom you talked, how they are progressing in the writing process with their current piece, and how they are doing using the particular skills they have been studying. Tell them that both you and they may not be good at this procedure at first, but that, with practice, everyone will get better at it. You will then be able to conference with more writers each session.

d) Conduct two conferences with the class listening. Coach each writer and yourself through the conference.

e) Tell the students to commence writing and conduct a few more conferences while they work.

f) For each student conference, record writer's name, topic, genre, stage, and skill use. Time each conference. As you and the writers gain experience, the effectiveness of the conferences will increase and times will decrease. Eventually a set of five to six Roving Conferences should require about 15-20 minutes.

6. **Group Lessons.** Many of the skills you teach are best presented to a group of students who share a particular need for that skill. You will have discovered that need by reading their manuscripts. The students should bring the manuscript with them to group lessons. You can introduce the lesson by saying, "I noticed reading over your manuscripts that you are having trouble with ..."or, "I see several of you have done such and such...and I wondered if we could show Mike and Ann, who wrote similar pieces, how to do that, too."

After a brief lesson, using literature for example or following a demonstration and a quick practice write, talk to the writers about their manuscripts and how they might incorporate the skill into their work. Your notes from a prior reading of their writing and diagnosing their need will help you direct them to the places in their manuscripts where the skill applies.

The lesson is for writers who are ready for the subject element or skill and are already trying to use it. The lesson is a conference as well. It is a one-on-one exchange with a writer about his work. Group lessons should not exceed 15-20 minutes.

7. **Group Conferences with the Teacher.** You might need to meet with a small group of writers who are not having success with peer conferencing. Schedule a meeting with no more than five of these writers. Ask them to come prepared, having read over their respective manuscripts. Conduct a peer conference with group members acting as responders for one writer. Guide them to ask the kind of questions and make the kind of comments that are useful to an author. Keep the focus limited to one target skill. Ask them to use the class cue cards of comments and questions.

Group Conference Model — Estimated time, 25 minutes.

Requirements:
- 4-6 writers with a common problem or goal.
- Table situated where you can see the rest of class.
- Record keeping device.

Procedure:
a) Explain to the class that you will be modeling a group conference. As in roving conferences, the writers must be prepared to discuss their writing. In the group conference, students will be called upon to help each other. Writers may leave the group as their problem is solved if the conference purpose is problem solving. You might leave the group once they are helping each other or are practice writing.

b) Later, when you conduct group conferences, invite writers to eavesdrop on conferences to review or preview some aspect of the writing process and craft that interests them.

c) The most common group conference is one for children who can't get started. Ask them to look at their personal inventory. Or, ask them to make a short list of things they know how to do, or things they like to do. Have them share their lists with each other. Share your list with them. Interview them in terms of their personal interests. Encourage them to tell about their favorite activities. As writers get ideas, they may leave to begin writing.

8. **Short Individual Conferences.** Formal teacher-student conferences can come at any stage of the writing process. They remain important response mechanisms in a writing class. They must be modeled, and both participants must be prepared to conduct the conference in an efficient and productive manner. They should be short, no more than 7-8 minutes. They should be scheduled. (Melissa Odom Forney, author and teacher, makes out small

appointment cards—like a dentist's—for her students' conferences. This is an example of another concrete mechanism to use with young writers.)

The writer's responsibilities are to:

- Give the teacher time to read your manuscript prior to the conference. This might be overnight.
- Attach a note telling the teacher on what the conference will focus: problems, confirmation, or what to do next.
- Be prepared to tell the teacher what you are trying to accomplish in this piece of writing.
- Be able to cite skills you have tried to incorporate in the piece.
- Be able to read the manuscript smoothly.

The teacher's responsibilities are to:

- Read the manuscript prior to the conference. Consider the focus requested by the writer.
- Prepare a response to that focus.
- Prepare a comment about the content.
- Note achievement and prepare to compliment the writer. Record anecdotal notes about growth and achievement on the student's Commitment Statement sheet.
- Select one major area of need in organization or composing skills to address in the conference.
- Select one editing area (punctuation, capitalization, spelling) to address in the conference.

Individual Conference Model—Estimated time, 10-15 minutes. Repeat the model several times during the year.

Requirements:

- A volunteer who will conference with you in front of the entire class.
- Volunteer's manuscript.
- Blank stickers.
- Record keeping device—The back of your Commitment Statement record sheet for that writer works well.
- A student volunteer timer and a clock or stop watch.

Procedure:

a) Sit next to the writer facing the class so you both can see the manuscript. Do not write on the manuscript. Attach stick-on notes for comments and questions.

b) Ask the student timer to start the clock and announce every two minutes of elapsed time.

c) The writer begins the conference with the name of the piece, its topic, genre, and stage of the writing process.

d) Talk to the writer about the content, invite him to read the parts where he thinks he did a good job, and give compliments. You must make it clear that the student cannot use the conference to read the whole manuscript to you. You have read it prior to the conference and are prespared to discuss it.

e) Discuss the writer's requested conference focus area. Provide verification, information, and help.

f) Show the writer the area in which you think he needs to work. Give information and provide additional resources. Thank the writer for sharing manuscript with you.

g) Ask the student timer for the total elapsed time.

h) Review the model with the class. Analyze the process — what took the longest time, which parts were useful, how it could be improved. Let the students know that you, too, are learning how to do this effectively and efficiently.

i) Schedule conferences with some other writers. Invite the class to listen in if they like. Remind the students of the time constraints.

Conferences should offer a writer encouragement and a reaction to the content and presentation of the piece. They should be an opportunity for clarification, elaboration, and help within those areas.

The most difficult thing in conferencing is curbing the temptation to correct all the things you see wrong with the student's writing. You must content yourself with correcting one composing or organizational area and one cosmetic area. Attention to, and discussion of, any more can easily overwhelm and discourage a young writer. You can note and record other areas in which the writer needs help. Use this information for lesson planning.

Summary

Well conducted conferences have the following characteristics.

- Young writers have opportunities to talk about their writing.
- Writers are encouraged.
- Teachers learn more about their students.

Conferences are also an excellent opportunity to keep track of young writers' progress. Each of the conference types can provide you with one or more of the following progress indicators:

- Demonstration of organizational skills
- Demonstration of composing skills
- Demonstration of mechanical skills
- The use of the writing process
- Genre attempted
- Length of time invested per piece
- Topic selected and the reasons for selection
- Ratio of started pieces to finished pieces.

This progress information is vital to your evaluation procedures for report cards, parent conferences, and portfolios. (See also Chapter X, Evaluation and Portfolio.)

Chapter VI

Revision

Writers at every level — from beginners to professionals — need to revise their drafts to bring them to publication quality. Developing writers revise primarily to clarify and add more information. Fluent writers, streamline their writing and remove clutter.

Young writers who are new to the writing process are often reluctant to revise because they view the task in a negative way. They associate redoing something with error and failure. Ironically, this attitude may be most common among good students who have a strong drive for perfection. This chapter presents techniques that will make revision a positive experience and help young writers overcome negative associations.

Revision is what writers do to their rough drafts when they get positive responses to the questions, "Can I make this clearer?" and "Should I include more information?" As they become fluent and proficient, they will ask themselves these questions as they write.

Once a young writer has had a potential reader compliment, comment, or ask questions regarding the clarity and interest of his piece, he must reread it himself and make some decisions. Writers remain in charge of their manuscript, but they should be encouraged to consider their potential readers.

The longer the time since the rough draft was written, the easier revision will be for them. *William Forstchen, science fiction author, historian, and assistant professor of history and education at Montreat-Anderson College, North Carolina*, tells young authors that a manuscript is like road kill — the first day it doesn't smell so bad, but leave it a while and it starts to stink.

Also, revision will be easier if writers have selected their own topics and are writing from personal experience. They have thorough and personal knowledge of the subject. When they hear their manuscript, they are likely to find incongruities and inaccuracies and to self correct.

Nonetheless, revision, remains a difficult task for most young writers. To revise successfully, the author must

- remember what the responders said.
- manage the physical aspect of adding and changing text.
- know what kinds of revision are possible.

This chapter details procedures, models, materials, and lessons that will help satisfy these requirements for young writers. The section devoted to kinds of revisions contains information about composing skills and conventions of style and usage as well.

Remembering Responses

Author's Chair inherently encourages revision because potential readers compliment and ask questions of a writer. Unfortunately, young writers may forget the many good comments and questions they hear in Author's Chair before they have an opportunity to work on their manuscripts.

The following technique will help writers remember comments and questions after they have left Author's Chair or peer conference. It will help them remember where in their manuscripts peer writers asked for clarification or more information. It also will help them remember the compliments they received for their use of writing skills — new and unusual vocabulary, a literary device, a vivid verb, paragraphing, great description, complete sentences, adjectives, adverbs, series commas, dialogue, etc.

What Works

1. **Author's Chair or Peer Conference Stickers.** (Modeling time is about 25 minutes. Repeat the model again in a peer conference format.)

Requirements:
- Stickers: 3/4-inch diameter, white, die-cut self-adhesive printer labels. Cut them into blocks of ten and give a block to each writer. (Note: These labels are available through a printer supply company. Request them in your supply budget.)
- Special chair or a chair labeled "Author's Chair."
- Two or three volunteer writers with rough drafts.
- Recording sheet to note the Author's Chair session as a conference for the volunteers. The writer's Commitment Statement sheet doubles as a recording sheet for conferences. Use the back for brief comments.
- Clipboard and paper to record useful compliments and questions.

a) Ask one of the volunteer young writers to read his piece in Author's Chair and direct the other students to listen for specific elements they would like to compliment. When the author has finished, responders may give compliments (start with two). Each complimenter gives the author a sticker on which he has drawn a smiley face or star. The sticker goes on the manuscript next to the complimented element.

Compliments, as modeled in previous Author's Chairs (see Chapter V, Author's Chair, Response), are specific and always precede questions and comments. They reflect current writing interests and skills under study in the class. Examples: "I like where you told how your dog always hides." "I liked how you used alliteration when you said crept cautiously." "That was a vivid verb when you said your balloon collapsed." "Your use of metaphor draws our attention to the theme."

b) Have the author read the selection again. Direct the audience to listen for specific places where they would like more information, where they have a question or comment concerning clarity, or where they think the featured skill(s) might be applied. When they hear one, they raise their hand to ask the question or make the comment. Examples: "How did that happen?" "Why did the monster do that?" "I can't picture when..." "Have you thought of telling more about...?"

c) Ask responders to write one or two key words summarizing their comments or questions on a sticker. Give it to the writer who places it on the manuscript precisely where the comment or question applies. This continues until the writer has several stickers. The number of stickers awarded depends on the grade level and experience with the technique. In kindergarten and first grade, use smaller colored stickers for compliments only. The children do not write on them.

d) As the volunteer writer leaves Author's Chair, encourage him to consider the sticker questions or comments. The writer must decide whether to address the issues raised and revise by adding information, changing words, moving sentences or paragraphs. The writer makes the decision in all cases, maintaining ownership of the piece.

e) Compile a list of the most valuable compliments and useful questions you recorded and distribute it to your students. They should keep the compliments in their writer's notebooks. Young writers can select some to make cue cards to use in future Author's Chairs and peer conferences.

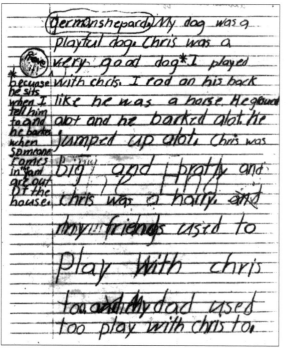

A third grader revised in response to a comment in a peer conference.

Using Author's Chair and stickers in this fashion accomplishes several things.

- Writers know exactly where and how they might revise their piece.

- Young writers' attitudes are changed. Children universally love stickers and they enjoy this Author's Chair experience. Writers who may have been reluctant to hear suggestions about their writing, may have been defensive in Author's Chair, or may have viewed revision as correcting errors, become eager to be "stickered." Revision becomes a positive exercise.

- You can locate and note where writers revise their rough drafts in response to other's comments and questions. This is useful when student writing is placed in portfolios and used for evaluation and parent conferencing

- The young writers in the audience focus on the writing and their task. They listen more carefully with the stickers in hand. They are eager to award them—even more so after they have been "stickered."

- Writers hear the application of target skills and the associated compliments. This increases their awareness and understanding of the skills and promotes the use of them in their own writing.

- Most importantly, the questions and comments writers ask of others will become the ones they ask themselves as they write. They become better writers as they internalize these concerns about clarity and information.

Managing the Manuscript

Here's the scenario. You are conferencing with young writers who show you rough drafts in desperate need of additional text to clarify or provide interest. The pages are solid text. The writers have received compliments and questions from peers, but they are frustrated and reluctant to revise. They have no space on their paper to do so. They need help managing their manuscripts.

What Works

1. **Skip Lines.** Start with the suggestions in Chapter IV, Drafting. The first thing young writers need to revise is space.

2. **Modeling Revision Strategies.** Show young writers how to add and move text. Adding and moving text within a manuscript is not an easy task nor is it an intuitive skill. Many teachers model the addition and moving of text while composing the Morning Message —a letter to the class about the day's work and special features written in their presence. If you present the model consistently in friendly letter form, young writers will have an image of that model. Learning friendly letter conventions will become a matter of practice. Use chart paper or an overhead transparency to demonstrate revision in your own writing.

   a) Adding single words, phrases, and sentences. Teach young writers to use the caret. (^) Model the use of the caret often in your board writing.

   b) Moving a single sentence. Show young writers how to move a single sentence by circling the sentence and drawing an arrow to the insertion point. A transparency master is provided to demonstrate adding a word and adding or moving a sentence. (See **Reproducible # 14**)

   c) Adding and moving large blocks of text. Introduce this strategy to students in the third and fourth grade (9-10 year olds). It needs to be modeled, as follows (20 minutes). Repeat the model several times in a year.

Requirements:

- A transparency of student writing made from **Reproducible #15**.
- Copies of the manuscript page for each student.
- Overhead projector, blank transparencies.
- Washable or erasable, colored felt transparency markers.
- Scissors, tape, crayons, colored pencils.
- 8-1/2 x 11-inch paper, cut into two-to three-inch slips.

1) Distribute copies of the sample student writing. Ask the children to read it quietly to themselves.

2) Project the transparency and ask a student to reread it aloud.

3) Ask the students if there is a place in the piece where they might ask the writer to add more information or to explain something in further detail — it will probably be at line eight of the sample manuscript (**#15**).

4) Ask the students to pretend they are the writer. Have they ever been lost at a park or seen this happen? What might they add to explain how the father found Miles?

5) Entertain a few ideas. Encourage them to put their ideas into several sentences.

6) Write some of their ideas on a clear transparency.

Examples:

- My Dad found Miles when they announced that there was a little boy named Miles at the security desk. He went to the desk and Miles was playing with three other kids.

- Miles was sitting on the edge of the water fountain waiting to be found. He was happy to see Dad.

- Dad asked the guards if they had seen Miles and they said yes.

7) Ask writers how they would add the new information to the manuscript.

- Some may want to color code the block of new text and the insertion site. Others may want to number the block of new text and the insertion site or use symbols such as triangles, stars, circles. Some may suggest writing the additional sentences in the margins and arrowing to the place they belong.

- Others may suggest cutting the manuscript and taping or pasting in the new material. (The disadvantage of this method is the page becomes longer than standard size and will need to be folded to fit in the student's writing folder).

8) Ask the young writers to add their sentences to their copy of the manuscript, using their preferred method. Provide strips, tape, and glue for those who elect to cut and paste. Using concrete and physical mechanisms is useful to the students who need to engage the tactile and visual senses in the learning process. This procedure encourages each writer to employ the mechanism of his choice for the management of his manuscript.

Invite your young writers who are at the response-revision stage to try this in their own manuscripts.

Repeat the model using a manuscript from a writer in your class.

1) Make a transparency of the volunteer writer's rough draft (with permission) Make copies for all the students.

2) Ask the author to read his piece from the overhead projection or

from the paper copy.

3) Invite the class to ask questions of the author and locate a place in the piece that may need clarification.

4) Give the author time to supply more information and to write the clarifying sentences on a new transparency or on the board.

5) Have the student demonstrate the technique he uses to add text to his manuscript.

Results of modeling

By working through this procedure with your young writers, they learn.

- that they can add as much text as they like anywhere in their manuscripts.
- that text is moveable.
- that writers use different methods to add to manuscripts.
- that drafts are working copies of their stories.

Kinds of Revision

Young writers need to see models of specific revisions. For any given writing skill, there must be opportunities for them to incorporate that skill in their writing after the fact. They need to see how they can revise first drafts in which their primary objective was to get their thoughts down quickly.

It is important to show young writers that real authors work this way. Invite an author into your class or school, and they will tell young writers that they go back to their manuscript over and over, adding, changing, crossing out, and moving words and sentences.

By your example, and through Author's Chair and peer conferences, young writers can learn how to add, change, cross out, and move words and sentences.

Additions

Adding to a piece of writing is the first revision to show young writers. Kindergarten writers can be encouraged to add to their picture stories. First graders can learn to add descriptive words, action, and feelings to their stories. The earlier we make revision an integral part of the writing process, the more facile and comfortable young writers will become with it.

Additions might be

- more coloring in the picture story.
- more elements to a picture story.
- more letters per word.
- more words per sentence.
- more sentences.
- more action in a picture story.
- feelings.
- concrete examples.

- cause and effect.
- explanations.
- specific nouns.
- proper nouns.
- descriptive words: verbs, adverbs, adjectives.
- sound effects.
- literary devices.

What Works

The estimated time of each lesson or model is approximately 15-20 minutes.

1. **Single Target Skill Additions.** In an Author's Chair or peer conference, instruct your young writers to listen specifically for the particular skill on which they have been working. They are to give compliments for the author's use of the skill and give the author a question sticker to remind him of additional application opportunities.

   a) Description. Writers have been working on expanding sentences with the use of description. Sample sticker questions: How long did you wait at the veterinarian? How deep was the wound?

   b) Specific Nouns. Writers have been working on using specific nouns. Sample sticker questions: What did the character wear, jeans or shorts? Which rides did they go on at Busch Gardens? The addition of such words helps a reader identify with the writer. The feeling of recognition—oh, I've been there, too! I eat raisins, too. I know that type—adds to the reader's enjoyment.

   c) Proper Nouns. Writers have been studying proper nouns. They can search their manuscripts for places to change a noun to a proper noun. This creates move vivid writing. Sample sticker questions: What is the name of the school you mentioned? You said the boys were eating cereal. Was it Rice Crispies?

   d) Expressing Feelings. Writers have been focusing on incorporating feelings in their pieces. Sample sticker questions: How did you feel when that happened? I would have been scared, were you? Did you cry? Was your sister mad at you? You must have been proud of that. A sample list of 'feelings' vocabulary is provided in **Reproducible #10.**

2. **Adding Text by Innovation.** Revising the simple text of a published work is helpful when older children are new to the writing process. It is particularly useful for children who are insecure in their writing and who might be helped by an existing structure.

   a) Use very easy readers from the library or a first grade basal reader. Most children enjoy reading the simple text that they remember struggling with "when they were young."

   b) Invite the children to select a story and to pretend they are the author.

   c) Ask them to revise it by adding more information, adding literary devices, adding phrases to the small sentences, adding transitions, etc. The children should be invited to come up with their own list of things they think will make the stories more interesting. Here is a sample.

Ann and Pat (Original Version)	Ann and Pat (Innovation Ideas)
Ann and Pat rest in the tent.	Are they camping? Where?
It is a red tent.	Canvas or nylon, how big?
A bear runs to the tent.	Where did he come from? Describe him.
It runs at Ann and Pat.	Why? Where? Sounds.
Can the bear get Ann and Pat?	Escape method, feelings.

3.   **Sentence Length Variation.** Good writing requires variation in sentence length. Having young writers count the words in each sentence of a page of rough draft will help them see if they are offering the reader variation. Many young writers follow the pattern of four to five word sentences with a simple subject and predicate.

> I have a dog. He is nice. His name is Sam. He lives in the backyard.

Ask young writers to count the words in the sentences on a page from literature. See how the pros do it.

Present a minilesson about adding to and combining sentences to make longer sentences. Expand with adjectives and clauses that answer the questions: when, why, how, where.

> I have a big, brown dog named Sam. He lives in my backyard. He is nice because he pulls me in my wagon.

Include the exercise of counting words in sentences as a revision task when writers meet in peer groups or independently complete a revision check list.

Substitutions

Revision by substitution is more difficult than addition for young writers. A greater variety of skills is needed, including a large vocabulary, knowledge of synonyms and verb tenses, and how to use a dictionary and thesaurus.

Substitutions might be

- synonyms
- phrases
- verb tense
- mood
- point of view. (See Chapter IX, Fiction.)

What Works

1.   **Verbs and Imagery.** Even before children are formally introduced to synonyms and the use of a thesaurus, they can begin to think of substituting more colorful or descriptive verbs to replace vague ones. If they ask their audience, 'Can you picture this?' in the response stage of the writing process, they will find ways to describe action using a greater variety of verbs.

A good place to begin is with *went*, a common and overused verb in children's writing. Present a short minilesson about the use of went. Write a simple sentence on the board or overhead projector and ask the children to tell you what they picture.

> The dog went down the street.

Some children will picture the dog running, others picture it slinking, or trotting. Cross out went and replace it with a list of verbs that create different pictures.

> The dog raced down the street. Or, The dog limped down the street.
> Or, The dog slinked down the street.

Follow up with Author's Chair or peer conferences during which children can ask authors for a clearer picture of the action whenever they hear the verb *went*. Invite them to find where they might have used it in their own writing. Can they substitute a more descriptive verb? Make 'Went Hunting' an editing function.

2.   **Comparisons Through Similes.** Writers have been studying similes. At Author's Chair or in peer conferences they might ask the author to make a comparison to something they know in order for them to get a better picture of the thing he is describing. Example: "My dog is big," becomes "My dog is as big as a lion."

3.   **Stay in the Time Zone.** *Linda Jackson, Abel Elementary, Bradenton, Florida,* reminds her fourth and fifth graders to keep verbs in the same "time zone" in a narrative. By that she means keep to the same tense. To illustrate, she uses a volunteer manuscript in which the character operates in both the present and past tense. The class changes these "time-warped verbs" to a consistent tense in the manuscript presented in an overhead projection. Later, staying in the time zone becomes a target skill to be checked in peer groups or partnerships.

4.   **Sentence Structure Variation.** Brainstorm a list of transition words and phrases with your young writers. Have them look in their independent reading material and find words such as *while, after, as, suddenly, soon, until, before, and when.* Ask them to try using these as the first word of their basic sentences.

> My dog eats bones. When he finishes them he hides them under the bed.

5.   **Shades of Meaning.** Building a vocabulary continuum will help young writers expand their understanding of a concept. Write one of the following on the board with a long line between the two ends of the continuum.

naughty	_____	evil
cold	_____	hot
small	_____	big

Have the class brainstorm or use a thesaurus to find all the words that fit into that continuum and place them along it. For temperature: *freezing, bitter cold, cold, chilly, cool, mild, warm, cozy, hot, boiling, roasting, broiling*

Students will need to discuss and debate the relative position of the words on the continuum. Is broiling hotter than boiling? Besides increasing their vocabulary, young writers will come to see that words are precise in their meaning and have different values. The English language contains more words then any other language. Writers can find the exact word they need for every subtle difference of meaning.

This exercise will encourage students with excellent vocabularies and take advantage of their knowledge and expertise to increase the vocabulary level of the class.

Invite writers to construct a continuum of their own. Assign one for homework.

Deletion

Deletion is an even more difficult revision skill than substitution. Writers, young and old, cherish everything they write. Young writers often equate quantity with quality. Encourage young writers to save deleted portions, suggesting that they might use them another time or in another piece. Do not expect young writers in elementary school to delete more than a word or a sentence.

Deletions might be

- repeated words.
- extra words.
- dialogue that does not advance the plot.

What Works

1. **Nattering on.** When children discover they can use dialogue, some of them go berserk. Characters talk about anything and everything. This is a natural stage of development for young writers. When these children tell you a story, they will tell you what each person said. (Modern kids use, "He goes" or "She goes" instead of "He said" or "She said." Keep after them to use said.) Some young writers may lose the thread of their stories in their enthusiasm for their characters' conversations.

We must not be too hasty to identify excessive dialogue as a problem in their writing. We make it a problem because we see the writing taking a long time out of a short school day. We anticipate conferencing over a long piece. We dread the possibility the writer will want to publish it.

Here are a few things to guide young writers whose dialogue has run away with them.

- Praise writers' use of dialogue.
- Ask writers to identify their main character, the plot problem and resolution (See also Chapter IX, Writing Content, Fiction.)
- Ask writers if the dialogue helps a reader know the character better.
- Point out to young writers examples of dialogue in literature that help the reader learn more about the character(s).
- Assign a book response that asks readers to find dialogue telling something about a character. What is it the reader learns about the character?
- Point out to young writers examples of dialogue in literature that show the movement toward the resolution of the plot.
- Ask writers to examine their dialogue to see if it shows the main character moving toward the solution of the problem.

- Assign a book response that asks the reader to find places where the dialogue tells how the character is gaining on the problem or goal.
- When writers publish these manuscripts, help them divide them into manageable pieces.

Reorganization

Organization is a high level thinking skill. It requires an ability to put events in sequence, arrange objects or symbols in order, sort information, make comparisons, group like things together, and manage space.

Reorganization requires students to see the inaccuracies in their organization and then do something about it. It is the most difficult revision skill of all. Don't despair. Start small and start early.

Reorganization might be

- moving words.
- moving sentences.
- changing order of paragraphs.
- changing beginnings or endings.
- changing the point of view.

What Works

1. **Locating out of Place (Left Field) Sentences.** Out-of-place sentences break the focus in writing. Writing cohesive, well focused paragraphs means staying on the topic or subject within paragraphs and keeping similar information together throughout the piece. This applies particularly to expository writing and non-fiction narratives.

When sentences are off a topic within a paragraph, they are considered non sequiturs. Young writers love the concept of non sequiturs, or "left-field sentences," as I call them. These are sentences that have little or nothing to do with surrounding sentences. When I introduced this concept to my fourth and fifth graders in Caldwell, New Jersey, their inclination toward hyperbole lead them to extend it to "coming out of the bleachers" for ideas or sentences that were way off the topic.

The easiest way to find left-field sentences is by listening for them. This can be modeled (20 minutes).

Requirements

- Examples of expository paragraphs containing non sequiturs (see sample paragraphs in **Reproducible #16**).
- Students' rough drafts.

a) Introduce the concept by providing examples. Read samples to the class.

Ask young writers to listen for sentences that are "from out in left field." Explain the meaning of "left field," alluding to baseball from which this slang is derived. In baseball, on-field strategy sessions take place on the pitcher's mound. Only the infielders participate —pitcher, catcher, shortstop, basemen. It would be inappropriate for the left fielder to trot in, from out in left field and join the conference — he doesn't belong. Left field sentences don't belong.

> Parrots are found in Central and South America. Rain forests are their natural habitat. Their diet consists chiefly of fruit and seeds. My Aunt Polly has a parrot. Parrots are noted for their colorful feathers.

The left field sentence about Aunt Polly should be deleted or moved to another paragraph where it belongs.

b) Invite young writers to build on this concept by making up outrageous examples of their own. Share them. Invite children to publish a book of examples of paragraphs with left field sentences.

c) Ask your young writers to listen for examples in their own writing when they meet in peer conferences. It is especially easy to hear them in an expository or non-fiction narrative piece. This will help them understand about unity of ideas within paragraphs.

2.   **Extra Ideas.** Extra ideas are an extension of left field sentences and represent a loss of focus. A young writer may start out to tell his reader about one thing and wander off to another idea. These instances are best identified when young writers read their pieces aloud to themselves or one another.

Encourage young writers to write the topic of their piece at the top of each sheet of the rough draft.

> This is about ghosts chasing kids. —This is about whales and what they eat. —This is about my gymnastics class.

When writers use graphic planners, such as webs and lists, you can ask them to go back and see what they started out to write. Then they should look in their drafts and see if something new has been added. Ask them what they might do with the new information. The new direction may turn out to be the one they want to pursue. Reorganization may be the solution.

3.   **Keeping Like Information Together.** Young writers may jumble information willy-nilly into an expository or non-fiction narrative paragraph or an entire piece. It is difficult for the reader to sort through it. Bits of information that are closely related need to be in close proximity.

When young writers listen to sentences that contain pieces of like information separated from each other, they become aware of unity and clarity. They learn to locate these stray sentences using auditory as well as visual skills (see following models).

Do not expect most of the young writers in your class to be competent at applying this skill. Few adult writers are. Do show your students that these are matters with which writers concern themselves. The more they know about the writing craft, the more likely they will be to write and write well.

Practice model: About 20 minutes. Repeat during the year.

Requirements

- Samples of writing that contain out-of-sequence text are provided in **Reproducible #17**. Make copies for each student.

a) Following a workshop session during which writers have worked on expository writing, call them together to discuss paragraphs.

b) Introduce the concept of straying sentences by asking them to think back to left field sentences. Tell them that straying sentences belong in the text but are simply out of order, making the reader work harder to receive all the information.

Auditory method.

c) Read this paragraph to your students. Ask them if they hear information that should be placed in closer proximity.

> Camels have long eyelashes that catch blowing sand. If some sand gets into the eye, a camel has an extra eyelid to get it out. The camel is designed to cope with desert winds. The extra eyelid moves side to side, like a windshield wiper, and wipes the sand away.

d) In this example the final sentence about how the eyelid works needs to be moved to directly follow the sentence about a camel having an extra eyelid. The best way to accomplish this is to move sentence three to the beginning of the paragraph where it serves as an excellent introduction. Or, leave it at the end to summarize the idea. Students need to see that topic sentences can come at the end of an informational paragraph.

e) Read the paragraph with the sentences rearranged as described.

Visual method.

f) Ask them to read text that is characterized by similar information interrupted by other text. Use the provided sample.

g) When they have identified the sentences containing related information, ask them how a writer might bring the two sentences closer together. Refer them back to Managing Your Manuscript lessons, earlier in this chapter.

h) Show them how to move the sentences closer. Ask them to move the stray sentences in the samples provided (see **Reproducible #17**).

i) This is an awareness lesson. Invite them to look for out of sequence or straying sentences in each other's work when they peer conference.

j) Post Straying Sentences as one of the target skills for the next expository piece.

4. **Red, Green, Blue, Yellow.** If young writers use a web, list outline, or map for their piece, it may be useful for them to color code each division of their topic. When they finish their draft, they can check their organization in peer conference or in a small group meeting with you. Ask them to read the draft carefully, placing a colored mark in front of each sentence to match the color of that information on the graphic planner. If a red sentence is in the

midst of green ones, they should move it to the red section.

Young writers should use the text moving technique they prefer (See Managing the Manuscript, this chapter). Do not expect smooth transition from one piece of information to another if a writer moves a sentence. This is a very difficult skill.

5. **Breakfast to Bed Narratives.** When children become prolific writers they often produce long, weak narratives. They tell about a field trip to a theme park by starting with getting up, eating breakfast, dressing, etc. This is a natural progression in their writing. Children need to write *long* before they write *well.* The best way to help them progress to more concise writing is to show them how to focus on the most important event in the narrative. Be sure this part is developed to the fullest in terms of clarity and interest (See also Chapter IX, Narrative Writing.)

- Where is this?
- Who is involved?
- What happened?
- What feelings were evoked?
- What did it mean to you?
- What did you learn?

Help young authors of long, weak narratives in the following fashion.

- Ask writers to reweb or build a time line of the story to identify specific events.
- Ask writers to identify the best part of their story. (See Chapter IX, Narrative Writing, "The Snake that Ate the Rat.")
- Suggest to writers that they bring their story to conference divided into chapters and that they underline the key event in each chapter.
- Encourage writers to look at the rest and see if there are parts that are not crucial to revealing the main event. Say nothing more.
- When the time comes to publish, help young writers divide the manuscripts into manageable increments for daily publishing work. Ask them to plan where they might have illustrations. Have them alternate between writing text and illustrating as they publish.
- Suggest writers explore other genres such as a letter, literature response, informational exposition.

These strategies help young writers become more concise. Do not expect them to use these strategies immediately. Publicize efforts or achievement whenever you can.

6. **Who is Telling This Story?** Narratives can be presented in different voices. The two with which children will be the most familiar are the first person voice: the main character talking as 'I', and the third person voice: the writer as narrator telling the story of the main character using 'he' or 'she'.

Many young writers start their pieces in the third person, but as they become more engaged in the writing they take on the persona of the main character and switch to the first person. That's great! They are really into it! On the other hand, it will confuse the reader. Writers must make the decision to write as a narrator or be the character and use 'I'.

Choosing to use the first person, I, creates a story restriction. The main character has to be in every scene. Anything that happens away from the main character must be told to him by another character. Otherwise the reader asks, "How did he know that!"

> I stormed out of the kitchen as my mom yelled, "You're grounded. Don't come out of your room 'til tomorrow." What were they planning? Were they going to punish me further?"

> Later that evening I heard a tap at my door. "Mary. It's me, Carrie. I'm not supposed to talk to you, but I had to let you know. You are being sent to Aunt Dora's. Dad agreed too."

> I couldn't believe it. Dad had let me down.

Ask the children to find other examples in their reading. (See Chapter IX, Writing Content, Point of View in Fiction.)

7. **Fiddle Dee Dee.** Children who have heard poetry and stories from an early age are attuned to the sound and rhythm of words. The order of words produces a rhythm in writing. One configuratlon of words that has a distinct rhythm is a double syllabic word and a single syllabic word, or, as I call it, a "Fiddle Dee Dee," pattern. Illustrate this pattern for your young writers to help them in choosing word order when combinations include an *and*.

Say the following aloud and ask your students to consider which sound best. Ask them to clap the syllables.

gerbils and mice	or	mice and gerbils
chicken and rice	or	rice and chicken
green eggs and ham	or	ham and green eggs

You can hear this Fiddle Dee Dee rhythm in names. Clap the syllables.

Tommy Lee Jones

Kitty Jo Carr

Billy Joe Barnes

Michael J. Fox

Ask young writers to find examples of names such as these and examples of the Fiddle Dee Dee pattern in their reading. Invite them to find combinations linked by *and* in their own writing and to test the sound, the rhythm. They might like to change the order of words in their own work to achieve this pattern.

8. **Word order.** Reading aloud is one of the secrets to improving writing. Develop young writers' awareness of rhythm by reading examples to them from children's literature. Ask them to identify sentences that sound choppy. Which sound smooth, which sound like poetry?

Examples:

I have six gerbils and six mice.

I have gerbils and mice, six of each. (rhythmic)

We need pliers and a hammer.

We need a hammer and pliers. (rhythmic)

We all went to the mall and played games at the arcade.

We all played games at the mall arcade. (rhythmic)

Ask volunteers to read individual sentences of their pieces and have the class listen for the rhythm. Analyze a sentence that sounds choppy. Can the order of the word by changed to make it smoother?

Summary

Show children, by example, that revision is a positive experience. When revision is modeled and made the focus of conferences,

- young writers discover that revision is a natural function of the writing life.
- young writers revise when they know how to do it. No writer wants to present unreadable text.

Talk to your students about revision in our lives, using analogies to improving sport skills, house remodeling, dress alteration, or ourselves. Remind your writers that "Good is Best's Worst Enemy."

Chapter VII

Editing

Editing is what writers do to prepare their writing for presentation or publication. In fact, the word "edit" is from the Latin *editus,* to publish. In this book, the term "editing" refers to proofreading—corrections of grammar, punctuation, capitalization, spelling, and paragraphing—to distinguish it from revision—rewriting for greater clarity and interest.

Editing is an important part of the writing process. While it does not change the quality of the writing, it does improve the quality of its presentation. As such, it enhances the reader's understanding and enjoyment.

Editing is comparable to a dressmaker ironing a newly finished garment: checking for loose threads, making sure that the buttons are sewn on tightly, the buttonholes clipped neatly, and the hem is straight. If, however, the garment is poorly designed and poorly tailored, these final steps accomplish little and certainly do not make it a desirable article of clothing. The same is true for writing. Writing craftsmanship and revision control the quality of a piece; editing makes it presentable.

Standards

Editing comes after revision and before publishing. Not all writing in your classroom writing workshop needs to be edited and published. You and your young writers should determine how much and how often work should be published. Publication editing standards should be established. They will vary according to the conventions for which young writers can edit independently.

Build a chart of several standards that represent increasing levels of editing development. Set a class minimum standard, but allow writers to choose the highest level standards they think they can achieve. For example, a group of writers in a second grade might choose a fourth grade editing standard. If they do, encourage them.

An initial first grade class standard might be that all published work must start with a capital letter, end with a period, and have the author's name on it. And grow to include:

- All published work must have 'I' capitalized.
- All published work must have content words spelled correctly.
- All published work must have a title.

A beginning fourth grade class standard might be:

- All published work must have a title, author, and date on it.
- All sentences must start with a capital letter and have end punctuation.
- The beginning sentence of the piece must be indented.
- All content words must be spelled correctly.

And grow to include:

- People's names must be capitalized.
- Fifty percent of misspelled words are corrected before publishing.
- Quotation marks are placed around what speakers said.
- Speakers are identified in dialogue.
- First paragraph of the piece is indented.

A sixth grade class publishing standard may begin with:

- All end punctuation in place.
- All verbs in consistent tense.
- Capitalizing names of people, states, and countries.
- Quotation marks and commas in dialogue.
- Paragraph indenting in all narratives based on time and speaker changes.

And grow to include:

- Each word of titles capitalized.
- Paragraph indenting in narratives based on setting and major action changes.
- Paragraphs indented at change of subject in expository piece.

Does this mean some published pieces will contain errors? Yes, it does. If you insist that all errors be eliminated before your young writers publish, and you take on the task of correcting all work, they will lose ownership and control and may cease writing. Remember that these are young students learning a difficult and creative skill. We cannot insist on perfection when they are in this developing stage of writing any more than we can insist of perfection in their art, sports, and music. Allow them a few stray lines, misplays, and wrong notes. Allow them a few misspellings and missing indents.

Teaching Writing Conventions

The conventions of punctuation, capitalization, grammar, usage, and spelling should be taught through application. Children's writing, editing and publishing needs drive their acquisition of skills. Young writers want their work to be read, understood, and enjoyed. They will discover that they must follow conventions to bring this about.

We learn more quickly when we need information or skills. Teach writing conventions as an adjunct to writing, not as the focus of writing.

Teaching writing with the focus on convention is comparable to teaching children columnar addition by instructing them on how to list the numbers so that the place values line up, to draw a line under the number list, to put a + sign to the left of the bottom number, and to place the answer below the line. After some drills, they will be expert in conventional notation for columnar addition but they still won't know how to add.

What About Parents?

Parents need to hear about your writing program. They need to know that you are teaching writing skills and the writing process. They must be educated to focus on the content and composing skill displayed in their children's work. It is essential that they are informed about the editing and publishing standards in your classroom and can put them in the proper perspective. A letter, such as this one, may help them understand the developmental nature of writing and the need for them to take an encouraging and tolerant stance.

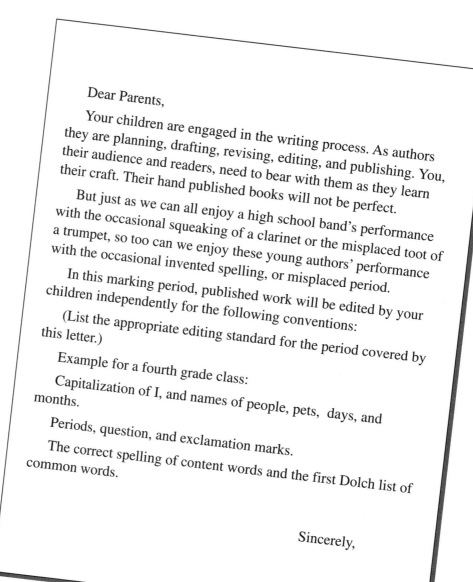

Dear Parents,

Your children are engaged in the writing process. As authors they are planning, drafting, revising, editing, and publishing. You, their audience and readers, need to bear with them as they learn their craft. Their hand published books will not be perfect.

But just as we can all enjoy a high school band's performance with the occasional squeaking of a clarinet or the misplaced toot of a trumpet, so too can we enjoy these young authors' performance with the occasional invented spelling, or misplaced period.

In this marking period, published work will be edited by your children independently for the following conventions:

(List the appropriate editing standard for the period covered by this letter.)

Example for a fourth grade class:

Capitalization of I, and names of people, pets, days, and months.

Periods, question, and exclamation marks.

The correct spelling of content words and the first Dolch list of common words.

Sincerely,

Editing Procedures

In this section you will find lessons and procedures that will help your young writers become competent editors in some basic conventions. They are based on how writers work and on children's natural abilities and limitations. They include:

- editing someone else's writing.
- editing by ear: end punctuation and following capitalization,
                     paragraphs,
                     repetitious words.
- editing dialogue.
- spelling.

Editing Someone Else's Writing

All writers find it easier to edit someone else's paper for the conventions they are studying or know. Given a long enough interval between the writing and the editing of their own manuscripts, mature writers might find most of their errors. But children live very much in the present and are not given to setting work aside and retrieving it later for reworking. The difficulty for young writers editing their current manuscripts is that the story or information is still in their head. They may even ad lib when they read the piece, adding missing words and punctuation that is not written.

When they read or hear another writer's piece, they find errors more readily. Spelling, paragraphing, punctuation, and capitalization conventions can be reinforced by having them edit other writer's papers. The editors will internalize the application of the skills and begin to use them in their own writing.

> When one of *Carol Collins' first graders, Palmetto Elementary, Palmetto, Florida,* wants to read a piece to her, she occasionally calls on another young writer to read the piece to her. The author stands at his classmate's elbow. The author may prompt the reader and even take the paper back to make corrections when the reader says the wrong word. Collins says this ploy helps young authors learn that their writing has to be legible and that their reader needs to be able to figure out what the words are. This puts pressure on writers to write legibly and pay some attention to spelling when they present their papers.

The following classroom procedures will help young writers become better editors.

What Works

1. **Class Edit Model.** Make a transparency of a young writer's manuscript (limit it to one or two pages) or use the samples provided in **Reproducible #18**. Alternatively, provide each student with a copy of the manuscript.

Select one convention appropriate to the grade and writing level. The easiest convention for young writers is capitalization of names. Discuss the convention and review its application. Students should be able to tell how it helps a reader.

Lead the students through an edit of the projected or copied manuscript for the convention selected. For each edit, writers must give the reason for the correction.

> Capitalizing names - (The first paragraph does not have an uncapitalized name) The word <u>Monday</u> needs to be capitalized because it is the name of a day. The word <u>bruno</u> needs to be capitalized because it is the name of a pet. The words <u>jefferson park</u> need to be capitalized because it is the name of a specific park.

Students using these samples will want to edit for other conventions they see misused or missing. If they have individual copies, invite them to edit for anything else they choose.

2. **Class Exchange Edit.** Following a writing session, call for the students to exchange whatever drafts are available. Journal entries, Picture Response drafts, science observations, or a page of any rough draft are suitable for this exercise. Decide on the focus convention and review its use. Give the students a two to five minute period to read each other's selection and edit for that one convention. They may ask each other for help reading a manuscript. Then ask for results, phrased in this way — "Who found a place that called for (convention)?"

Keep the emphasis on the success of the editor finding a place to apply the convention, not the failure of the writer to follow the convention. Model desirable responses. Student editors are to say, "I found a place where..." or, "I found that the word..." rather than the accusatory, "He left out..." or, "She didn't..." or, "He forgot to...."

Discuss the function of an editor. Suggest that editors make corrections on the paper as they find places that need correction. They should write over lower case letters to capitalize them, add large periods or end punctuation marks, circle words possibly misspelled, and write a suggested spelling of the word above it.

Do not use valuable writing workshop time teaching young writers proof marking symbols. Rather, devote the time to the practice of editing and making the corrections as they go. If editing with corrections is practiced early on, in the spirit of helpfulness in a writing community, writers become used to it and do not balk at other writers making marks on their papers.

3. **Edit While We Wait.** Use wait time for students to reread their own manuscripts. Every time a writer reads his work there is an opportunity for revision.

> *Debbie Steube, Abel Elementary, Bradenton, Florida,* meets with rotating groups of her second graders during writing workshop. She has established the practice of an Edit by Ear session (see following sub-section) for the waiting group while she settles the rest of the class to their work. The group edits for one convention such as a period at the end of sentence. They also help each other with spelling. The group members read their papers to one another while they wait for her to join them. This helps the group prepare for the conference or lesson as they have had a chance to read their papers aloud.

4. **Group Edit With the Teacher.** A group meeting of five or seven children with the teacher may be helpful at the start of editing training. You will start

by having everyone read his own paper. Then, working with one student as a model, begin editing for a convention that can be checked by Editing By Ear — periods, sentence start capitalization, series commas, or paragraphing (see following sub-section). Review the skill. The student reads, and you make the sound signal. Ask the other writers to join you in finding the periods or paragraphs for the first writer and in giving the sound signal.

After a few minutes, you will find the others becoming impatient for their turn to be the author-reader. Ask them if they think they can do the editing you modeled with a partner. They will be willing to pair up with each other now. At the start, they may have refused because they thought they were all going to do it with you.

Remain with the group after you have helped the first student and encourage them. Stay only until you see they are functioning independently.

5. **Editing Board.** Review the conventions you want young writers to practice in their editing work. List these on the blackboard along with any content requirements of current pieces. Ask students who are ready for the editing stage to pair up and edit each other's papers for these items. Ask them to put their first names on the board after each item as they accomplish it. This gives them the opportunity to get up and move purposefully and to get public recognition for their accomplishment. The concrete nature of the task enhances the editing experience.

6. **Editing Committees.** Assign young writers, on a rotational basis, to editing committees. Each committee edits peer manuscripts for a single convention. Manuscripts must pass through each of the committees before publication. If each committee member finds even one place to apply his skill independently, you should consider the exercise worthwhile.

Set up the first two rounds of committees for children capable of the task who will likely experience success. Later, form groups in which experienced members can help and teach other student editors through discussion about the specific convention use.

Set up a record keeping sheet for editors to enter their initials under each convention when they find and correct errors in that convention use. Use this sheet to enter children's initials during a class exchange edit as well. Publicize the great editing going on. Let young writers know which of their peers are good at editing for specific conventions.

- In a second grade class, committees might edit for the writer's name and date on his paper, capitalization of title words, periods at end of sentences, or a content word spell check.

- In a fifth grade class committees might concentrate on end punctuation, capitalization, content word spell check, Dolch word spell check, paragraphs, capitalization of all names, or dialogue punctuation.

7. **Editing Committee Materials.** Younger students are more enthusiastic about editing when they utilize concrete objects to aid in the exercise.

For example,

- Younger edit committee students like to have small red file labeling sticker-dots to use as Stop Signs to indicate where periods belong.

- Student's editors can use different colored pencils for different conventions.

- Young editors can use a rubber stamp of a set of lips and a red ink pad to surround what came out of speaker's mouth, the first step in dialogue punctuation.

- Teachers might provide their student editors with badges or green visors marked EDITOR.

8. **Editing Committee Time.** Editing committees meet in formal sessions or accept papers at any time. Editing committees do not have to meet simultaneously, but in younger grades students enjoy the shared task with special materials to enhance the experience. In higher grades, writers may submit their manuscripts to a committee member during writing or free time.

The most important thing is to provide sufficient time to do the task. If you make time for this activity, young writers will know you are serious about the quality of their work.

Editing By Ear

It is easier to hear where end punctuation belongs than to see where it belongs. Noam Chomsky's research in the 1950s[1] tells us that children acquire the syntax of their native language in the early months of infancy and are born with the ability to do so. By the time they reach school age they understand the complexities and nuances of the language in which they have been raised. It is this understanding that makes editing by ear possible. The use of aural skills to edit for punctuation, organization, and repetition is described in the following sections.

1. **Editing By Ear for Sentence End Punctuation and Beginning Capitalization.** (About 25 minutes for first and second graders; 20 minutes for older students. Repeat the model several times during the first semester.)

Have you ever seen Victor Borge, comedian-pianist, perform his punctuation routine? He reads a short selection of prose, using an array of vocal sounds and hand gestures to indicate each of the punctuation marks required in the piece. of course, the sounds are silly, and the piece is overloaded with punctuation to increase the hilarious possibilities.

This routine can be adapted as a model for Editing By Ear. Present it to developing writers as early as first grade. In first and second grade classes, you may want to restrict the exercise to only one end punctuation—periods. Older students can keep track of questions and exclamations as well.

[1] Chomsky, Syntactic Structures, p. 52.

Requirements:

- A Big Book of fiction or fact. Select one with the full variety of end punctuation.
- Author's chair.
- An easel and a pointer.
- Predetermined peer partnerships with assigned places to meet.

a) Gather the class in front of an easel. Older students may remain in their desks or gather in front of Author's Chair.

b) Tell them you are going to show them an easy way to edit for end punctuation and capitalization.

c) Ask the students to read chorally with you from the Big Book. Encourage them to do it with feeling. Read declarative sentences with a slight voice drop, exclamations with a rise and more volume, questions with a rise and pause. As you reach the end of each sentence, point out the end punctuation. Often a student will point out that the next sentence starts with a capital letter. If none does, do so yourself.

d) Continue with the choral reading until you think most of the students get the connection between the end punctuation and the sound of their voice. With older students, continue until you have covered all the types of end punctuation.

e) Now take the Big Book from the easel so that the students cannot see the text, and read it aloud to them. As you read to them, ask students to snap their fingers or cluck with their tongues when they hear the end of a sentence. Invariably, some students will cluck and snap at random for the novelty of it. Acknowledge that urge, and invite them to practice the snap and cluck for a moment or two. Then quiet them and proceed.

f) Point out how your voice sounds when you reach question marks, periods, and exclamation marks. The class may suggest two new signal sounds for questions and exclamations. Great!

g) Now, invite a young writer to read his piece to the class. The class will listen for periods, question marks, and exclamations marks and make the agreed signal sounds. The writer may have a pencil with him to add end punctuation he has left out.

h) You will observe that the writer usually reads with greater than usual feeling and will start to look up expectantly when he reaches the end of sentences, anticipating classmates' clucks or snaps. Remind the writer, if he adds some end punctuation in response to the signal, to start the next sentence with a capital letter.

i) Invite a second student to read a manuscript. Repeat the procedure.

j) Now invite all the writers in the class to try this kind of editing in peer partnerships or groups. Give your young writers a few moments to read their pieces to themselves so that they can read smoothly. Remind the class that the job of the reader is to read the piece with feeling. The job of the listener is to give the signals and ask if the writer has a capital letter after the end punctuation.

k) Do not expect one hundred percent accurately edited work. This is a trial and error session.

l) Rove around the class encouraging the partnerships.

m) After five to eight minutes, stop and ask the writers to put their initials on the top of the other writer's paper after helping to find the end punctuation.

n) Ask partnerships if they found any missing end punctuation — Who found places that they could clap or cluck? Invite the student to share the sentence and end punctuation. Let your students know that it was great if they found any. What good editors they are!

o) Remind the writers that they will have a chance to do this again. Ask them to think about end punctuation and capitals the next time they write.

A second grade teacher told me of an editing problem in her class and wondered how to cope. She had followed the principle of writers editing each other's work but had asked them to edit visually. She considered the independent editing a failure because many children were putting a period at the end of every line of each other's work. Their papers looked like this:

> I went on my bike to.
> the park my mom took.
> me and my brother I.
> got hurt I fell off my.
> bike on the side walk.
> and skinned my arm.
> and knee.

This is a good example of how young children tend to interpret information literally and concretely — in this case, the instruction to put a period at the end of each sentence. They thought of the end as a physical location and viewed the word string on each line as a sentence. They thus placed periods on the right hand side of the paper where each string ended. The key factor was that these young writers did not yet understand the abstract notion of a sentence.

In this situation, the teacher said to me, "This doesn't work. It's a case of the blind leading the blind." She was prepared to drop class editing until she had taught lessons with worksheets about subject and predicates. I convinced her instead to work on choral reading and to Edit By Ear for periods. I modeled the procedure for her class. She pursued it and had enough success to continue with independent editing.

2. **Editing by Ear for Paragraphs.** We think of paragraphing as an organizational skill and may teach it in conjunction with the prewriting or planning stages of writing. I have found, however, that young writers understand more about paragraphing and cohesive paragraphs when they learn about them in conjunction with editing. When developing writers know the reasons for paragraphing, they more readily apply them in the editing stage than in drafting.

Just as children can be trained to hear end punctuation, they can also learn to hear where new paragraphs start and when sentences are off the topic. Before they can do this, they must understand paragraphing concepts.

Paragraphing skills should be introduced to developing writers as they start to extend their writing to include development of ideas, when they are working on organization based on webbing (usually around third and fourth grade).

You might teach paragraphing to the whole class or to a selected group whose writing indicates they are ready.

Why Paragraph?

Conduct a ten minute discussion and brainstorming session about why writers divide their manuscripts into paragraphs.

Ask the class to look at paragraphing in trade and text books. What seem to be the reasons for the indents? The students will probably come up with several of the following reasons for paragraphing and you can offer more of your own.

- Paragraphing is for the reader.
- It helps us know when the author is about to tell us something different than in the preceding paragraph.
- It helps us identify a change of speakers in dialogue.
- It is a place to rest our eyes.
- It is a place to return to if we are interrupted in our reading.

Ask your writers to write the list of reasons in their writer's notebook.

When to Start a New Paragraph?

Use children's literature to introduce your young writers to paragraphing conventions. An introductory discussion and analysis of paragraphing using a children's book takes approximately twenty minutes. Repeat the analysis with small groups as the need arises.

Requirements:

- Two texts; one narrative and one expository. Examples of both are provided in **Reproducibles #19 and #20**. Make transparencies of them.
- Fiction paperbacks, class literature, science, and social text books, or *Ranger Rick Magazine.*

1) Find out what the students already know about paragraphing. Ask the young writers if they know when to paragraph. Brainstorm a list.

2) Invite them to look in their fiction paper backs, literature texts, science and social studies text. Ask them to find the indents and read the paragraphs. Project the sample texts to point out an indent. Can they see the reason for some of the indents?

3) Guide their responses to form a list such as the following one and give the writers a copy of this list. They might keep it in their folders or paste it in their writers' notebook. See **Reproducible #21**.

When to paragraph:

- at the start of a piece
- at a change of topic, a new clump of information
- at a change of time
- at a change of place (setting)
- at each change of speaker
- at every major change in the action
- every five to seven lines if none of above apply.

Editing By Ear For Paragraphs.

Once your young writers understand the whys and whens of paragraphing, they are ready to learn to Edit by Ear for paragraphs. The practice may take 20-30 minutes. Repeat several times during the year.

Requirements:

- Class list of when to start paragraphs or copies of **Reproducible #21.**
- Book of fiction*, or the narrative and expository examples, in **Reproducibles #19 and #20**, or
- Two student writers — one with a narrative piece, one with expository.
- All students with rough drafts of either types.
- All students assigned to peer partners.

*(One of my favorite books for this exercise is *The Mushroom Center Disaster* by N. M. Bodecker. Atheneum, NY, 1976. The easiest paragraphing for young writers to hear is setting changes, and this book has so many.)

A fifth grader's use of star stickers in Paragraphing by Ear with a peer. (Special Ed.)

Procedure:

a) Read a narrative selection to the class. Ask them to keep an eye on the When to Paragraph list in front of them. Ask them to clap when they think a new paragraph starts. Verify and ask them what reason applies. Continue through a page.

b) Read an expository piece to them. Ask them to listen for paragraphs. Tell them that this is not as easy as for narrative. The expository text, sample **# 20**, has conspicuous changes of topic. It is a good example to use for this modeling. Ask them to clap when they think there should be a new paragraph. Ask them why each time.

c) Invite a student to read a narrative to the class and ask the students to clap when they think they hear places for paragraphing. Again, ask them what the reason is for a new paragraph applies.

d) Repeat the procedure, this time inviting a student to read an expository piece to the class.

e) Remind the young writers that it is easier to hear the paragraph changes than to see them. Invite them to try this in peer partnerships. Instruct writers to add a paragraph symbol ¶, a large P, or a star sticker to the manuscript where their partners thought they heard the start of a new paragraph.

f) After five minutes, ask for a status report. Ask writers, "Who was able to find a place for a new paragraph?" Have them tell the reason for the new paragraph. Remind them to say, 'I found a place where a new paragraph is needed because...' instead of, 'She forgot...' or 'He didn't...'

g) Close with the question, "How did you do?" and the reminder that they will get a chance to try this again. Suggest they be aware of the paragraph rules as they work on their writing.

Results of using paragraphing by ear

When writers approach paragraphing through the editing stage of the writing process, they learn about focus and organization using aural skills. The more learning styles that students use to understand a given concept, the more likely they are to internalize that concept.

Editing Dialogue

Dialogue conventions can be taught quite well through editing. The usual way young writers start to use dialogue is by having characters talking with few *saids* and in a continuous fashion. When they read it aloud, we have no problem following it, but in written form it is very difficult to follow. The first editing young writers should do in dialogue is simply to put quotation marks **around what** each person said: what came out of the character's mouth.

What Works

1. **Who is Talking?** Introduce editing dialogue to young writers using a concrete and appealing way. Have them draw a set of lips, in red pencil or marker, at the start of what came out of a character's mouth and at the end of it. Some teachers have a rubber stamp of lips and a red ink pad for editors to use to punctuate the quote.

The conventions of dialogue include quotation marks, commas, and capitalization. They are complex, as you can see from the following Dialogue Progressions, and they should not be taught all at once.

DIALOGUE PROGRESSIONS

Stages of Development in Usage and Editing.

1. Jim said that he had a cat. Mom told him to feed it. (characters talking)

2. Jim said I have a cat. Feed it. I can't. Why not? (use of *said* and direct quotes but speakers unidentified)

3. "Jim said I have a cat." "Mom said feed it." (use of quotation marks—but not quite in right place)

4. Jim said "I have a cat." Mom said "feed it." (quotation marks but no commas or capitalization of quote)

5. Jim said, "I have a cat." Mom said, "Feed it." (addition of punctuation, without paragraphing)

6. Jim said, "I have a cat."

   Mom said, "Feed it." (addition of paragraphing—indenting)

7. Jim said, "I have a cat." "It is hungry."

   Mom said, "Feed it." "Here is cat food." (indenting and more than one sentence quote, but quotation marks incorrectly placed around each sentence)

8. "I have a cat," said Jim.

   "Feed it," said Mom. (indenting, quotation marks, punctuation, plus a new format—the *said* after the quote)

9. Jim said, "I have a cat. It is hungry. It is waiting for me by the door."

   Mom said, "Feed it." (indenting and more than one sentence from speaker)

10. "I have a cat," said Jim, "who is hungry." (indenting and interrupted speech)

11. "I found a cat!" shouted Jim. (indenting and *said,* replacement for effect)

Use children's literature to illustrate the use of dialogue form as the writers become aware of it.

In grades two and three, some writers can locate characters' speech and stamp red lips, or place quotation marks around it. In grades three and four, some writers can independently edit, putting quotation marks around speech and paragraphing by ear when they hear speaker changes. In grades five and six, some can edit to indent speech, start the quotation with a capital letter and perhaps add the comma between the quote and the word said.

2. **Replace Some *Saids*.** *Said* should be replaced only when the author wants to show that there is a definite reason for dialogue to be spoken in a particular voice. For example, if two characters are trying to be very quiet, they might whisper. Or, if characters are yelling at each other they might call, yell, or shout.

A wholesale replacement of *said is* unnecessary and undesirable. Read some fiction and you will see that the repetitive use of *said is* not a distraction.

When young writers are using dialogue freely, you can introduce them to words that may replace *said* for specific effects.

The following lesson takes 25 minutes.

a) Gather a basket of the most appealing fiction books you can. The children should be involved in this task. They are to search for books with lots of dialogue (talking) in them.

b) Ask pairs of writers to scan the books and write down all the words professional writers use to replace said. Have several writers prepare a list for the whole class, reproduce and distribute it. Or, set up your class computer for children to access a class Dialogue File and let them enter their lists. Because this is so much more effective than handing them a prepared list, I have not included one in this book.

c) Ask several children to share the words they found. Draw their attention to the way that said replacements reveal the manner in which the speaker has spoken.

d) Point out to your developing writers that better writers avoid using ad verbs to modify said as in: said loudly, said softly, said furiously, said sarcastically. Instead, they use more descriptive speech terms such as: *yelled, whispered, croaked, screamed, snarled, whined.* Tell them also that an important guiding principle of writing is to get rid of extra words and that said replacements are an opportunity to do this —*whispered is* preferable *to said softly.*

Humorous adverbial qualifiers of *saids,* parodying the dialogue style of Victor Appleton in his *Tom Swift* books, are called "Tom Swifties."

"I missed the target," said Tom, aimlessly.

"My pulse is racing," said Tom, heartily.

"I can't crack my knuckles," said Tom, disjointedly.

"Give me CPR," said Tom, breathlessly.

Invite older students to invent some.

Teach young writers that the important goal in dialogue is to reveal characters' personalities and advance the plot. The manner in which characters speak and what they say is crucial to achieving that goal.

Encourage writers in peer conferences to target replacing *said,* when the manner of speaking is unusual.

3. **Eliminate Some of the** *Saids.* If a writer's characters are developed to the point that the reader can identify them by the things they say and do, then a writer need not identify the speaker in every line of a dialogue. The reader will be able to follow the conversation because he knows the characters. (See Chapter IX, Fiction, Writing Content, Dialogue.)

For example, after the author introduces Sally Pippin and clearly establishes that she detests the twins, he might write "I'm not going to lift a finger to help those vile twins," without adding, *said Sally.* When children write long dialogue exchanges, ask them to read their stories with some of the saids eliminated. Can a reader still follow who is talking?

Getting Rid of Repetitious Words

Hearing repetitions is relatively easy for young writers. The repetitions they are quick to notice, if they are in the habit of listening to each other's manuscripts, are the narrative cue words—*Then, And then, And,* or *So.* These cue words are a natural writing development in young writers who are indicating to their reader or listener that there is more to come in the sequence of their story.

Other repetitious words include 1, *he, she, they,* and *said.*

When writers overuse words, readers notice. We need to show writers how to replace these repetitions or eliminate them.

What Works

1. **Listen For Repeaters.** (About 15-25 minutes. Repeat in groups as needed.)

It is difficult to find repeated words in our own writing because we tend to read what we think we said. Student editors can find the repeated words in other writers' pieces more readily than in their own. If a young writer tends to repeat words, be sure he has the opportunity to have a peer editor check it for that very thing.

Introduce this concept when you see repetitions occurring in the students' manuscripts.

Requirements:

- Sample of text with repetitious words. Samples including all types are provided in **Reproducible #22**.
- Students with rough drafts and stickers.

a) Tell the young writers you want to help them with something they might have noticed in Author's Chair or peer conferences.

b) Read a sample text to them containing repetition you think they are ready to address in their own writing.

c) Ask them if they notice anything. How did they feel about hearing the same word over and over? Did it break their absorption in the story as they become aware of it?

d) Show them a copy of the text or use it as a transparency.

e) Discuss and brainstorm ways writers get rid of repetitions. These will include crossing them out or changing them.

f) Ask young writers to make this a target skill in peer conferences.

2. **Pronouns and Proper Nouns.** Many children will point out to another writer that they are repeating a character's name too much. They might offer the suggestion that the author replace it with *he* or *she*.

Or the reverse may be noted — that an author is using *he*, *she*, or *they* too much and the reader loses track of who is doing what. The writer needs to substitute the character's name for the pronoun occasionally. This becomes another specific exercise that young editors can do independently.

3. **Getting Rid of *And, And then, Then* or *So*.** When writers start sentences with *And, And then, or So*, they do so for legitimate reasons. They are inviting the reader to continue. It also helps them keep the sequence in their own mind as they write narratives. Here is one way to deal with it.

AND (10-20 minutes) Invite some writers who habitually use many *Ands* to read their piece in Author's Chair. After they finish, invite them to try reading it again, leaving out the starting *Ands*. Ask the audience if they could still follow the story. Point out that authors usually do not use And to start a sentence, much less every sentence. Use literature to verify this. Invite the young writers, in peer pairs, to find starting *Ands* in their own writing and to see how it sounds if they leave them out.

AND THEN, THEN, or SO (10-20 minutes) Young writers use these sentence starters to move the reader forward in time. When they do, they are ready for lessons about transitions that establish time sequence. Tell them that using *And then, Then,* or *So* is legitimate but repetitious and boring to the reader. It is time to learn how the pros do it.

The following model uses narratives that you and the students construct. Repeat the model at least once in the year.

Requirements:
- Fiction books for each student.

a) Ask your students to construct narratives describing their day from waking up until they came to their classroom.

b) Construct one of your own on the board or using an overhead projector. Use lots of Thens, And thens, and Sos.

c) After ten minutes invite one or two of the young writers to share theirs.

d) Ask the students to look in their library books or literature based reading series. How do the pros move their readers forward? Have them look for beginnings of sentences that refer to the passage of time. Help them get started by sharing one you found in a book. Remind students about their work on paragraphing when the time in the story changes.

e) Construct a class list from the words or phrases they find. Later, turn the list into a chart or publish it on the class computer with each student adding the ones he has found. Writers should keep this published list in their notebook or folder.

Some Transitions Establishing The Passage of Time

That day	Later that evening	When they were done
Suddenly	On Wednesday	Two days later
Afterward	Meanwhile	Finally
Soon	At last	Next
After they ate	While she slept	Years later
Immediately	At once	In the morning

f) Now substitute some of these for the *And then, Then,* or *So*s in your modeled narrative. Point out to the young writers that, not only is the repetition eliminated but, the reader has a clearer understanding of the sequence of events and what happened when.

g) Suggest that writers check their own or each other's manuscripts for *And Thens, Thens,* and *So*s. Have them ask themselves or each other about the time involved. Is it a day later, the next morning, after school?

Invite the writers to find and replace these repetitious words in their manuscripts when they peer conference. Make it one of the target skills associated with a piece.

Results of model and practice.

- Young writers will edit each other's manuscripts when they know exactly what they are looking for and they can use aural as well as visual clues.

- Writers who successfully edit each other's papers for a given convention will eventually internalize that convention and apply it to their own writing. They will anticipate fellow editors looking for these conventions in their writing and begin to look for them on their own before peer edits.

- Every opportunity that young writers have to read their writing to another writer leads to revisions for clarity, self editing for conventions, learning from other writers, a greater feeling of ownership, and further development of a sense of writing community in your classroom.

> Do not be concerned that the young writers will overuse these transitions. Invite them to use them to the point of ridiculous. This is only practice. They will begin to use them more judiciously as they mature as writers.

"Ants are carrying their larvae. They're living in a leaf. They are in a web-like structure. Ants have an abdomen like we do. They have a thorax. They have a head like us." (First Grader)

Spelling

Many great professional writers are poor spellers. Conversely, many great spellers are poor writers. But in spite of a plethora of examples confirming that great spelling does not equal great writing, parents, students, and teachers often focus on this most visible cosmetic aspect of writing. If developing the ability to communicate in writing is our goal, we must find ways to overcome the focus on spelling as a prerequisite for writing and relegate it to its proper place, as part of editing.

In the editing stage of the writing process we can concentrate on strategies to provide the conventional spelling that readers need to decode and understand written text.

Professional journals, writing process textbooks, and teacher's instructional magazines abound with information about teaching spelling. Here, we are concerned only with strategies students can use to edit their manuscripts for misspelling in preparation for presentation and publication.

Tell your students that readers spotting misspelled words in writing is like when a person listening to you talk notices that you have a piece of spinach stuck on your front tooth. He understands what you are saying but is constantly distracted by that little piece of spinach.

Spelling standards should be established in all writing workshops. Typical standards might be:

Grades 1-3

Topic words you took from a book, i.e., *Content Words,* must be spelled correctly.

Your name must be spelled correctly.

Grades 3-5

All Content Words must be correct.

All Dolch Words must be correct.

Two out of every five misspelled words must be corrected. The teacher will correct the remaining words. Or, the rest of the words will remain in inventive spelling form.

Resources

Use environmental resources—wall word banks, lists.

Try to sound out words.

Ask other children.

Ask teacher how to spell words.

Use a word bank.

Use a picture dictionary.

Use a dictionary or computer spell checker.

What Works

1. **Locating Content Words.** A reasonable standard in any grade is to expect topic-related words to be spelled correctly. The source of these words is usually environmental print, in the case of students writing about a class social studies or science topic, or informational books that the students have used in research.

Conduct a class editing session for Content Words only. (About 15-20 minutes. Repeat as needed as a whole class or group activity.) Apply the principles that writers should edit for one thing at a time, should edit someone else's paper, and should do it aurally if possible.

Requirements

- Children's expository writing—informational—likely to contain Content Words.
- Transparency of the following examples of text with content words. (See **Reproducible #23**.)
- Informational books students have used in their research.
- Picture or word dictionaries.

a) Introduce the concept of Content Words by projecting or writing on the board and reading the examples. Ask students to identify the topic and Content Words—words that are related to the topic—in the first two paragraphs.

Examples:

> Climate is the average weather over the whole year. A climate may be warm and humid, or cold and dry. Some climates have lots of rain and some have periods of drought. Some climates have precipitation in the form of snow.

> Kittens are baby cats. They purr. They have fur and whiskers. They have pads on their paws and they have claws that they can pull back in.

b) Ask those writers who are ready to edit expository manuscripts to exchange papers and read each other's text. Ask writers who do not have an expository piece to use the third paragraph of the projected example text.

c) Ask the writers who have a peer's manuscript to write on the top of the paper what they think the topic of the piece is. It may be the title of the piece which is fine. The writers using the sample may write the topic on a blank piece of paper.

d) Have them find as many words as they can that are related to the topic and underline them on the manuscript. (The writers using the sample can list them.) They should confer with the author if necessary or with you if they are using the sample provided. Preferably they should work with a young author's paper because there is no guarantee that the words in the samples provided are to be found in environmental text or books currently in your room.

e) After a minute or two, call on one or two students to share what they have found so far. This encourages some non-starters who have not figured out what to do.

f) When almost all students have located at least two content words ask them to return the manuscript to its author.

g) Direct the authors to check the spelling of the content words using informational books, dictionaries, or the environmental text in the room. Ask the children using the projected text sample to use any resource they can.

h) Make this procedure a target skill for editing peer conferences.

> I was invited into a second grade class in which the students had written a piece about their trip to a zoo. The prewriting and planning work had resulted in excellent pieces. There was evidence of revision which the class had been working on prior to my visit. The authors were going to publish these pieces, and the teacher had collected them. She was fully prepared to edit and correct the spelling and punctuation herself for the publishing they would do in computer lab. She told me a few of her advanced writers had been able to punctuate with periods.

> She had invited me in to demonstrate Editing by Ear for end punctuation, which I did. As the young writers worked in pairs editing each other's papers, many of them began asking us how to spell words. I suggested we make a list of all the animal words and require that the children take the responsibility for correcting the zoo trip content words. The children all helped construct the list and eagerly worked on correcting each other's papers. This was something they could do on their own and they were proud of it. The teacher said she would

start providing content word lists for her students since it worked so well. I left her with the reminder that the children should help construct the list.

2.   **Use Designated Spellers.** Make use of your good spellers by asking them to act as designated spellers on a rotational basis. Model the procedure writers should use to employ a designated speller.

   a) Ask young writers to take their word bank, individual writer's spell checker notebook, or whatever recording device the class uses to the designated speller.

   b) They are to ask politely if he could spell the word *needed.*

   c) Tell students to say the word they need and put it in a sentence to help the designate speller identify the word and to give the correct spelling.

   d) Write it in the recording book. Thank the designated speller.

   If the designated speller can't spell it, they are to try another strategy.

3.   **Class Spelling Edit.** In her elementary classes, *Melissa Odom Forney, children's author and former teacher;* periodically asked her young writers to display their rough draft manuscripts at eye level all around the room. She provided for this with trays, bulletin board space, wires with clips, etc. All writers were invited to read the pieces during free time over the next few days. On the third day, they were invited to take yellow highlight markers and mark words they thought were misspelled. The authors checked the highlighted words using the variety of spell-checking resources available.

This procedure requires that you have established a working community of writers who help and trust each other. They will have had prior experience with fellow writers editing their manuscripts.

4. **Great, Big, Juicy, New Words.** Children want to know how to spell and they love big words. When they ask for the spelling of a big, new word they need, write it on a stick-on note and fix it to their desk for the day. Encourage them to use it when they talk about their writing and as often as they can. If they keep a word bank, have them enter it there as well (See following What Works, #5).

   Mary Compton, Gulf Gate Elementary, Sarasota, Florida, offers her students the gift of a new 'mega word' as she reads over their shoulders in Roving Conferences. She spots a place where a more advanced synonym could go and offers it to the writer. She writes in on a stick-on note and leaves it on their desk. She says they love the gift of a mega word and use it during the day. Some ask to make it a spelling word.

5.   **Personal Word Banks.** Word banks are collections of words a writer uses or needs that are personal to his interests. When children ask for an uncommon word, one that is not displayed on the wall or easily located, spell it for them, and enter it in their personal word banks. Word banks can be organized in variety of ways.

   •   on cards with a hole punched in the corner, collected on a key ring.

   •   in a Zip-Lock plastic bag.

   •   in a card file.

   •   in a spelling resource booklet, such as the Quick-Word handbooks published by Curriculum Associates. They come in three levels and contain basic word lists with blank lines for the addition of personal words. These are kept in the writer's folder.

- on an 8-1/2 x 11-inch oak tag or press board sheet, written on self adhesive labels and stored in the writer's folder.
- in small, hand sized, spiral bound notebooks (3rd grader and older). The students need to place stickers on every few pages and label A through Z. Let them figure out how many pages per letter they can get from the total pages of the book.

6. **Class Word Bank.** In grades K-3, use the lower half of your classroom walls, sides of filing cabinets, desks, and cupboards to post laminated word cards. The cards should be attached with Velcro, tacky clay, magnets, or fixed with clothes pins to wires strung beneath blackboards or bulletin boards.

In kindergarten and first grade, a small picture of the word on the card helps children locate words. The children locate them with each other's help and take the word to their desks to copy from an excellent model. This wall word bank helps young writers develop independence for the spelling of common words. Add to that the concrete aspect of the activity so necessary to young learners, as well as the chance to get up and move about, and the unquestionable value of the practice is clear.

7. **Use Computer Spell Checkers.** An interesting and useful attribute of computer spell checkers is that the worse the spelling, the longer the drop down list of choices for the writer to consider. Spell checkers do not automatically replace misspelled words with the correct one. The writer must make an educated guess as to which word on the drop down list is the correct one. He must study the word list to locate the one that looks right. Spellers who are not good at sounding out words may be able to spot the word by its visual correctness.

The drop down lists often contain families of words, variations in suff1xes, and sound-alike words. These can help poor spellers identify the correct spelling.

8. **Use Alternative Words (Synonyms).** Show the students the strategy of finding a substitute word they can use when they are stuck on a word they can't spell.

If you can't spell

friend, use *pal.*

cafeteria, use *lunchroom.*

elementary, use *primary.*

occasion, use *event.*

commitment, use *promise.*

restaurant, use *dining place.*

February, use *month after January.*

One of my fourth grade classes wrote and published books based on this idea. One student's book was titled, *Help for Lousy Spellers.* Two students working together compiled, revised and edited class contributed rhyming couplets. One contribution was, "If you can't spell pickerel, use trout. If you can't spell mackerel, cross it out." The books took a great deal of thesaurus work and neatly covered a required curriculum item, Synonyms.

9. **Use Spelling Dictionaries.** Spelling dictionaries are available for all ages of writers. Younger writers love picture dictionaries with words collected by category. Curriculum Associates publishes three levels of word finder dictionaries. These are lists of words including the root word, prefixes, suffixes, plurals, and variations of the word without definitions. They are less intimidating for young writers than a regular dictionary. They often contain spaces for students to create their own banks of words used frequently.

10. **Provide a Wealth of Spelling Resources.** Many teachers include a laminated list of the Dolch words in their young writers' folders. A list of the 240 words most commonly used by elementary student (Heath Publishing) and a list of homonyms is useful as well.

11. **Personal Help.** After the final edit by a young writer, underline words that are so misspelled they are indecipherable by a reader. Make a list of these words, spelled correctly, — but not in the same order that they occur in the manuscript. Give the list to the writer and ask him to use it to correct the underlined words.

12. **Final Spelling Edits.** After a young writer has corrected Content Words, Dolch words and the percent of misspelled words that were his responsibility, edit your share of the child's manuscript before publication. If you find a few misspelled words that are in the content of Dolch category, indicate to the author that there is a misspelled word in a line by placing SP in the margin — but do not locate the word for the writer. Being able to locate misspelled words is as important as knowing how to find the correct spelling.

Results of modeling and using multiple resources for correcting spelling.

- Young writers who are poor spellers are encouraged when the emphasis on spelling shifts to a cooperative editing function.
- With an arsenal of useful strategies, young writers experience greater success in spelling edits.

Chapter VIII

Publishing

Young writers love to publish. Whether the read their piece in Author's Chair, publish a small handmade book, or hang their work on the family's refrigerator, they are proud of the accomplishment. Publishing is a natural part of the writing process, and opportunities for publishing must be part of the classroom writing community.

Although publishing may seem like the end of the writing process, in another sense it is a starting point—publishing is a great motivation for writing. Hand published books made by classmates, ready to use blank books, and the classroom computer offer children strong invitations to write.

Invite your young writers to publish early in the school year. Their early published works need not leave the classroom, but should be displayed and shared. Later, after editing standards have been established and editing procedures have been modeled, published work can go out into the world.

Classroom Publishing Considerations

- Kinds of Publishing
- When and How often to Publish
- Editing Standards (See Chapter VII, Editing)
- Typing and Printing Considerations
- Educating Readers of Hand Published Work

Kinds of Publishing

To publish means "to bring to the public's attention, to announce." Think of all the ways this may be accomplished.

- bulletin board
- newspaper
- flyer
- radio
- Author Days
- TV
- record on tape
- books
- letters

- newsletter
- read aloud to an audience
- scrapbooks
- class collections

The publishing stage of the writing process offers a wealth of opportunity to practice the four language arts — reading, listening, speaking, and writing.

If we avoid the trap of evaluating everything students do, publishing will be an enjoyable celebration. Participation, practice, and self-satisfaction must be encouraged.

What Works

1. **Newsletter.** In place of Show and Tell, the students in *Mary Compton's Second/Third class, Gulf Gate Elementary, Sarasota, Florida,* publish their news. They write brief news items on greenbar paper, peer conference for clarity and editing, and place their revised draft on a Write and Tell clipboard. During the next few days, they work at the class computer independently. They access the newsletter file, type in their name and news item, use the spell-check, save their text, and close the file. Every few days, Compton checks the file, formats the text into two columns, and prints it out. The students read the newsletter on their own. At the start of the year, Compton edits the newsletter only for punctuation contributing to clarity. Within two months, pairs of students take over the editing of the newsletter.

2. **Class Collections on a Theme.** Class collections are the easiest way to publish. Each student's contribution is small, no more than a page. Call the collection an anthology and encourage young writers to use that term. Young writers edit each other's pages and publish in pencil. The book stays in the classroom. During the year, young writers reading the class collection may make any additional edits they have learned.

Display these books and encourage writers to read their contribution to peers. If a writer has used a skill under study, read it to the class along with examples from children's literature. Show the children you value their work.

> The fourth graders in *Pam Willingham's class, Palmetto Elementary, Palmetto, Florida,* often make class shape books when they study a topic in science or social studies. Pairs of students prepare pages, publishing them on the shape paper. The pages are laminated and assembled using one or two key rings. One of their class collections is an illustrated glossary of weather-associated vocabulary published on cloud shaped pages.

3. **Traveling Class Book.** Start a class story and send it to a succession of schools across the country. Enclose a cover letter describing the project, asking succeeding schools to add a specific amount to the manuscript and to send

The Compton Newsletter

Stamps

France doll
by R.
This is my France doll.
This doll is very fragile.
Her name is Casey.
I got this doll from my
step dad.

by J.
This is my stamp
collection. I have
stamps from all over the Her
This is a hobby I like.

The Bean
by J
This bean has been growing
for five days.

Helmet
by
This hat is called a helmet.
It is part of my dad's hat
collection. It was made 110
ago in 1885.

Star Shimmer
by J
I brought my new toy.
Her name is Star Shimmer
and she's a star dancer.
When you pull the string
she flys. She is fun and pretty.

Star Trek cards
by S
I have star trek cards and
basket ball cards, and
baseball and I've been
collecting for 2 years

The Chameleon
by
I brought in a minor chameleon.
His name is dinosaur. He's from Africa.

Second and third grader writers' independent computer use.

it on. Ask them to do this within a prescribed and reasonable amount of time.

Ask the class that finishes it to return it to your class. Provide a self-addressed manila envelope for them to do so. Read the returned book to your class and ask them to comment on the content and style.

The United States Post Office will deliver it to:

> A Second Grade Class
> Any Elementary School,
> Town/City, State, Zip code. (Specify the name of the town,
> state, and zip code)

4. **Tape recordings.** Using children's work in the classroom shows them that we value what they have to say and what they do — that we value them. Some of their manuscripts can be recorded on audio cassettes for classmates to use in independent listening centers. They can be accompanied by the corresponding hand-published books. They can be placed in students' writing portfolios. They can be used in parent conferences to show writing progress.

5. **Buddy Classes.** Older buddy classes serve as audiences for young writers. Buddy classes work best when younger students read their manuscripts to older students. Older students need to share writing with students closer to their age unless they have specifically written for a younger audience.

Procedures should be modeled by both teachers involved. How to assemble, where to sit, length of activity, materials needed, and objectives should be worked out at the start of the year. Alert older students to the shorter attention span of the young students and have them limit their reading to fit that span. Partnerships should be defined and refined early.

Older children may act as scribes to help a younger class publish a sentence or two. Acting as editors for younger writers helps them with their own writing.

6. **School Audiences.** Schools contain audiences for children's work — secretaries, nurse, principal, physical education teachers, volunteers, media personnel, janitorial staff, older children. Young writers cannot monopolize their time, but they should have access to them for brief readings. Young writers might share a small piece — no more than eight sentences. Older writers might just show their published work and read one of their favorite lines from it.

Many school principals have an open door policy for young writers to come in for a brief reading of their work. Others have a time slot set aside for this with a sign-up clipboard on their door.

> *Mike Rio, Principal, Palmetto Elementary, Palmetto, Florida,* regularly receives young authors to hear their work. He established a Principal's Outstanding Author Award, a gold leaf, printed colored ribbon that young authors receive when they read their manuscripts to him. Their name and the title of their work appears in the school newsletter as well. He says, "We started the Author Award to encourage students to write at every grade level and to get excited about it. Attitudes developed at an early age have a big influence on future endeavors."

7. **Author's Days.** Some established classroom writing communities set aside a day each quarter, or semester, to celebrate authorship. Young authors read

their works, read favorite passages, or recite poems from the work of an author they have studied, read letters from authors, visit buddy classes to read their work, perform dialogues, or invite parents and friends to the readings. Illustrators show their work. Students give writing lessons to the visitors. Students may serve refreshments. Every student is involved. The scale of the celebration depends on how often it is held. Some are held in conjunction with a school-wide Author's Conference to which a children's author is invited for assemblies and workshops.

Media specialists establish a check out system for student, hand published books during a special week — Library, Education or School Young Author's Celebration Week.

8. **Hand Published Books.** No matter how simply constructed, books for children to hand-publish should have a Title page, an About The Author page, and attractive covers (pictures of sports, animals, vehicles, children engaged in activity, etc.). Blank covers should be available for children who like to illustrate their own.

I stamp the back inside cover with the words, "I've read your book and I liked the part... " This sets the tone for the reader's response. The reader is more likely to write something positive before they say, "They let you publish this with these words misspelled?"

Note: You may want to establish an editing standard for young author's published books that are used for classroom independent reading. You can require that all words must be spelled correctly and all punctuation and capitalization corrected. This will mean that, after independent editing, you reserve the right as publisher to correct the rest, preserving the author's wording.

A parent volunteer can keep your class supplied with hand publishing books. (Directions for construction of hand published books are described in the following section.) Fifth graders and older students can make their own. If several teachers need books, you might cooperatively set up a publishing center run by volunteers to supply all the classes.

Involve the art teacher in illustration. The art teacher is a resource for your writers as they plan the layout of their books. Art teachers are facile with handling process and projects and can help you with publishing management strategies for your classroom.

Easy To Make Book Using Recycled Materials

Required Materials

- Recycled cereal boxes, front and back panels, cut to 8-1/2 x 5-1/2 inches.
- 8-1/2 x 11-inch recycled copy paper, one side blank, cut in half.
- 8-1/2 x 11-inch new copy paper, cut in half.

- Three rubber ink stamps:
  WRITTEN by
  ABOUT THE AUTHOR
  I've read your book and I liked the part ...
- Glue sticks, glue tubes, or rubber cement
- Duct tape
- Stapler
- Scissors

Directions

Cut cereal box front and back panels to 8-1/2 x 5-1/2-inches. Cover with used copier paper cut as shown. Or cover with magazine pictures.

Cut <u>used</u> copier paper in half for inside end sheets (fly leaf). Stamp "About the Author" and "I've read your book........" on the blank side of half the sheets (back inside end sheet)

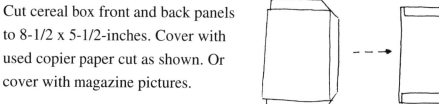

Cut <u>new</u> copier paper in half for text pages. Stamp "WRITTEN by" on them for title pages.

Staple six blank sheets between two sheets of used paper (used surface out) Use the ones stamped, "I've read your book..." as the back fly leaf..

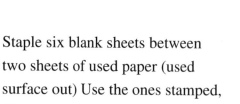

Make a sandwich of the covers and the stapled innards — the stapled edge protruding about 1/4 inch.

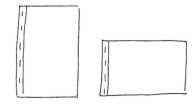

Bind with duct tape.

Note: It is important that the stapled edge of the innards extends past the covered cardboard covers so that you can see the staples before you bind the book.

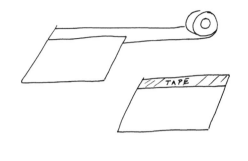

Open the book and place glue on the front fly leaf. Close the book and press cover to fly leaf. Repeat for back cover.

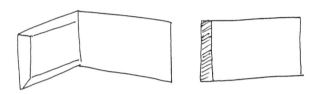

These books can be assembled in a vertical and horizontal format. Younger writers, with larger handwriting, may need the wider-paged horizontal format.

Other book types

- Shape Books
- Flip Books
- Slit Books
- Pop Up Books
- Shape Books
- Step Books
- Triaramas

Teacher magazines and educational materials retail stores abound with creative ideas for handmade books. Beverly Eisele, in *Managing the Whole Language Classroom* (1991, Creative Teaching Press, Inc., Cypress, CA 90630), gives excellent directions for making flip books, slit books, rainbow books, triarama, step books, and shape books.

Each kind of publishing should be modeled. If you invite writers to present their work in a shape book, provide the material and directions to make one. If a bulletin board is cleared for presentation, show writers how to frame their finished piece with colored paper or bordering material.

9. **School Publishing Center.** A school publishing center is a recycling center as well. Two of the ingredients of handmade books are cereal box cardboard and used copy paper. Young writers purchase their books with a cereal box. Office staff and teachers contribute the used copy paper.

Three or four volunteers can keep a school's young writers supplied with books. A publishing center for supplies and distribution will need to be organized and maintained.

How to Set up a School Publishing Center

Explain the idea to the staff and principal. Make sure enough teachers are committed to using the service. Volunteering falls off if the center is underutilized.

- Get your administration's backing.
- Explain the project to the PTA. Obtain funds for materials and volunteers to staff the center. Materials needed are new copier paper, glue, duct tape, and the ink stamps. The rest of the material is collected by recycling paper, magazine pictures, and cereal box cardboard.
- Find a site for the center. You will need counter or work space, and cupboard storage space. The center will need a large paper cutter to cut cereal box panels into book covers and to cut copy paper in half.
- Set up a training session with the volunteer who will manage the center. The volunteer manager needs to keep the center stocked with materials, train volunteers to assemble books (assembly can be done at home), schedule volunteers to fill teacher requests for books, organize the work area, and deliver the books to teachers. This will take three to six hours a week.

When and how often to publish

When

In ongoing writing workshops, young writers publish their books as one of their regular activities. Children can publish during independent work time, indoor recess, at lunch time, and at home.

Publishing conferences can be handled in groups, during writing workshop and independent work time. Demonstrate page layout and text division on one writer's manuscript for a group of students ready to publish. Publishing Center volunteers can be trained to help students with book layout.

Publishing takes time. It is the responsibility of the writer with the help of the teacher. That help comes in the form of presentation guidance, materials, and opportunity.

How Often

A schedule for publishing depends on the length of writer's manuscripts and the method of publication. Work out with writers what percent of their work they can realistically publish. Typing or copying are tedious tasks.

In younger groups, publish often. Pieces are short. Have writers share in Author's Chair, read to a buddy class, display on bulletin boards, place in a class collection, or hand-publish in a book. Very young writers do not copy over but cut out their pictures and word/sentences and paste them on more substantial pages of a class book or display.

Make a distinction between books to be shared informally and those to be used in the classroom for reading centers or the class library. Set different editing standards. Young writers can publish the former types directly from the revised and edited rough draft into a booklet covered by color, construction paper. First, second, and third graders might publish in this fashion several times per marking period.

A second grade teacher told me her students want to publish everything. She was dubious about publishing so much, especially if it were not well written. Here are a few suggestions I shared with her.

a) Vary the publishing medium: frame by color paper and place on bulletin board or hang on a line, place in a class collection, print by computer, copy into a folded paper booklet, record on an audio tape, copy into a cardboard-covered book.

b) Explain about different editing standards for published work as a source of reading within the classroom, work going home, or work simply kept by the writer in portfolio or folders.

c) Establish two check points for all pieces before publication:

- The manuscript must be checked by an editing committee before publication, and the manuscript must be read to you by a classmate of the author.

- If a classmate can read the text, and the committee says it meets the established editing standards, the work may be published.

Young writers might publish one book a year suitable for reading material in the classroom library. This will entail extra editing, planning illustrations, dividing the text, and copying the rough draft into a dummy book. The teacher is responsible for a final spelling, punctuation, and capitalization check. The young writers or a volunteer can then copy from the dummy book into a more substantial hard cover book. One of these hand-published books a year is a reasonable goal for first, second, and third graders. It should not be the only published work produced in a year.

In older groups, one-fifth of their manuscripts is a reasonable publishing goal. Again the publishing technique should vary — alternate oral and written presentations. Some classes set a publishing goal of one written and one oral presentation each quarter. This represents a good balance and a reasonable goal when long manuscripts are the rule.

Editing Standards

Teachers are concerned about standards and the quality of work children do. They are also concerned about young writers developing a strong sense of authorship. Setting editing standards, teaching editing skills, and providing lots of opportunity for young writers to practice will improve the quality of their written work.

Do not take on the task of ensuring that all the children's published work is mistake-free. Besides using valuable time that you might better spend reading children's manuscripts and preparing for conferences, you will erode their sense of ownership and lose the important engagement that such ownership produces. Be sure the message they hear is, "You need to consider your reader. Do you need help?" not, "This is no good. I will make it right."

Strike a balance you can live with.

- Ask writers if they would like you to do a final spell or punctuation check after their work has been edited independently.
- Suggest to young writers that they might want to edit again for end punctuation after they have published.
- Ask young writers if a classmate was able to read their manuscripts.
- Refrain from changing a writer's words or message.
- Have realistic expectations about children's published work.
- Encourage excellence.

Typing and Printing Considerations

1. **Long Manuscripts.** If young writers balk at publishing when faced with the prospects of copying or typing a long manuscript, let them choose from other modes of presentation. Some of these are a diorama, a book cube, a poster, a book jacket, an audiotape.

Writers, who want to publish but are truly overwhelmed by volume, need help in breaking the manuscript into increments. Call a group publishing meeting for all writers with long manuscripts and show them how to read their pieces to find places that would be a natural break for a page or an illustration. Alternating text with illustrations breaks the tedium of scribing. Help them estimate how much text will fit on a page and mark off in their manuscripts each page break with a crayon line. They can then publish one page at a time.

Dividing the piece into chapters and publishing a chapter at a time may be the solution. Scribing or typing help from volunteers might be made available.

2. **Computer Generated Text.** Many young writers have the opportunity to type their text on classroom computers or in computer labs. If they plan to publish it in a cardboard covered book the easiest way is to publish it in the 8-1/2 x 11-inch format.

They can also generate the 8-1/2 x 5-1/2-inch pages of text for the horizontal hand published book format by typing half pages of text and putting a one inch margin on the left and right.

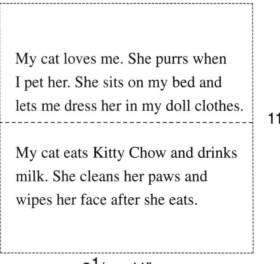

My cat loves me. She purrs when I pet her. She sits on my bed and lets me dress her in my doll clothes.

11"

My cat eats Kitty Chow and drinks milk. She cleans her paws and wipes her face after she eats.

8¹/₂ x 11"

Assemble and staple the innards of the book, substituting the writer's computer generated text for the blank pages. Add blank pages for illustration if needed. Bind as usual.

Computer generated text can be pasted into prepared books. In first and second grade classes teachers often type children's work consisting of a sentence or two. The sentence strips are cut and pasted on the blank pages.

> *Peggy Koplitz, Gulf Gate Elementary, Sarasota, Florida,* uses a volunteer to type her first grade students' sentences from their picture stories. The children cut them out and paste them below the original picture. They often revise their drawings, adding more color or elements while they await the printed text. These published pieces are tacked to a portable, eye level bulletin board called the Reading Wall. Young writers read their pieces to each other from the Wall.

3. **Hand Printing.** Hand published books should be printed, not written in cursive. Essentially all of the text we see daily is printed.

Young writers should publish their work in pencil. This allows the writing community to continue editing the work after publication. Readers are encouraged to take a book to the author and point out edits that can be made. Members of the writing community teach each other and take responsibility for the quality of published work from all the writers.

4. **Publishing Mistakes.** When young writers copy their rough draft to the publishing medium they frequently make mistakes that were not in the draft. Or they simply make the same ones over. Let them mask the mistake with liquid eraser or a self-adhesive label and write over it. This will help them understand that they can change their writing at any time in the writing process.

5. **Line Guides.** Provide line guides for hand publishing on the unlined pages of the prepared books. Darken the lines of several sheets of loose-leaf paper with a black magic marker. To accommodate your various writers, on some sheets darken every line and on others darken every other line. Cut the papers to fit the vertical and horizontal format of the hand made books. Laminate these sheets for young writers to slip behind the blank pages of their books. This will help them keep their printing level.

Educating readers of hand-published books

Based on the remarks of teachers who share their writing process concerns with me, they often are daunted by the outside world's reception of children's published works. Adult readers may immediately focus on cosmetic aspects such as spelling, punctuation, and capitalization instead of on the content and quality of the writing. Here are some ways to cope with this.

What Works

1)   **Don't send early publishing home.** Display it and use it in the classroom. Invite parents and family to see it at the first conference or parent's night when you can explain the writing process and the role of early editing and publishing.

2)   **Send a letter** to parents at the opening of school telling them about the

writing process. (See sample letter in Chapter II.)

3) **Send a letter** about hand publishing, editing standards, and independent editing with the first hand-published book to go home. (See letter provided in Chapter VII, Editing.)

4) **Use Homework Response.** Children take a rough draft home for a conference with parent, guardian, or any adult reader, drawing attention to the target skills and focus of a piece. (See Homework Response in Chapter V, Response.)

5) **Be sure to stamp** "I've read your book and I like the part... " in the back of hand published books to guide readers to focus on the good things the writer has done.

Summary

Publishing makes young writers feel like authors. They take pride in their work. Children who are tactile and product oriented love the feel of the small books.

Adults are no different. In many of my one to two year staff development inservice assignments, I require teachers to write a book appropriate for their grade reading level. They go through the writing process — prewriting, drafting, Author's Chair, peer conferencing for response, revising, editing, and publishing in a hand made book. They face the same problems, need the same lessons, and ask the same questions as young writers. On the day of presentation, all of them want to read their books. They are as proud of them as the children are of theirs.

Help your students publish early and publish often. Help them publish Class Collections, shape books, small books, big books, short books, long books, stories, and fact books. Celebrate writing!

Chapter IX

Writing Content

Young, developing writers are most comfortable with personal narratives, personal expository writing, description, and fiction. As they gain confidence and experience with composing skills and conventions associated with these styles, they will increase their range to explore practical and purposeful genres such as letters, literature responses, opinion pieces, informational pieces, news reporting, as well as aesthetic genres such as play writing, poetry and lyrics. Fluent writers work through the more specific expository forms— persuasion, journalism, reviews—and more complex levels of fiction, plays, and poetry.

This book defines developing and fluent writers by the level of their knowledge and use of the writing craft, not by grade or age. College remedial writing classes are filled with developing writers, and fourth grade classes may have a fluent writer or two in them.

Many of the teachers I have met through my inservice workshops are themselves developing writers and readily admit to a paucity of knowledge about the writing craft beyond conventions and a few composing skills.

Try this experiment. Make up a quiz about writing that you could give to your class at the end of the year. Use multiple choice, true and false, and fill-in-the-blank answering modes. But do not include any questions about capitalization and punctuation, spelling, and grammar. Save the test and compare it to one you construct at the end of a year spent building a writing community.

Teachers seriously interested in teaching the writing craft come to understand that their ability to do so is limited by the depth of their knowledge of the subject. They undertake to augment that knowledge by studying writing content along with their students. A good starting point is the list of books about the writing craft for developing writers of all ages at the end of Chapter II.

Writing Content is comprised of style and genre characteristics, composing skills, and writing conventions. Together with the writing process, these elements form the basis of a curriculum for elementary school writers. This chapter presents an outline of essential writing content elements. References are provided to the associated writing process chapters where some are covered more fully. Following the outline is an extensive discussion of specific styles and genres.

Style and Genre Characteristics

Each writing style and genre has a set of attributes that characterizes the form and gives it its essential nature. These characteristics must be understood in order to build a curriculum for teaching the styles and genres. Lesson and models for most of them are presented in this chapter. Literary response, journalism, and letter genre information can be found within the various writing process chapters.

Descriptive Style

- Organization based on choice of attributes and order of presentation of the elements of scenes.
- Consistent sequence of element presentation: from left to right, background to foreground, top to bottom, from center outward.
- Based on observation, memory, and imagination.
- Evokes the five senses: See, hear, smell, feel, taste.
- Substance is the vocabulary of attributes; size, color, position, shape, texture, temperature, composition, age, sound source, intensity, quality, etc.
- Elements of scene: visual; action or movement; reference to sound; feelings engendered or a reminiscent factor.
- Use of comparison: bigger than a football field, louder than a rock band, shaped like an egg

(See details under Descriptive Writing, later in this chapter.)

Narrative Style

- Personal Narrative
- Informational Narrative
- Fictional Narrative

(See details under Narrative Writing, later in this chapter.)

Expository Style

- Personal Exposition
- Informational Exposition
- Persuasion

(See details under Expository Writing, later in this chapter.)

Book Review or Literature Response

- Organization is based on hierarchy of specific ingredients.
- Title of book
- Author of book
- Genre or form of the book.
- Brief summary — if fiction, don't tell the resolution of the plot.

- Recommendation — who would like it?
- Where we can find it?
- Why you liked it or your favorite part.
- Comparison to another book within the same genre.

Journalism

- Organization is based on hierarchy of ingredients: Who, What, When, Where, Why, How. (Reserve Opinion for Editorials)
- Leads and focus.
- Contains firsthand observations.
- Descriptive elements are chosen for impact in support of headline.
- Interviews and quoted sources.

Letters

- Organization is based on either narrative or expository schema.
- Follow conventions of form and format.
- Business letters are brief and to the point — the main point covered in the first paragraph.
- Manners guide writer in friendly letter to consider reader first.

Poetry

- Organization is based on meter and rhythm, rhyme, shape, narrative sequence.
- Writing is condensed.
- Evocative nature of language.
- Strong feelings and imagery.
- Presentation is by performance as well as printed text.

Composing skills

These consist of organization, conveying meaning, and style and usage. Composing skills are covered throughout chapters about the various stages of the writing process and, in this chapter, as they relate to styles and genres. References to the respective chapters are included in the following skills outline.

Organization (Chapter III, Prewriting)

- Sequence based on chronology as in narrative writing.
- Sequence based on hierarchy or importance of ideas as in expository writing.
- By comparison.
- Alphabetically.
- By viewpoint (See also Fiction)
- Genre-specific order.

Conveying Meaning (Chapter IV, Drafting, and this chapter)

- Going from a graphic planner to a draft.
- Maintaining the focus.
- Building cohesive paragraphs.
- Considering sequence.
- Using transitions to establish time, consider alternatives, link cause and effect, refer back, extend an idea, or summarize.

Style and usage

- using specific nouns
- using active verbs
- using consistent verb tense; parallel construction
- using literary devices — alliteration, hyperbole, onomatopoeia, simile, irony, metaphor
- selecting the order of words with an ear to rhythm or patterns
- constructing sentences in a variety of forms and lengths
- revealing character personality through dialogue
- creating tone and atmosphere
- creating tension in fiction
- creating strong imagery
- using dialogue to present information.

Conventions (Chapter VII, Editing)

These consist of capitalization and punctuation rules, letter formats, and spelling conventions.

Capitalization

- The word 'I'
- Names — all kinds
- At the start of a sentence
- YELLING!

Punctuation

- End punctuation
- Series commas
- Commas in direct address: Tom, Yes, No, Oh,
- Punctuation convention in dates
- Bibliographies
- Dialogue
- Underlining and parentheses
- Abbreviations.

Personal and Business Letter Form

- Return address
- Greeting
- Body
- Closing.

Spelling

- Inventive or temporary spelling
- Spelling rules
- Strategies for correcting misspelled words.

Descriptive writing

Writers, like scientists, artists, philosophers, and comedians, are observers of the world. They notice and record their observations, enlightening and entertaining the rest of us.

Children are naturally great observers. We can help them record their observations by revealing the substance and structure of descriptive writing (A basic function of teaching is to reveal the underlying structures, patterns, and substance of a concept.)

The substance of description is made up of the elements of a scene and their attributes. Elements of a scene are physical objects, inanimate or live, that can be observed. Attributes are the properties of these elements that are perceived through the five senses. They are observed directly, remembered from experience, or imagined.

The structure of description determines how we describe a scene. It is about the choice of which elements and their attributes to present and the manner and order in which they are presented. (Fluent writers make these choices based on the emotive value of words as well as the image they create.)

Description is a great place to start a writing program. It is basic and applicable to all other writing. Descriptive writing makes use of children's natural curiosity and observant powers. Encourage these traits and help them build a rich vocabulary of descriptive language.

Descriptive Attributes (A copy of this list is provided in **Reproducible # 24.**)

size: actual and comparative — larger, as big as...
color: red, green; tone, hue; comparative — reddish, brown like chocolate...
shape: round, oval, cubic, square, columnar, tubular, triangular...
movement or action: gliding, slithering, flapping, explosive; comparative — faster, more frenzied...
symmetry: horizontal, vertical, radial
texture: smooth, rough, bumpy, lumpy, soft, fuzzy, slippery; comparative — stickier, slickest...

number: specific—six, ten; general—many, some, several; comparative—more than, fewer...

composition: wooden, metal, plastic, cloth, glass, concrete, cardboard, paper. . .

smell: smoky, putrid, floral, acrid, burnt, sweet; comparative—like raspberries. . .

taste: sweet, salty, acidic; comparative—like licorice, fruitier...

function: use location: for inanimate objects—place, time

habitat: for living things: underground, den, water, ocean, desert...

direction: left, right, up, down, backward, sideways, forward...

orientation: horizontal, vertical, parallel, perpendicular...

state: liquid, solid, gas.

temperature: forty-six degrees, three below zero; comparative— hotter than, coldest...

weight: ten pounds, seven grams; comparative—as heavy as, the lightest. . . age: specific—five years old, eighteen months old; nonspecific— old, new, ancient, antique; comparative—older than Methuselah. . .

special features: writing, designs, knobs, buttons...

Descriptive Structure (See **Reproducible #25**)

Choice of Elements and Attributes (based on the five senses, memory, and imagination)

People and objects seen: who, what, number, position, age, condition, size, shapes, features, all attributes.

What is happening: people, animal, and object movements, weather conditions.

Sounds heard: type, source, magnitude.

What it feels like: textures, mood, atmosphere, ambiance.

Smells: types, source, magnitude.

What you are reminded of: other places, other people, other events.

Form and Presentation Order

Scenic: From left to right, from top to bottom, from foreground to background, from center to perimeter. The choice of order depends on the nature of the scene described, but a writer must be consistent.

Events: Chronological order.

Portrait: No prescribed order, although visual attributes and motion usually are presented first. Most important attributes first.

Comparison: Use comparisons through simile and metaphor to help your readers better picture the scene.

Follow the "**Don't Hit Your Reader Over the Head**" principle. (See Expanding and Developing Ideas in Chapter IV, Drafting.) Instead of "My dog is very big," try, "My dog barely fits in the front seat of our car."

What Works

1. **I Spy Attribute Field Trip.** Take a field trip around the classroom, the school halls, or the school yard to find examples of descriptive attributes.

   a) Give each student a clipboard and a copy of the attributes list provided in **Reproducible #24**. Modify the list content or length depending on the age and attention span of the class. Read the list together and discuss comparative attributes. Ask students to star three to six attributes that appeal to them.

   Model one or two entries on your clipboard. Show it on the board. For example, size by comparison. Instead of describing something by its exact size, say:

   It's the size of a loaf of bread.

   It's small enough to fit in my hand.

   It's slightly larger than an egg.

   b) Walk writers around the area selected. Young children need to get up and move about often. You can turn some of this stretch and move time into academic exercise.

   c) Gather in a central place with prearranged seating and share entries.
   Color — a red bulletin board, a gray and yellow book bag, a dark green leaf. Shape — a leaf that looks like a hand, a round shell, a square sign.

   d) The page of attributes with their entries goes in their writing notebook.

2. **Descriptive Writing Analysis.** Give each young writer a copy of the Descriptive Structure provided in **Reproducible #25**. Provide each child with a story in multiple copies or in a reading series. Read the story together and help the students analyze the author's descriptive writing for the variety of ways to present a scene.

   Some possible results.

   • The author uses a sentence about what is seen.
      Three bowls of porridge were cooling on a large wooden table.

   • The author describes a smell.
      The room smelled of flowers, apples, and porridge.

   • The author tells of some action in the setting.
      The curtains flapped in the breeze and the napkins flew off the table.

- The author is reminded of something else.

  It felt like a library, hushed and still.

- The author refers to a sound in the setting.

  The loud snoring from their bedroom puzzled them.

- The author makes a comparison.

  The porridge was as thick as pea soup.

3. **Verbs.** (See also Dialogue in Fiction, later in this chapter.) Ask young writers to write a description using a family photo or a picture they have selected from the classroom file. They are to base their description entirely upon what is happening in the picture. Before they write the description, ask them to list all the action words, verbs, that apply to the picture. Model one for them.

- playing
- stealing base
- pitching
- throwing
- yelling

> This is my family playing softball at my Aunt Suzy's house. My brother Tom is the one pitching. He always throws too low. We were all yelling at him to play fair. My sister Audrey is leading off second base, trying to steal third. She didn't make it, Tom picked her off.

4. **Attributes.** The day before this activity, ask young writers to bring in an interesting or colorful item.

   a) Make copies of the attribute list provided in **Reproducible #24.** Select a large object for your demonstration (globe, basket, toy). Give classroom items to students who did not bring one in. If they complain they don't like the object, remind them they could have brought in their own. If they trade without disruption, ignore it; they are problem solving.

   b) Read the attribute list with your class to see which ones are applicable to the demonstration object.

   c) Using the attribute list as a reference, write a class description of the demonstration object. Try for a variety of sentence types, avoiding elementary constructions such as: "It is round. It is blue." Rather, try for interesting sentences such as: "The globe is round with a metal frame around it. Most of the surface is blue for ocean."

   d) Ask the writers to describe their own object. Ask young writers to restrict their sentence starts to only one each of: *The, There, It,* and *I.* Ask them to use some of these starters: *Where, Not, All, Some, Beginning, Most, You*; and any others they can come up with as they observe the object. Write these two groups of words on the board for their use.

   e) The object of the practice is to use as many attributes as possible; the focus is not on composing or convention skills. The exercise is not evaluated.

   f) Allow 10-15 minutes for sharing. Results go in the writer's notebook in the Practice Writing section.

   g) Repeat this activity with photos children bring in, or select from the class file of pictures.

5. **Colors.** As Diane Ackerman says in *The Natural History of the Senses*, (see Bibliography at end of Descriptive Writing section), we have a rich vocabulary of descriptive words for our visual sense compared to limited ones for smell and taste. Shades of color are virtually limitless, and most of them have a name. Many color names use a comparisons to natural elements such as flowers, trees, and woods - *periwinkle blue, coral, primrose, lemon yellow, mahogany, sky blue, orchid, ash blond, etc..*

Provide color word resources for students. Ask your art teacher for other sources in addition to the following:

- Crayola Crayon: box of 64
- Paint chips: Dozens of cards each with an array of 6-8 named shades of one color are available at paint and hardware stores.
- Carpet samples: Sets of 4 x 4-inch squares, in an array of named colors and shades.
- New car color charts.

6. **Shapes.** Integrate geometry and writing by using plane and three-dimensional shapes as the source of descriptive vocabulary. Include the study of symmetry as well. Once you have introduced geometric shapes to the children in math, take your writers on a short class clipboard field trip to find these shapes in the natural and architectural environment. Set a limited goal of finding and describing two to three geometric shapes. Model writing about geometric shapes.

> I saw a triangle made up of the ground, the stairs, and the slide.
>
> The stop sign in front of the school is an octagon.

7. **Onomatopoeic Sounds.** Compared to sights, we have a limited vocabulary for sounds. It is extended by words that imitate the sound; *Splash, whir, pbzzt, kerplop...* (See Literary Devices in Fiction, this chapter.) Young writers love Peter Spier's book, *Crash! Bang! Boom!* (see bibliography at end of Descriptive Writing section.) They can use it as a dictionary of sounds.

Sounds can be described by their source and intensity as well as their quality. Take the class outside for a sound field trip armed with their clipboards. Ask them to identify two or three sounds, describing them in quality, source, magnitude, and recording their reaction — Is it coming from the building, the trees, the playground? — Is it high pitched, humming, loud, annoying, soothing, relaxing, irritating, puzzling, melodic?

8. **Attribute Books.** Attribute books focus on one attribute and give illustrations of it —*red* is for apples, *red* is for fire trucks, *red* is for embarrassed. Or they focus on one object and give all its attributes — *apples* are red, *apples* are round, *apples* are delicious.

Writers of all ages enjoy making attribute books. They can present them as shape books, too.

9. **Picture Prompt.** Encourage descriptive writing that captures young writers' thoughts, feelings and opinions.

For visual prompting of descriptive writing, ask children to select a picture from the class file. Ask them to select three or more attributes that they think are appropriate to the picture content. A sentence for each of the attributes chosen will be the target skill. Ask them also to make a statement about what they think about the content. Model this with a picture you have selected.

Example: The picture is of a garden. Attributes selected are color, size, and shape.

> The flowers in this garden are mostly pink and white. Some of the flowers are tall and form a border behind the smaller ones. The garden edge is wavy and makes a big curve across the lawn. I would love to have a garden like this in my yard.

10. **Other Descriptive Work.** Integrate description with vocabulary development using brainstorming and children's literature as a source of picture images.

- Describe what's going on in a picture (Action words).
- Describe how the person in a picture might be feeling (Feelings).
- Describe what the person in a picture might be saying (Dialogue).
- Describe using comparison (Similes).

A second grader uses a simile.

```
Meridith M.                    IN PROGRESS

I  like   the   way   the
artist   did   the   sky.
It   looks   like he wetted it
with   a   brush  sweep of
water. So  when   he   painted
with   water   colors  ti
it   sped   like   melted
butter   on   hot   tost.
I love   the   backround.
```

11. **Scientific Description.** Observation with description and classification (sorting), are two of the most important skills in science. If we do nothing else in elementary school science but help children to become adept at these two skills, we will have prepared them for science study the rest of their lives.

You can effectively integrate science and writing by making the observation of materials, living organisms, behavior, and habitats the focus of your writing program for a portion of the school year. Attributes will be the basis of this work.

Marleen Wallace, Abel Elementary, Bradenton, Florida, and her third graders start out with buttons and move on to leaves, animals, and habitats. Students select ten buttons from a large collection. They sort them into two, three, or four groups. They orally defend the logic of their groupings. They are encouraged to use the language of attributes.

Next, they select four different buttons. Wallace models a student data collection sheet made of four columns, with a row for each of the attributes they mentioned in their classification work — number of holes, edges, size, color, composition, surface features, miscellaneous. They list the attributes of each button using one or two words only.

Later they write a paragraph about the attributes of each button. Initially, her students write simple sentences such as, It is blue. It has two holes. It is flat. She asks them to share their paragraphs.

Next she gives a short lesson about complex sentences and Sentence Start Variation (see Chapter IV, Drafting, Sentence Variation) which goes something like this.

She asks the students to put two attributes in one sentence using *and*. "Which sounds best? It is flat and thin or It has four holes and thin? Whoops! That doesn't work. It has four holes and is thin."

"Can we start a sentence with the attribute? Which ones sound best doing that? The edges are smooth. or, The color is blue. Whoa! That sounds stilted. Is that the way we say colors?"

"Can we use a comparison? What does it look like to you? This button looks like a quarter."

The young writers work on revising their paragraphs based on the lesson. They peer conference, compliment each other, and help each other find places to enliven their descriptions. They save this work in their writing folder.

12. **Portrait Capsules.** The object of a portrait capsule is to compose a one sentence description of a person engaged on some activity, using rich, image-forming vocabulary, trying to involve more than one of the five senses. Model this for young writers.

Requirements
- Large art prints (borrow from art teacher or media specialist, or collect your own).
- Pictures of people in a scene from the class picture file.
- Thesauruses.

Procedure (10 minutes for modeling, 15 minutes for practice and sharing.)

a) Place the picture on the board or on an easel where all the young writers can see it.

b) Tell the students the objective of the practice write is a one-sentence description.

c) Invite them to contribute vocabulary for the description. When an unexciting descriptive word is offered, ask several students to look it up in the thesaurus and suggest some alternatives. Let the class select the alternative word.

d) Compose the sentence using their input and your own.

> A girl with heavy gold earrings, a long blond braid, and wearing too much makeup, was holding onto a little kid with a big, sticky, swirly red and white lollipop.

Throw in a word about series commas as you write it.

e) Distribute pictures from the class file or other art prints. Art prints are an excellent resource. While using the prints, the writing students are introduced to fine art and artists. This is another example of killing two birds with one stone for efficient use of time in the writing workshop.

f) Invite writers to make up their own portrait capsule.

g) Share them. All participants can compliment vivid vocabulary.

h) Variation: Place pictures for all to see and have students try to match the portrait capsule with the associated picture.

13. **Atmospheric Capsules.** Model a capsule sentence that describes the

atmosphere of a place. The objective is to cram as much as possible into one sentence and try to involve more than one of the five senses. Use pictures, as with the portrait capsule model, or brainstorm a list of places students have been. Encourage thesaurus use.

> The cafeteria stunk of hamburger grease, peanut butter, and sweaty
> kids just in from the playground.

14. **Comparison.** Imaginative comparisons are a wonderful way to create the imagery necessary to put readers into a scene as the author sees it. A prompt to a writer in Author's Chair, in peer conferences, and in conference with you, such as 'What did it look like to you?' What did it seem like to you?" may help young writers compose a fresh and vivid comparison.

> There were more cars than at the mall.
> They were crawling like ants.

Similes, metaphors, and analogies are the names of the devices used for making comparisons. (see Fiction, later in this chapter for lessons on literary devices.)

15. **Process Description.** Describing a process is an element of the writing craft that older developing writers might find challenging. Fiction writers will tell your students that describing a fight is a useful exercise in process description. Dick Francis, adult mystery writer, is a master at this. Read excerpts to students from any of his earlier books about the horse racing scene.

Showing the movement of a character through a scene is another difficult process. The reader needs to picture important movement. The movement of a scene within a young writer's story may be acted out in front of the class — the author directing. The written version of the scene can be compared. This will help a writer add the necessary description of movement.

Ask young writers to find examples in their independent reading and to share them with the class (see Dialogue Tied to Action, Fiction, this chapter).

Making something or performing a task are typical examples used as models for process description. Look for examples that interest your students. Have them make a list of processes to describe (see also Expository, this chapter).

A Word about Adjectives

Notice that the discussion, lessons, and models about descriptive writing all focus on the use of descriptive language in relation to the function of imagery. I have deliberately avoided the use of the word 'adjective.' Descriptive language includes the use of nouns, verbs, adjectives, adverbs, and their phrases. When we focus on adjective — calling them 'describing word' — we may inadvertently lead young writers to limit their description to the use of adjectives. Descriptions become filled with *large, red, fuzzy, wool mittens catching big, round, white snowballs, etc.*

Adjectives are fine if they perform a meaningful function in the description. Is the adjective specific? Is it appropriate to the meaning we want to convey? Or is it worn out and trite? Warn writers to avoid a redundant adjective — one which describes an attribute already implied in the noun it modifies, such as *green grass, sandy beach, white snow, furry kitten.*

The best descriptive writing is kinetic and active — writing in which the reader sees characters and scenes as if they were in a film rather than in a static picture. Action words, verbs, are the key to achieving this kind of vivid descriptive writing. Help your young readers focus on what is going on, what is happening.

Spend time with your young writers, pointing out how authors of children's literature use descriptive language. Read to them often and relish the imagery.

Recommended Professional Reading

Ackerman, Diane. *A Natural History of the Senses*. New York: Random House. 1990.

Spier, Peter. *Crash! Bang! Boom!* Garden City, NY: Doubleday and Company Inc. 1972.

Narrative Writing

Narrative writing is characterized by the passage of time. The writer relates a series of events, usually in chronological order. Those events can be real or imaginary, that is, the narrative may be non-fiction or fiction. Both tell a story, the difference is a matter of plot.

Fictional narrative has a plot consisting of conflict and resolution or a goal and attainment. Non-fiction narrative does not have a plot but is based on a central theme or idea that is revealed through the sequence of events. A narrator may be used to provide information by telling the story of an animal, person, or event.

Personal narrative and fiction are the forms to which young writers usually gravitate and at which they most easily can excel. The major characteristics and considerations of narrative writing:

Personal Narrative
- Personal focus: the main event or idea in the time span of the narration.
- Organization based on the passage of time and sequence of events.
- Transitions of time and place.
- Graphic planners include lists, timelines, storyboards, and webs.
- Content based on first hand observation and memory.
- Descriptive writing evokes the five senses, movement, and comparisons.
- Feelings of author revealed.
- Point of view usually first person.

Informational Narrative
- Organization, transitions, description, and graphic planners — same as for personal narrative.

- Focus: the subject of the narrative — animal, person, place, event.
- Content based on facts and details, knowledge, and observation.
- Point of view usually third person.
- Feelings of author may be revealed.
- Writing can be lively and expressive with vivid description, literary devices, and emotive language. Non-fiction need not be dull.

Fictional Narrative

- Organization based on the passage of time and a sequence of events involving a plot.
- Graphic planners based on character, setting, and plot. (see also Chapter III, Prewriting)
- Transitions related to time, place, and events.
- Content based on writer's imagination, memory, and observation.
- Descriptive writing evokes the five senses, attributes, movement, and comparisons.
- Utilizes literary devices such as alliteration, simile, hyperbole, metaphor, onomatopoeia, personification, anthropomorphism.
- Six basic plots: Lost and Found, Character with Problem or Goal, Character versus Nature (survival), Good Guys vs. Bad Guys, Mystery or Crime and Solution, Boy Meets Girl.
- Theme and moral: Hard work pays off, beauty is only skin deep, don't judge a book by its cover, etc.
- Tension created by: deadlines, readers knowing something a character doesn't, setbacks, and anticipation of a major event (foreshadowing).
- Character development through what he says, does, looks like, thinks, or others say about him.
- Dialogue used to reveal characters and advance the plot.
- Point of view: first person or third person (main character's perspective) throughout, or alternating between two main characters, usually by chapter.
- Beginning 'hook': Struggle, goal, or conflict revealed or strongly hinted at in the first paragraph.
- Use of definition, for example, *the reel, the thing that holds the line, came off...*

Personal Narrative

Developing writers normally find personal narratives the easiest to write. The source of a writer's ideas is his knowledge and memory of the topic. The writer will be in control of the content. This will encourage engagement and foster ownership. Personal narratives should be the starting point of your writing process workshop. They are excellent vehicles for teaching the application of writing craft skills. The writer can concentrate on word choice, composing skills, and form because the content information is within his grasp.

Early attempts at personal narrative may often be too brief and undeveloped, or too long, with nattering on and side tracking. In the first case, young writers need to know that readers are interested in their story, and in the second, writers need to know that their readers might wander off just as they have done in writing the piece.

The following lessons and models will help young writers enliven and improve their personal narratives. Later they will use these skills in other genres and styles.

What Works

1. **The Snake That Ate a Rat.** All good personal narratives are built around one central idea. This is focus. I use an analogy to help young writers build personal narratives. I tell them that a narrative looks like a snake that ate a rat. I draw it for them.

At the mouth and head of the snake, I write who, what, where, and when. That's the start of the tale. The belly, with the rat inside, is the biggest part, the most exciting part of their story. Most of the writing should be about the exciting part of their story.

I fold a sheet of paper representing their manuscript and mark off the start, about two lines; the belly part, most of the paper; and the ending — the tail of the tale— another two lines.

I ask students to tell me of any trips or adventures they have written about. When they identify them, I urge them to tell me what was the best part of those events, days, or trips. "Don't tell me all about the car trip and how you were bored — I'll be bored too. Tell me about the very best part. Tell me everything about it that made it the best part."

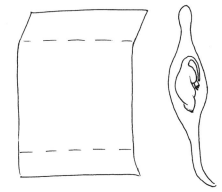

The tail of the tale is small. A good ending tells how you felt about the exciting part. It sums up the event or tells what you learned from the experience. (See also Chapter IV, Drafting, Endings.)

2. **How Did You Feel?** Find appropriate selections in famous historical speeches ("Give me liberty or give me death." Patrick Henry), passages in

fiction ("It is a far, far better thing that I do, than I have ever done; It is a far, far better rest that I go to, than I have ever known." Sydney Carton in *The Tale of Two Cities,* Charles Dickens), letters to the editor, and editorials that illustrate how writers express their feelings about events and people.

Brainstorm vocabulary about feelings to make a word bank. Young writers should keep the list in their notebook and add to it (See **Reproducible #10).**

Have some volunteer writers tell how they felt about the central event in their narrative. Ask writers to include how they felt about events or actions of people in their personal narratives. Make that the target skill for the piece.

3.   **What Did I Learn?** Many personal narratives are about events or actions that have helped us learn something. Ask young writers to share a personal event in which they learned something about themselves—they love being the leader, they are afraid of heights, they sunburn very easily, they are squeamish about baiting a hook, they excel at joke telling. Or, in which they learned to do something—sing a song, jump rope, fish, swim, ice a cake, iron, ride a two wheeler, box, use a computer, cook. Make that learning event the focus of a piece.

4.   **What Is This About?** Encourage young writers to write on the top of every page of their manuscripts, in one or two words, what their topic was when they planned the piece. If they are following a timeline, storyboard, or list, they can write, on the top of every half sheet (paragraph), the word from the portion of the plan about which the paragraph pertains.

Finding left field sentences (see Left Field sentences in Chapter V, Response) will help writers see where they have wandered off. Finding those wanderings can serve as the target skill in peer conferences and Author's Chair.

Use Homework Response (see Chapter V, Response) and assign the responder the task of asking the writer about each new piece of information, "What has this to do with the topic?"

5.   **Tell Me More.** In a group conference, you might demonstrate the technique of finding a word in one sentence and writing another sentence about that word. Repeat several times to divulge more information.

> Last week my cousin took me fishing. We caught three fish. (Original piece)

> Last week my cousin took me fishing. We caught three fish. I caught the biggest one. (Next version)

> Last week my cousin took me fishing. We caught three fish. I caught the biggest one. It was a trout. (Final version)

Writers who are stingy with their narratives may not be accustomed to anyone listening to them. They also might not know how to add additional information. They will need work in manuscript management and revision techniques. (see Chapter VI, Expansion in Drafting, Chapter IV and Adding Text in Revision.)

Refer also to the following additional techniques applicable to narrative writing:

•   Smooth transitions in narration to get rid of Ands and Thens (Chapter VII, Editing).

- Narrative planners — Chapter III, Prewriting, Graphic Planners.
- Descriptive writing — Description, this chapter.

Informational Narrative

Fiction often predominates when we choose books to read aloud to elementary school children. Unwittingly, we communicate to children that fiction books are fun to read and non-fiction books are not. If young writers' first writing work in non-fiction is report writing, that message is reinforced.

Read well written and lively non-fiction to your students. Show them that it can be as exciting as fiction. Show them that non-fiction can have suspense, adventure, and humor.

Many young writers exhibit an unquenchable thirst for facts and begin their quest to satisfy that need for knowledge as soon as they can read. Encourage these young writers to write about factual information.

What Works

1. **Nature and Discovery.** Make watching nature or science documentaries on television a home work assignment and show some in your classroom. Ask your young writers to listen particularly to the narration. How does the narrator weave in facts? Remind them that the narrator is reading from a script that enhances the video — someone has written that script.

2. **Pet or Bird Watching Journal.** Set up a journal beside your classroom pet cage for interested students to observe the pet and write a few sentences about what it is doing. Ask them to think like the pet, talk to the reader of the journal, or try to copy the style of a TV nature series narrator. Model an entry for them.

> The gerbil, which is a herbivore, picks up a sunflower seed with his paws. He sits up, and his tail acts like a brace to keep him from falling over. He uses his sharp front teeth to crack the covering of the seed. Seed covers fly as he quickly goes through the handful of seeds.

If you have no classroom pet, ask the students do some bird watching in the playground or observe their own pets or birds in their yards. They might write a few sentences about what the pet or bird does, weaving in a fact they know about that animal.

3. **Where or How I Learned That Fact.** A narrative about a field trip, an adventure, an event, a place, or a person can tell how the writer learned a fact. *How I Learned* ... books appeal to fact gatherers.

Show your young writers by example that not all stories have a plot and that some of them can be filled with factual information.

Fiction

Many children come to school with a sense of story. They may have had stories read to them, seen movies and TV or heard family stories and events described. Some are able to tell a story or relate an event using the narrative form.

In school we read stories to them. They read picture books, easy readers, chapter books. They write personal narratives and informational pieces. They write about the things they know, the things they do, the things they like.

Then, when we say to them, "Now let's write fiction," some of them go berserk. They write stilted stories filled with fake characters mouthing boring dialogue. Or worse, they create breakfast to bed narratives of colorless characters. What happened?

What happened was we assumed that children who hear and read fiction can write it. We would never assume that a person who can read music or enjoys listening to it can compose a concerto. Such an assumption is no more valid for reading and writing.

Some children have the impression that fiction is an esoteric form of writing vastly different from their narratives about their lives and experiences. In order for them to write effective fiction, young writers must be shown the similarities and differences between their personal narratives and "real books," as they are wont to call fiction.

They need to understand that fiction, like their personal narratives, is about characters with real emotions, in real settings, experiencing real events. While fiction writers create these characters, settings, and events from their imagination, they are based on their real life experience or study. These components cannot seem fake or unbelievable to the reader. Readers of fiction expect characters to whom they can relate, the tension or suspense of conflict, and a resolution of that conflict. Writers of fiction must deliver all these.

As any professional writer will tell you, good fiction is more difficult to write than any other genre. But, because it has the least constraints and allows the use of our imagination and different writing styles, it is also one of the most fun. Young writers love to write fiction. Help them improve their stories with information and lessons about fiction writing.

I am treating fiction here, under narrative style, because children's pieces are dominated by that style and it is what drives every story. Even so, you will note descriptive and expository elements in many of the lessons and models presented. As writers develop, descriptive and expository styles play an increasingly important role in narrative writing.

Fiction is constructed from the following components.

- Characters — Main Characters, Minor Characters, Character Development.
- Dialogue — Reveal Character, Advance Plot.
- Setting — Time, Place, Mood, and Atmosphere.
- Plot — Six Basic Plots, Plot Motivation, Setbacks.

- Point of View — First Person, Third Person
- Beginnings, Transitions, and Endings.

Characters

The main character is also known as the hero or heroine, or the protagonist. In stories with good guys and bad guys, the villain, or antagonist, may be a main character such as the wolf in The Three Little Pigs. Minor characters are the others in the story who interact with or help the main characters. They are used to enhance and help reveal the main characters' personae. Sometimes they are referred to as foils. Examples are Cinderella's stepsisters.

Writers reveal their characters through five means:

- what they say
- what they think (a book's advantage over stage or film)
- what they do
- description
- what the other characters say about them.

What Works

1. **Discuss Characters.** Find examples in the children's reading and writing of main characters, heroes and heroines, villains, minor characters. Talk to them about the characters' roles. When you read to them, draw their attention to passages that reveal characters through the five means listed in the previous paragraph. Ask them to identify such passages in their independent or class reading. Invite them to try these ways to reveal characters in their writing. Have them enter the five ways in their notebooks.

2. **Literature Response Character Analysis.** Instead of requiring a standard book report, make locating examples of character revelation the focus of a book response. Readers select a character in their independent reading and list everything they can find about the character. They record the page number where they found the clues the author used to reveal the character. They sum up the character in their own words.

3. **Writer's Notebooks.** Ask young writers to create a bank of characters, including names, that they can use in future writing. Brainstorm with them to start the bank.

Example:

- Biff, a gravely voiced, school yard bully.
- Uncle Tom, who lives in Maine and raises sheep.
- Ashley Sturbridge, a computer whiz in their homeroom.

The telephone book is a good source of first or last names when children

```
3/H          Meridith Morris
The Tale Of Jonny Town Mouse
Beatrix Potter
     Timmy Willie doesn't
like the town. Afraid of everthing.
He was nervouse in the hamper.
In longs to be back home

Page 15  He awoke in fright
              trembled
Page 16  dogs barked.....
21 T.W almost fright
33 The noise upstairs made soard....
34 appetite failed....
34 felt faint
44 grew thin
```

A second grader's Literature Response.

are stuck on naming their characters. Show young writers how important the choice of name is to the character's image by having them repeat the names of some of their favorite characters. Have them study portraits (art prints) and make up plausible names for the people. A Thaddeus Fletcher will conjure up a different image than Tom Smith; an Abigail Billingsly, a different image than Patsy Kelly.

> Writers are required to get permission from classmates if they want to use their names in a story.

4.   **Character Traits.** Character traits are abiding personal qualities. They can be physical, psychological, and social. A sample list is provided in **Reproducible #26**.

- Brainstorm a list of character traits with your young writers. List them on chart paper. Encourage children to name traits they have or their friends have. Ask them to name traits of characters in their reading and enter them on the chart throughout the year.

- For a science-writing activity, send the children to the library, or to lunch, with a clipboard. Have them watch and listen very carefully to another person and record any repetitive gestures or habits they see. They might see things such as excessive blinking, talking with lots of hand motion, facial expressions, or finger nail biting. They might hear sniffs, or throat clearing.

- Ask them what they make of their findings. Encourage them to discuss their findings with other scientist-writers. The skill of observation is important, for artists, writers, and scientists.

- Keep all this information in writer's notebooks.

5.   **Characters From Art or Photographs.** (15 minutes) Give copies of the trait list, **Reproducible #26**, to each student. Model a character sketch, with writers in the class contributing ideas to make the character come alive. Have them refer to the trait list. Physical description should be just a fraction of the overall presentation. Write the sketch on the board or an overhead transparency projection. Tell them anyone may use the class character later in a story.

In a subsequent twenty minute session, invite your writers to select a portrait from a collection of art prints and photographs. They will try to invent a character from the person in their picture and write a brief character sketch about him in their writer's notebook.

Or, do this as an oral exercise. Each writer should take the time to study a portrait and then introduce the character to the class as if it were someone they knew personally.

6.   **Visualizing a Character.** Many young writers find that a drawing of their characters helps keep them in mind as they write. Encourage writers to draw their characters at any time during drafting and revision. Have them keep the drawing with the rough draft and use it for their illustrations.

7.   **The Character Game.** (20-25 minutes) Make a set of character occupation cards from samples in **Reproducibles # 27** and **#28**. The object of this

game is to write a paragraph that reveals a character's occupation and character traits using clues and using the five ways authors reveal characters. Writers may not use the word on the card.

The other writers will use the clues to name the occupation and tell what they think the character is like. As writers, we do not want to hit our readers over the head with information but rather to let them figure things out with a few clues from us. Children love this concept and expression and can apply it in their writing. (See Chapter IV, Drafting, "Don't Hit Your Reader Over the Head.")

a) Reproduce and cut the occupations series provided. For a longer lasting set, reproduce them on card stock or laminate the pages before cutting.

b) Give out cards randomly in the morning for the Character Game to take place in the afternoon or give them out one day and write the next. If writers are not able to use the cards, they may select their own character and occupation. Some kids will trade. That's fine. All writers should have a character about whom they can write.

c) At writing time, list on the board the five ways writers let their readers know about characters. Give examples that do not hit the reader over the head. Give young writers 10-15 minutes for the practice writing. Write a paragraph yourself, as a model, on the board or on an overhead transparency projection.

d) Share the results. If students cannot guess the occupation from the character's traits, suggest that the writer try adding a few more clues. Ask students what clues they heard and which of the five means to reveal character were used.

Carol J.   9/22/94

The man in the gray sweat suit blew his whistle. He told the kids to get in line.

A second grader's character game practice write.

e) Have the children save the paragraphs in their notebooks. Repeat the game again later in the year and ask the writers to compare the paragraphs. Encourage them to evaluate their own progress.

Dialogue

Some children have an innate sense of dialogue. They are the potential playwrights of the future. Others seem to get mired down in inane dialogue that neither reveals their characters nor advances their plot. Following are some ideas that can help young writers with their use of dialogue.

Be sure to separate the mechanics of dialogue, an editing function, from the concept of dialogue as a writers tool for revealing character and advancing the plot. Teach the mechanical conventions of dialogue in conjunction with editing and at the level of the writer's use. (See Chapter VII, Editing, Dialogue.)

What Works

1. **Revealing Character Traits Through Dialogue.** (15 minutes) The objective is for young writers to practice using dialogue to reveal a character trait.

Brainstorm a list of possible single trait characters with your young writers.

Use the traits they charted in an earlier lesson. Examples: a school yard bully, a tired football player, a nervous airplane pilot, an irate coach, a nasty school crossing guard, a friendly school crossing guard.

Ask everyone to write one line of dialogue in their writer's notebook that reveals the trait and character. Model one on the board. Invite some writers to share theirs.

> School yard bully — "Give me your lunch money or I'll punch you out."
>
> Nervous plane pilot — "Check the fuel line, check the fuel line! We're near to landing."
>
> Irate coach — "You lily-livered babies better pull yourselves together for this next half or I'll have you running so many laps you'll be tripping over your tongues!"

2. **Model and Practice with Play Format.** (35 minutes) The objective of this model and activity is to help writers use dialogue that advances a plot, and reveals characters through what they say.

Brainstorm with young writers to form likely pairs of characters.

> traffic police and speeder
>
> doctor and patient
>
> librarian and reader
>
> waitress and diner
>
> bank teller and bank robber
>
> zoo keeper and parrot
>
> Santa Claus and one of his elves
>
> coach and player

a) Have peer partners make up a small vignette to act out in front of the class. Ask the participants to try for dialogue that 'hooks' the audience, makes us want to find out what happens next. Limit the dialogue to two lines apiece. Model one vignette for the class with a student.

Sample Vignette

> *Coach: Tom, Listen. This next batter is dangerous. Are you sure you know what pitch you are going to throw him? (Coach is worried.)*
>
> *Tom: I threw to him last year and he whiffs low and outside pitches. I think I'll throw him a couple of them. He'll go for them. No problem. (Tom is a confident fellow.)*
>
> *Coach: OK. Mix it up, though. If you get by this hitter we have the game and maybe the conference title. (Coach is worried and ambitious.)*
>
> *Tom: No sweat, Coach. (Tom is very confident.)*

b) Show them how to write the dialogue as in a play so each actor can see his lines. Use a color code so that each actor can find his lines in a hurry. Write the character name or draw a box around it in that color.

c) Let each pair perform their vignette.

d) Do not evaluate these exercises.

e) Invite young writers to try a play on their own or with a group.

3. **Dialogue Tied to Action in Story Form.** (25 minutes) The object of this minilesson is to show writers how to reveal their characters during dialogue. What the character is doing helps give information and move the plot forward as well.

a) Read aloud examples in literature where a character's actions or movements are described during the dialogue.

b) Have the students look for examples in the books they are reading or a literature series textbook. Share them. Note the way writers insert action description in the dialogue similar to stage directions in a play that tell actors what to do as they say their lines.

c) Brainstorm a list of activities in which two or three characters might be involved while they are in conversation.

- a coach showing a technique to several players
- a mother helping her kids with homework
- carpenters building a house
- spies snooping through computer files
- kids painting a mural
- a card game or board game with several players

d) Create a class model of conversation consistent with one of the listed activities. Ask young writers to focus on adding descriptive sentences about what the participants are doing, or what objects or tools they are using, during the conversation.

> "Where are you headed?" called Cheryl, racing her bike to catch up with Pat.
>
> "I'm going over to Lou's house," Pat said over her shoulder. She pedaled faster, hoping to leave Cheryl behind.
>
> "Wait up!" Cheryl yelled. "Do you think I could come, too?"
>
> Pat pretended not to hear her.

e) Invite writers to try one of their own. Share the results.

f) Suggest writers try this in their own writing.

g) Make this a target skill for their next narrative piece.

Setting

Setting involves time, place, weather, and mood or atmosphere. To reveal those elements, writers depend on descriptive writing, calling on all the senses to convey an image to the reader (see also Descriptive Writing in this chapter). Illustrations may complement the text and give information about character, setting, and ambiance, but they do not replace descriptive writing.

What Works

1. **Discuss Settings.** Read examples that contain descriptions invoking all the senses. Read from children's hand-published books as well as children's literature. (Doing so indicates to young writers that we value their published work.) Have students name the setting the author describes.

2. **Class Compilation of Settings.** Create a log or chart for young writers to enter the settings they identify and find in their reading. Ask them to list a few words or phrases the author used to reveal the setting. An example of an entry is:

> (Setting is a swamp) The kids jumped from hummock to hummock. Carrie slipped and her sneaker was lost in the muck. From *The Last Camp Out*, by Maurice Bowles. (Doug Fahey, grade 5)

3. **Literature Response Setting Analysis.** Make locating all references to setting in your students' independent reading the basis for a book response. Students should list pages and quote the author, tell what sense the author appeals to in each setting description, and what form the description takes — comparison, sensory based description, action.

4. **Establishing the Setting in Historical Fiction.** A reader knows a story's historical time setting by the clues the author gives him. The elements used depend on the location of the story and plot. Have your class study a piece of fiction set in the past and find the clues the author gives. This hunt could be the basis of a literature response journal entry.

Ask young writers to sort the clues into categories. Here are some they will find.

manner of speech, jargon, slang	names
clothing	customs
vehicles	manners
money	food and drink
tools	

Weaving these clues into a story is an exercise all aspiring writers should try.

5. **The Setting Game.** (30 minutes) The objective is for young writers try and use as many senses as possible in describing a place.

a) Make setting cards for the class using the series provided in **Reproducibles # 30 and # 31** or brainstorm with young writers for their own list. Some examples: morning on a farm, at the circus, the school lunch room on Friday, the beach in the evening.

b) Use the same procedure as in the Character Game (see What Works # 7, Character, this chapter). Ask students to write a brief paragraph in their practice books describing the scene, using clues, involving as many senses as possible, without using the words on the card.

c) Share and have others guess the place and time. Have the children save their paragraphs and repeat the game several times during the year. During self- evaluation they can analyze and evaluate their progress.

6. **Mood.** (15 minutes) The objective is to create an awareness of the vocabulary authors use to create mood or atmosphere in a story. Young writers practice creating mood or atmosphere in a practice write and in their own manuscripts.

Around Halloween is a good time to do this when students are absorbed in the idea of scariness, spookiness, and all the accouterments of the occasion.

a) Read a scary story or a sad story to the class.

b) Reread the story, and ask the students to raise their hands when they hear a word or phrase that they think helps create the mood of the book. List them on the board or have a student secretary take notes for a class chart to be made later.

c) Call attention to the verbs as well as nouns and adjectives used to create the atmosphere.

d) Invite writers to try this. Offer a sentence they might modify to create mood. For example,

> Original sentence: The cat went across the lawn.
>
> Results from class modification: The skinny black cat slunk slowly across the dark lawn.

Here is a sample list of base sentences that can be modified to create and communicate the noted moods.

> Lolly read her report card and took it home. (unhappiness)
> Mike heard his gymnastics scores announced. (elation)
> Sarah and her friends approached the house. (nervous, scared)
> Enrique and Pascal said they could find the trail. (confident)
> The trees around the campsite made sounds. (mysterious)

A fourth grader's setting game practice write.

7. **Weather.** Incorporating information about the weather is another way to create the atmosphere in a story. It would be pretty silly to describe a bright and beautiful day if you are trying for gloom and doom.

Combine writing and science with the study of weather and the use of weather to create literary atmosphere. Ask young writers to find reference to weather in their independent reading.

Have writers start a weather page in their writer's notebook to build a bank of phrases and sentences for future use. Professional writers use phrase books in this manner. Find one to show the young writers. They come in paperback, and you can get them at most book stores.

8. **Say Something.** Some children depend on visual cues to trigger their imagination. Invite writers to go into the class file of pictures and find a picture of a place. They can paste the picture on a page in their writer's notebook and say something about the setting. The focus can be on description of the place or the mood.

9. **Illustrate and Publish.** The act of illustration requires a visualization of characters and setting. Ask the writers to check with potential readers if their illustrations are consistent with the characters and settings set forth in their book.

Plot

Here are the six basic plots that have been used by all writers, from Shakespeare to Judy Bloom. They are in the public domain and young writers may use them without fear of plagiarism. They are expressed in problem and solution form.

- Lost and Found—person or object is lost and recovered.
- Character versus Nature—character survives a natural calamity.
- Character with a personal problem or goal—character solves it, reaches goal, or changes attitude or feelings.
- Good Guys versus Bad Guys—good guys usually win.
- Crime and Punishment or Mystery and Solution—character solves the mystery or crime and the culprit is caught.
- Boy meets Girl—problems or misunderstandings arise; characters resolve differences or clear up misunderstandings.

A copy of this list is provided in **Reproducible #31.**

These plots occur singly or in combination. Different motives, the reasons for the characters' actions, drive these six plots. Getting even, love and hate, rivalry, ambition, rebellion, self-sacrifice, sleuthing, and problem solving all drive the characters and events.

While the plot of a story provides the initial tension (Will the character reach the goal, solve the problem, find the missing link, solve the crime, win the heart, survive the storm?), added tension can be created through the use of setbacks and other devices.

What Works

1. **Minilesson About Plots.** Introduce the six basic plots to your students as they begin to write fiction. Introduce each one with an example from their reading background. Examples:

Lost and Found is the plot of *The Incredible Journey.*

Character vs. Nature is the plot of *Jaws.*

Character with Problem is the plot of *Freckle Juice.*

Good guys vs. Bad guys is the plot to *The Three Little Pigs.*

Crime and Solution is the plot of *Nancy Drew Mysteries.*

Boy Meets Girl is the plot of *Rapunzel.*

2. **Identify Plots in Reading.** Invite young writers to find these plots in their personal reading. You might make six plot charts for children to record the titles of books they are reading according to plot. They will notice that some of the plots are used in combination. This is excellent. Have them enter the title on both charts.

Provide students with a copy of the list of plots to keep in their writing folders. (see **Reproducible #31**.)

3. **Establish the Plot Early.** The conflict, goal, problem, or what the main

character wants, should be set up in the first sentence, paragraph, or page, depending on the length of the piece. If not stated outright, it should at least be hinted at very strongly. (see Beginnings, this section, for more information.)

Spend a half hour with your class finding out how early in a story authors reveal the conflict, goal, or problem. Use a collection of fiction books, as you did with the study of character and setting, or ask students to look at the fiction they are reading independently. Have them read the first sentence, paragraph, and page to find the plot set up. Invite them to share their findings by reading the passage aloud. Ask the class if they can identify the plot.

4.   **Three Sentence Synopsis.** To emphasize the three primary ingredients of a story—character, setting and plot—practice summarizing familiar stories in three sentences.

Examples:

Piper eliminates town's rats.	(Character and setting) beginning.
Town won't pay.	(Conflict or problem) middle.
Piper lures town's kids away.	(Plot resolution) resolution.
Pigs build houses.	(Character and setting) beginning.
Wolf destroys two of them.	(Conflict or problem) middle.
Wolf foiled and boiled at third house.	(Plot resolution) resolution.

Review the TV movie blurbs from your newspaper's weekly TV guide. Circle the ones you can present to the class. These are one sentence summaries naming characters, setting, and plot.

> *Bless the Beasts And Children—Six* misfits from a boys ranch-camp try to free a herd of buffalo marked for slaughter.

> *The Blob—*Formless red slime lands in Pennsylvania and engulfs people; teens try to warn scoffing adults.

> *Goliath Awaits—*An oceanographer finds a colony of survivors living in a luxury liner sunk by U-boats decades before.

Ask young writers if they can make a one sentence blurb about their own stories.

5.   **Minilesson About Story Timelines.** Most young writers' stories are presented in a simple linear form, events taking place in strict time sequence. (More fluent writers might use flash back or, as in detective stories, work back from the main event—the murder or crime.)

Read a short story, available in multiple copies, with the class. Or use the sample provided in **Reproducible #32**. Taking your students' suggestions, construct a timeline of the events of the story using the black board or on a long strip of paper taped to the board.

Next, have your students construct a timeline for a story they are reading independently.

Encourage young writers to use the timeline graphic planner detailed in Chapter III, Prewriting, when they are planning their next story.

6.   **Plot Resolution.** When young writers are having difficulty with endings, analyze some stories with them. Collect very easy to read, well illustrated books enough for each student or small groups of students. (Your school

librarian will help you find them.) Over two days, have the students read the books and identify the plot and the resolution. From their shared findings build a class chart or reproducible list of plots and their resolutions.

Examples:

> Lost and Found—object or pet was found by using an ad in the newspaper.
>
> Character with Problem—Kid made the softball team after she got a neighbor to pitch to her every evening for a month.
>
> Crime and Solution—By setting a trap, Encyclopedia Brown found out how the goldfish were stolen.

7. **Multiple Endings.** If students cannot find an ending to a story, suggest that they write three endings (solutions to the character's problem) and get some peer responses to help them decide which to use. Rather than writing three new endings, writers will often rework the original.

8. **Breakfast-to-Bed Stories.** Fourth grade girls especially love to write stories that go on endlessly. They want to include every last detail of the characters' lives. There is nothing wrong with this as a phase of development. We tend to view it as a problem because we contemplate the hours of editing and publishing it will require. We, therefore, discourage such verbosity.

Take a positive view of this trait. Be pleased that young writers can produce such a quantity of writing. Focus on the writers' use of target skills within these long pieces. Help them find places to improve their writing using the minilessons provided in this book. A long story will offer them many opportunities to apply the lesson materials.

Four natural feedback mechanisms at work in the classroom writing community will help Breakfast-to-Bed authors refine and shorten their manuscripts.

- Exposure to Author's chair and peer scrutiny will alert authors to the lack of reader interest in their unnecessary details.
- Publishing the piece may give the author an indication of its weakness, either in copying it to publish or by its poor reception after publication.
- Conferencing, in which you encourage writers to find the best parts, the most exciting event, or identify its plot and resolution, will help them identify their story's focus.
- Self-evaluation, particularly concentrating on the best part, often leads writers to recognize and delete the worst parts.

9. **Creating Tension.** Writers want to keep their readers turning the pages. They hook them into the story with the promise of an adventure. Then they must keep them interested. Writers want their readers to keep wondering, "What happened next?"

Writers build tension or suspense in several ways.

a) Time Pressure. The character has a limited amount of time to accomplish a goal or solve a problem. Examples of this are Rumpelstiltskin, and Hansel and Gretel. Other time pressure ideas:

- Forces of nature—tide coming in, impending storm...

- Deadline dates — preparations, contest entry deadlines, athletic training, mortgage payment, bomb set to go off, harvests before the rain, frost, onset of winter...
- Arrival of holiday — birthday or Christmas gifts to make...

b) Setbacks. The important part of plot is the series of setbacks the main character faces in trying to resolve the conflict or attain the goal. In well developed fiction, there are often three or more of them. The series of setbacks make up the middle of the story. The main character overcomes each successively more difficult setback — the last one in a grand way that brings the story to a satisfactory close.

Tell your writers a really dumb story with no setbacks. Be sure to say it with feeling as if you really think it is a great story. For example:

> Once upon a time there was a kid who lived in Iowa. He wanted a pony so badly. He asked his mother, "Will you get me a pony?" She said yes. He got his pony and lived happily ever after.

Wait. Watch their reaction. Ask them what they thought of the story. Agree with them that it stunk. Then tell them a new version.

> Once upon a time there was the kid who lived in Iowa. He wanted a pony so badly. He asked his mother, "Will you get me a pony?" She said no. He told his grandfather that, if he would buy him a pony, it could count for five birthdays and five Christmases. Grandfather said no. Then Grandfather said, "If you will work and raise the money for the pony this summer, I will buy the saddle and feed, and let you keep it in my barn." The kid worked hard all summer, picking berries, selling worms, helping with mowing, and such, until he had the money. He and grandfather went to buy the pony. And they all lived happily ever after.

Now ask the students what they thought of the story. Which of the two stories did they prefer? Ask them to identify the setbacks the kid faced: Mom's *no*, Grandfather's *no*, Grandfather's challenge to raise the money on his own.

Ask students to find evidence of setbacks in their independent reading. They are the events that temporarily prevent the characters from solving their problem. A list might include injury, weather, losses, mistakes, misunderstandings, and mishaps.

> Sports injury during training for a goal.
> Loss of horses or wagon wheel during the pioneer's trek west.
> Loss of crops through weather or locust.
> Flat tire in a bike race.

Suggest creating a setback as a target skill for their next story and identifying them in peer conferences.

c) Reader Is In On a Secret the Character Doesn't Know. Tension rises when the reader learns something through the narration that the character does not know. The reader becomes anxious for the character.

> The saddle girth is frayed and ready to break.

A villain is hiding in the house.

A trap has been laid.

You might read this example to your young writers.

> The lean and hungry wolf waited in the woods. When the dark of the night faded into the gray of early morning, he crept across the yard and into the barn.
>
> Piglet woke to the sound of his mother in the kitchen. She called to him to come down and gather the eggs for their breakfast. He dressed quickly and went down to the pantry to fetch the egg basket.
>
> A fine mist covered the farm and the barn cast a huge shadow over the yard. The barn door, left ajar for the chickens to come and go, was damp from the mist. Piglet slid the door open and stepped inside.

d) Anticipation of a Major Scene. Characters set up the tension through their dialogue about The Big Event or their warning, "Wait until Aunt Harriet gets here!" They are anticipating another character's arrival or action. This suspense ploy is used in the *Miss Nelson* books by Harry Allard and James Marshall.

Encourage young writers to identify the ways authors of their independent reading create suspense or tension. Ask them to chart them and try to incorporate them into their writing. Make their identification a target skill in conferences.

Point Of View

Point of view refers to how the author of a story speaks to the reader, through whose eyes the events are viewed and reported. Young or developing writers need to concern themselves with two basic points of view:

- The third person, wherein the author acts as a narrator who knows everything and tells the reader what the main characters are thinking and doing. The author uses *he, she*, and *they* to tell the story.
- The first person, wherein the author tells the story from the main character's point of view. The author uses 'I' to tell the story.

What Works

1. **Point of View Shifts.** Young writers may start their stories in the third person, calling their characters by name, then suddenly switch to *I* and become the main character. It may happen when writers are using their own names and that of a friend in the story.

This is great! It reflects that the writers are really into their story and characters. Isn't it wonderful they are so engaged with their work?

With a small amount of discussion, writers who exhibit this level of engagement will find that they are confusing their readers. The point of view must remain consistent. Finding places where the point of view changes can become a focus in peer conferencing and in Author's Chair.

2. **Which Point of View?** Ask young writers to find books in which the point

of view is the third person narrator, and some in which it is the first person, I. Discuss with the group which they prefer and why.

- An advantage to using the first person is that the reader more easily identifies with the main character.

- A disadvantage of the first person account of a story is that the main character needs to be present in every scene in order to relate the events. To overcome this problem, writers have minor characters tell the main character about events he or she missed. Invite students to find such an occurrence in their independent reading.

- Another disadvantage of the first person view is that there is no tension as to whether the main character is going to survive. He obviously survived to tell the tale. Therefore, a writer generally would probably not use this point of view for a spy thriller, or danger-ridden adventure story.

3. **Change the Point of View.** Ask students to try changing the point of view in a paragraph from *I* to *he* or *she,* and visa versa. Make a transparency or individual copies of the sample paragraphs provided in **Reproducible #33**. This can be done orally.

4. **Write a Story in the First Person.** Invite writers to try the first person point of view in a fiction piece. They are probably familiar with using *I* in personal narratives.

Beginnings, Transitions, and Endings

A visiting author told the young writers in my class that they had to hook their reader in the first sentence. The students thereafter referred to their beginning sentence as "the hook." In peer conferences they analyzed and critiqued each other's hooks. They researched fiction and non-fiction to find effective hooks.

The concept hooked them! Mimicking professional style and craft is a good approach for young writers to take in finding story starts, as it is in all aspects of writing.

Charles Shultz, through Snoopy as the ever-hopeful author, gets a lot of mileage out of "It was a dark and stormy night," the opening of Bulwer-Lytton's work, *Paul Clifford.* This particular hook is regarded as so trite that it has engendered a yearly national contest in which writers submit purposely overblown and trite paragraphs mimicking Bulwer-Lytton's style—all tongue-in-cheek.

Nonetheless, Madeleine L'Engle used "It was a dark and stormy night" to begin *A Wrinkle In Time,* and she won a Newberry Award for her story. Studying the way authors start their stories can be helpful to young fiction writers.

What Works

1. **First Liners.** (30 minutes)

   - Arrange a session in the school library to examine fiction books.
   - Work out a procedure with the librarian for the students to reshelve the books they examine. For example, students might have two to three long colored slips of paper with their name on the ends to put in the place of the books they pull from the shelf.
   - Students bring their writer's notebooks.
   - Students write the first sentence of as many books as they can in the time allowed.
   - Reshelve books and return to the classroom.

   In a subsequent 20 minute session, analyze the story starts and sort them into categories. Ask students to write the categories, one to a half page, in their writer's notebook.

   Throughout the year, have the students add favorite opening sentences from their independent reading to the category page. Remind them that the upkeep of their notebook is part of the writing evaluation process for the grade they earn.

   Sample of first sentence(s) categories: (See list in **Reproducible #34**.)

   - The author introduces the main character by name.
   - The main character, named, is thinking or doing something.
   - The author describes the setting (place).
   - The author tells the setting (time).
   - The author sets up the conflict in the first sentence.
   - The character is talking. An event is in progress.
   - Combinations of any of these.
   - A letter or note.
   - A prologue telling of an event in past that sets up the story.

   Writers who have no difficulty starting their stories find verification and confirmation in seeing story starts like their own—"I already write like a pro!" This increases their self-confidence. Those writers who have trouble writing that first sentence now have a resource.

2. **Transitions.** Fiction is narrative writing, and narrative writing is characterized by the passage of time. A writer helps the reader follow the story's events, in time and place, by using transitions that mark the start of new paragraphs. For example:

   - The following morning...
   - Meanwhile, back at the ranch...

- When the picnic was over, we went back to town.
- In three weeks...

For a lesson about transition of time and place, refer to Chapter VII, Editing, When to Start a Paragraph.

3. **Endings.** Some young writers have trouble bringing their stories to a close. Commonly, this is because

- They might not want them to end — they're enjoying the process and their story.
- They have become bored with them.
- They have lost the thread of the story and gone off to side issues from which they cannot reach the resolution of their original plot.
- They have not identified their plot and therefore don't know the resolution it requires.

Teachers become anxious when writers don't finish pieces. Adults are more concerned about closure than children. Ask any professional writer about unfinished work. They all have plenty. Not all ideas pan out. Some turn out to be just plain bad ideas.

Instead of spending time and energy getting these young writers to finish these stories, we need to spend time and energy helping them learn why they are not able to complete them.

How to Help

(a) Young writers who write on and on are having so much fun with their stories we should be grateful. Work with these writers to ensure they are incorporating the skills and ideas under study. Have them mark skill use in their manuscripts. Review the plot with them and ask them about their plans for the resolution. Say no more.

(b) The writers who have lost interest in their story probably picked a topic of minor interest to them. Perhaps they selected it for the wrong reason — a friend was doing the same idea, the idea came from TV or a book, and the writers did not have sufficient experience or information to back it up.

- Ask such writers to go through the story as it stands and mark the places where they did a good job on anything such as vocabulary, conventions, or dialogue.
- Help them identify why the story fizzled, and let them know that this happens to professional writers as well.
- Ask them to write a sentence at the top or bottom of their manuscript, giving the reason they are abandoning the piece.
- Have them save their work in the back of their writer's notebook or in the class's designated storage for old manuscripts.
- Watch for a repetition of this difficulty.

(c) The writers who lose the thread of their story need to identify its original plot and corresponding resolution, to refer back to their graphic planner, to recall the events they were planning to use to reach the resolution, and to locate where they went off on a side trip.

- Suggest that they may want to cut out and save the side trip part of the manuscript in case it contains something they can use again.
- Have them meet with a peer and tell how the story will end. If the interest and engagement with the story is still high, they will probably finish it.

(d) Writers who can't seem to find the right ending need to review the basic plot types and their corresponding resolutions. They might also try writing several endings and select the one that works best. Encourage writers to visualize the ending of their story early in the planning stage. Suggest that they draft the ending early on. This will provide them with a goal to reach for and help them keep their story on track.

Some students may become chronic non-finishers. This is a different situation. These writers need help focusing on a small project they can complete. (See also Chapter III, Prewriting.)

Additional Reading

As teachers, we need to make it a continuing professional habit to read about writing. Our ability to teach the craft is limited by our knowledge of it. The books on the subject written for children contain the essential aspects, are fast reading, and will help you focus on specific areas to research at more advanced levels. (See Bibliography at the end of Chapter II.)

Expository Writing

In this book, the term *expository writing* refers to a writing style characterized by ideas, opinions, information, directions, explanations, and argument, supported by substance. Unlike the time-based narrative style, exposition is based on a hierarchy of ideas, a sequence of steps, comparison, or a specific form appropriate to the writing purpose. All expository writing must be focused and unified to be effective.

Most of what we say, hear, write, and read is exposition. A *Keep off the Grass* sign, an explanation of why our homework is late, instructions for playing Monopoly, a newspaper column, a recipe, an invitation to a party, a textbook — all are exposition. Most communication of practical importance is exposition.

Expository writing goes by many names: essay, report, theme, review, and non-fiction. We must be careful not to use the terms fiction and non-fiction as synonyms for narrative and expository styles, since narration can be either fictional or non-fictional. For example, a narrative about a family outing is non-fiction; a narrative about the adventures of Peter Rabbit is fiction. We can best avoid confusion by referring to each kind of writing by its specific genre name, such as personal narrative, literature response, book review, opinion paper, business letter, invitation, fiction, science fiction, poetry, etc.

Personal Exposition

Personal writing is the best place for young writers to start in expository writing. Emerging writers will naturally do this — kindergarten children and first graders draw pictures of things relative to themselves, and their messages are about themselves.

> This is me and my mother. —This is my dog. He is smaller than me. — This is my house. It has a big tree in front. — I love my cat. She licks me and lets me hug her. It feels funny when she licks me. Her tongue is all prickly.

Developing writers should start in the same fashion, writing about what they know, feel, believe, perceive, and want. The focus at the start of a school year should be on personal writing in order to engage the student writers and give them lots of practice writing from their interests, knowledge, and experience. All your lessons about composing and conventions can be taught using personal exposition and narration as a vehicle for their application.

Later in the year — once your young writers are familiar with the workings of the classroom writing community, have experience with the writing process, and are writing freely — they can branch out into expository writing that requires research and considerations of new facts and ideas. Their writing about new concepts and ideas will help them think them through.

What Works

1. **Introduce Yourself.** Ask writers early in the school year to write a paragraph that will introduce them to the rest of the class. Help them make of list of possible topics to include, such as where they are from, what they like to do, what they are good at, the music they like, favorite kind of books, food preferences, earliest memories, or anything they feel they want their classmates to know.

8/24/94

I would be perfect being a sales-men (becous) I am nice, And (becous) I like to sell things to pepole. Also I'm youst to selling things to pepole from all the (grage sals) I was in last year, And I like pepole.

A third grader tells about himself.

Save the piece for further development. Do not evaluate these early pieces.

2. **What Do You Think?** Expressing opinions should be modeled early. Young writers' expository writing should not be confined to informational pieces. Science writing, learning journals, and book recommendations provide some opportunities for young writers to express opinions.

• Model how to state an opinion and back it up with reasons.

> I think we fourth graders shouldn't have to share the playground at recess with kindergartners. They take too long on the slides. They hog the swings. We knock them over by mistake and then we get in trouble.
>
> I think the Goosebumps books by Stine are the greatest. They are just scary enough to give you goosebumps but you don't have nightmares.
>
> I think the smaller meal worm is going to turn into a beetle before the bigger one. It is already turning dark and that's what happened just before David's meal worm turned into a beetle.

• Brainstorm topics. Help students come up with more weighty issues than food and TV preferences.

Sample opinion topic list from a fifth grade class in Sarasota, Florida.

- lunchroom rules
- homework load
- computer access
- food preferences
- music preferences
- phys ed
- allowances
- clothing styles
- school bus schedule

Challenge writers to write the reasons for their opinion without the use of the word *because*.

Have students publish short opinion papers, no more that a paragraph, for a class *What Do You Think?* book. Class collection books are the easiest publishing projects and should be utilized early in the year. Conduct a class exchange edit for the several conventions that comprise the class editing standards.

3. **Everyday Stuff.** Kids are knowledgeable on a variety of subjects for early expository writing. When studying the elements of expository writing they might use these common, universal topics for the practice writing sessions.

- Money — United States coins
- Playing cards
- Books as objects
- Toys
- Playground games
- Grocery store
- Television programs
- Weather
- Vehicles
- Vacations

4. **Personal Expertise.** Most students have expertise in some area. It might be in a sport, an art, a hobby, travel, a craft, a game, a chore, or a TV program. Whatever it is, they should be encouraged to write an informational piece about their expertise. A requirement might be to include a number of words that are unique to that topic — words the ordinary person on the street would not know.

Model this idea for young writers. Ask someone in the class who takes music, art, craft, or sport lessons to compose a piece on the subject with you in front of the class. Underline the new vocabulary. This practice, noting words associated with a topic, is a precursor to note taking (see What Works #7, Informational Exposition — Gathering Information, later in this chapter).

Informational Exposition

Teachers often ask children to write about a subject following total immersion, extensive study of a theme or class topic that includes multimedia presentations and hands on projects. Writing about the topic is one way for children to demonstrate what they do and do not understand. Preparation for this writing should include a choice of genre, time to gather information, time to talk about their findings, help with organization, and models of finished products.

Choice of Presentation Form

Children should have as much choice as possible in the way they approach topical assignments. The object is to have them exhibit understanding of the concepts and retention of factual information about the topic. Individual students will recall different aspects of the topic depending on prior knowledge and their interest in the topic. You might require that specific information about the topic be included in all presentations, but the choice of form should remain with the students. Some of these choices:

- oral presentations
- poetry
- non-fiction narratives
- reports
- newspaper articles
- fiction
- dioramas
- charts, maps, posters
- flip books and shape books

Gathering information

Gathering information may not seem like a writing activity, but it is. It is a vital part of prewriting, which itself is a key to writing. The drafting and revision of this book took me fourteen months, but prewriting was a three year process. During that time I was gathering information, planning the organization, and rehearsing the content. We write best about what we know. Knowledge building is a writing prerequisite.

What Works

1. **Scrapbooks.** Informational writing comes more easily to young writers who have immersed themselves in a topic. A long term scrapbook project helps children become expert in a subject. Let everyone in the school and community know the topic and sub-topics your students have chosen. Publish them in the school newsletter. Have students write letters to request materials and collect data. Engage the help of the media specialist. Pictures also are a source of information for developing readers. Compiling a scrapbook is a way to gather information.

Bring community resources to your classroom for as many aspects of the topics as possible. A variety of purposeful writing will arise out of the quest

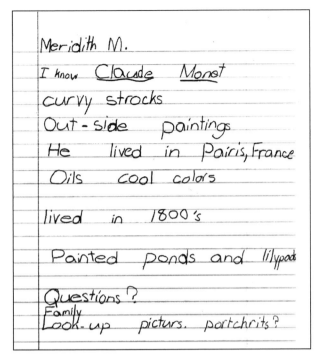

Meridith M.
I know <u>Claude Monet</u>
curvy strocks
Out-side paintings
He lived in Pairis, France
Oils cool colors

lived in 1800's

Painted ponds and lilypod

Questions?
Family
Look-up picturs. portchrits?

A second grader's list of
What I Know So Far.

for information — letters, interviews, invitations, captions in the scrapbook, a chronicle of the quest. Writing about the topic should come about naturally.

I just love the expression, "He hasn't two thoughts to rub together." For all the work we do on critical thinking skills, when you get right down to it what contributes best to thinking is having a wealth of information at your beck and call. We can't build analogies without specifics to compare. We can't generalize from two samples. We can't evaluate without criteria and comparisons.

2. **What Do I Already Know.** Have students make lists of what they know already about the topic or the aspect they have chosen to investigate. Some lists are single word lists, others are sentences. Writers find it easier to develop webs after they see the range of a topic as it is displayed in a list.

3. **What's the Best Place To Start?** Young writers should start their research in easy picture books about their topic. Reading the text should not interfere with finding information. Fiction and non-fiction can be used. Captions provide excellent information. The first readings should be done without attempting to take notes.

I advise all researchers, young and old, to go straight to the non-fiction section of the Children's Room in the public library and find the easiest, illustrated book on their topic. Read it quickly and you will find you have a clear overview of the topic. The writer has even presented a possible outline of the topic's main points in the form of a table of contents. Focus on the most interesting part of the topic and find other children's illustrated books about that. Look also for fiction about the topic. After you have narrowed the topic for your investigation, proceed to other resources, such as magazines and audio-visual materials. Use encyclopedias as a last resort.

When some high school students told me they would be embarrassed to use the children's library, I advised them to take a little kid along or take the children's book into the adult section to read it.

4. **Pocket Sized Fact Books.** Young writers may like to use small, hand made fact books to record the information they gather for their piece.

Mary Compton, Gulf Gate Elementary, Sarasota, Florida, shows her class of second/third graders how to make small folded paper books out of one piece of unlined copy paper. The pages are 1/16 of the sheet. She says these little books encourage the children to record facts briefly and discourage them from copying from encyclopedias. The students read easy, illustrated non-fiction books and they shorten the information to fit in their books. They naturally paraphrase the material they find.

Here's how to fold the paper to make a small, fit-in-the-pocket Fact Book.

Fold a blank sheet of paper in half vertically, like a hot dog roll.

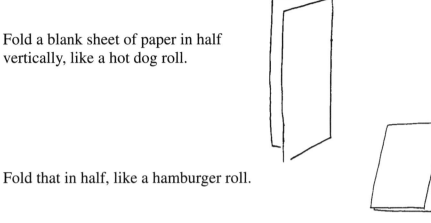

Fold that in half, like a hamburger roll.

Fold that in half, like a half a peanut butter sandwich.

Open the sheet and hold it vertically, facing you.

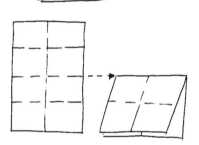

Fold it in half as shown.

cut

Cut down from the folded edge halfway, to the first folded crease, as shown.

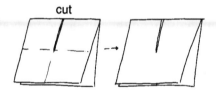

Unfold it and refold it lengthwise, like a hot dog roll. Pinch it together to make the center hole shaped like a diamond.

Push it even closer until it forms a plus mark, +.

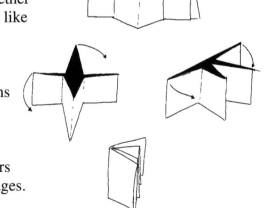

Fold two sides around the others to make a little book of four pages.

Have your students write their names on their Fact Books and the topic for which they are going to hunt for facts.

5.   **The ABCs of the topic.** When young writers write an informational piece, ask them to start an ABC (alphabetical) list of all the words associated with the topic. Their classmates can help. For example, Horses—*Appaloosa, bridle, cast a shoe, draft horse, equestrian, foal, gelding, horse, Indian paint, jockey, Kentucky Derby, loco, mare, etc.*

Small books result from this practice, as well as the development of schemata—background knowledge associations that help a reader comprehend written text. The concept of *horse* is extended.

6.   **Field Trip Preparation and Report.** The value of field trips is enhanced by preparation. The technique used by these first grade teachers works at any grade level.

> *Nancy Erwin and Jean Shannon, Abel Elementary, Bradenton, Florida,*
> help their first graders get the most out of field trips by providing information
> about the place before the trip. The children make small fold-over books.
> They write in them before and after the trip.

Page one: What I think I will see.

Page two: observations. Parent chaperones carry a clipboard and write what the children observe and tell them about during the trip. They write the child's name next to an entry. On their return, they type the observations and the children cut their respective items from the sheet and paste them in their booklet on the observation page.

Page three: What I remember from the trip.

Page four: What else I want to know (composing questions).

7.   **Note Taking.** Young writers need to know how to gather information from print sources. They need to know what they can use as it is written and what they must put in their own words. For example, a sentence such as "Whales are mammals" is in the public domain and may be used as it is written. By contrast, "All the whales sighted off the coast of Maryland that October morning were cows with nursing young." This is a creative statement and can not be copied without citing author and source.

Note taking is one of the most difficult tasks for students. Identifying topic and content words is a first step. If students have had the opportunity to write informational pieces based on personal expertise, they will be familiar with the concept of vocabulary unique to a topic. An editing standard of correcting content words reinforces the concept as well. (See Chapter VII, Editing, Content Words, Spelling.)

a) Content Words. Help young writers identify content words in informational text. Use highlighting markers and a natural history article from *Ranger Rick Magazine,* or any other age-appropriate material. Ask students to read the article, tell what the topic is, and underline any words they think are specific to that topic. Share findings (See "Spelling," Chapter VII Editing, for more details about this technique).

b) Reader-Teller to Listener-Writer. (Model this procedure with your class first.) One technique for joint research is the use of read-tell and listen-write partners. In this technique two young writers incorporate the four language arts as they search for information about a topic under study. The Reader-Teller silently reads a paragraph in an easy, picture book on the topic and tells his partner what it is about. The Listener-Writer writes down what he understands his partner to have said. They can converse to make sure they have the information correct.

c) <u>What Am I looking For</u>? It is helpful for students to decide what they are looking for before they begin their research. Have them refer to their lists of what they already know and make a new one of what they would like to learn. Two questions or items are sufficient to start.

d) <u>Model Note Taking</u>. In fifth and higher grades, model note taking with an overhead projector transparency of grade level material on a topic under study. Or use multiple copies of the text. Predetermine with the class what kind of information they are seeking. List some questions to be answered.

Read the material to the students, a paragraph at a time, and ask them to identify important information and key phrases. Underline them on a clear transparency placed over the text or have the students underline it on their copy. Express your thoughts aloud about the information as you write your notes on a blank transparency or on the board. Ask the students to write their own notes from the information they thought was important.

Collect the notes and text and set them aside for a few days. (Diagnose the class for those students who will need more modeling and practice.) Give the notes back after a week, and ask the students to write a few sentences on the topic using only their notes. Invite some students to discuss the topic in front of the class using their notes.

Repeat the note taking model several times in the year. It is a difficult skill and will require a great deal of practice.

Time to Talk

Once writers have gathered some information about the topic, they need time to talk about it with other writers. They need to compare notes, trade information, and discuss the genre they have selected for their presentation.

What Works

1. **Small Discussion Groups or Peer Groups in a Timed Meeting.** The objective of the discussion group is to trade information and hear what others have to say about the overall topic. An agenda for the discussion, in the form of three or four questions to address, will help the group accomplish its objectives.

Help your students compose three or four generic questions that will lead to trading information and discussing the topic. Chart the most useful questions. Make the list available to all the students. Use class secretaries to do this.

Examples of some questions the groups might use:

- What do you find most interesting about the subject?
- What confuses you about the subject?
- What else would you like to know?
- What bits of new information did you learn about the topic?
- How do you suppose people such as scientists, historians, etc. originally found out about this topic?
- What part of the topic do you like the best?
- If you could ask the experts about the topic, what would you ask them?

The groups should be small, no more than four writers. Set a definite time limit. Concrete proof of their interaction is a must — a recording or written notes will serve.

2. **Tell One Fact.** Everyone in class tells one fact they learned about the topic. If a student says "They took my fact," ask the student to find another one while the fact telling goes on, and assure him that you will return to get his fact. Variations on the same fact are fine.

Summary — Informational Exposition

Report writing is one of the most difficult tasks students face. Students need to know a subject in some depth before they can write intelligently and effectively about it. We only make report writing a frustrating exercise and invite plagiarism if we fail to provide the immersion, resources, and prewriting time to acquire knowledge of the subject. Ask any parent, and they will document the tears, the photocopying, and the help they give to produce a school report. That should not be necessary. When it is, it is a clear indication that the report writing assignment was premature.

Take informational writing step by step. Teach young writers how to gather data, discuss it, take notes, gather more data, ask questions, find the area within the topic that interests them most, select a genre for their presentation, plan, draft, discuss some more, revise, and finally produce a significant document. The main objective of the first report writing should be teaching students how to do one. Once students know how to do all these things, they can begin to use writing as an important learning tool.

Persuasive Exposition

Persuasion is the art of making a reader change his mind. We write to ask readers to change their plans or actions. We may aim at a practical result — vote for us, contribute money to a cause, or buy something.

Student government elections and school fund raisers offer young writers an opportunity to practice persuasive writing. Settling differences, changing classroom rules, and seeking privileges all call on persuasive writing skills. A typical persuasive piece is divided into three sections. (See also Chapter III, Prewriting, Planning Techniques.)

- a statement of proposition or opinion including acknowledgment of the opposition's stand and showing why that opposition is false or weak

- arguments
- best summarizing argument (clincher)

The elements of a persuasive piece usually take up the following space: 20% statement and acknowledgment; 70% arguments; 10% clincher and summary.

Arguments include:

- facts
- concrete examples and case histories
- comparisons/analogies
- authoritative quotes
- statistics

The clincher is the very best argument, saved for the ending.

What Works

1. **Analyze Ads.** Separating fact and opinion is a mainstay in most schools' curricula, and teachers have developed many fine lessons about advertising and propaganda. These lessons lay the ground work for persuasive writing.

An analysis of advertisements shows the basic approaches to persuading us to buy products: appealing to our vanity, placing us in association with celebrities, saving us money, promising us better health.

Use TV, magazine, and cereal box advertising as sources of study. Ask your young writers to find the words, phrases, and sentences that reveal the author's approach to persuading them to buy a product.

2. **Class Model of Persuasion.** Before you ask young writers (fourth graders at least) to write a persuasive piece, model the formula for your class. Fold or line chart paper to reflect the space allotments. (See diagram in Chapter III, Prewriting, planning techniques.) Develop a class persuasive paper to suggest a playground or cafeteria rule change. Draft each of the sections. Ask students to think of as many arguments as possible to fill in the reserved 70 percent of space. Leave the chart paper up for two to three days as an invitation for more arguments.

Example of a persuasive piece (fifth grader)

> Mom, you should let me have a horse. I know you will say no at first because we have no place to keep it. But Kristin told me I can keep it at her grandfather's farm with her two horses.
>
> If I had a horse I would take care of it. Grandma is always saying taking care of a pet develops responsibility. You could buy me the horse for my birthday. I'll spend my own money to buy stuff for the horse. I know I can get a saddle secondhand from a kid in my class. And you were the one who wanted me to take riding lessons anyway.
>
> Having a horse will give me a lot to write about in writing workshop and I will get better grades. Don't you think it would be worth a try?
>
> Your daughter,
>
> Jody

Expository Writing Content

Organization

Expository writing can be based on sequential order, as in directions; a hierarchy of ideas based on importance, as in informational pieces and persuasion; or other genre-specific orders, such as stating the title and author early in a book review. Show young writers how to organize their exposition through models and analysis.

What Works

1. **Sequential order.** Before asking your young writers to describe a process, have them bring to class recipe books, game directions (cereal boxes often have a printed set on them), or directions for assembling a bike or toy, or for programming a VCR. Let the students who brought something read it to a partner who did not.

Discuss the similarities in the different directions. Make a list of all the words the children find that lead the reader, cook, player, assembler, etc. through the process — for example: *first, next, before this, then, after that, finally*. When the students write their process descriptions, be sure they each have a copy of this vocabulary of step transitions.

Alternatively, for a more concrete example, do this practice writing following a hands-on art or science project. During the activity, have an assigned recording secretary ask students individually what they are doing and in what sequence. The secretary should enter their responses on the board.

When the task is complete, ask the secretary to read his notes from the board and invite the students to go over the secretary's notes and make revisions. If the activity was a group task, the historians for each group can record the order of the process and read it back to the group members who can help revise it.

Talking about the task as it is performed will help students remember the sequence and how to do it again. After completing the project, take five to eight minutes to discuss the steps in the process or, conduct the discussion on the following day.

Brainstorm with your class for some other processes besides making a peanut butter sandwich or brushing your teeth.

Sample brainstormed list.

- how to add a column of figures.
- how to take care of a pet.
- how to take a book out of the school library.
- the life cycle of a chicken, meal worm, butterfly.
- how to get from your house to school.
- how to write a book

- how to read a road map.
- how to put the chain back on your bike.

2. **Hierarchy of ideas.** Help young writers determine the order of ideas in an expository piece by using a web for the organization. (See Chapter IV, Drafting, From Graphic Planner to Draft.) Whether the web is constructed about the topic prior to drafting sentences or is formed after the information has been gathered and written in a list form (preferred for younger students), the students can look at the sub-topics and decide on a logical place to start. They should number the sub-topics in the order they think best.

They should ask themselves and their peers:
- What would a reader want to know first?
- What is the big idea?
- Where do I want to start?
- What do I know the most about?

When writers make their choice, do not try to change it even if you know it is not the logical place to start. Leave them in control of their writing. This is practice. They will hear and see other young writers' pieces; they will read expository pieces with a writer's awareness. They will improve.

3. **Comparison.** Young writers need lots of examples of, and practice at, using comparison as a way to organize expository writing. As they use the ideas described here, you will want to help them with the vocabulary of comparison, the ..*er* and ..*est* words. This would be the time to incorporate these words into their spelling rules work.

The use of comparative words can be applied as a target skill to specific pieces, science writing, and math. Descriptive writing depends heavily on it, including the use of simile and metaphor.

> The term 'comparison' means the setting forth of both likenesses and differences. To ask students to compare and contrast is redundant, but widely used.

a) Analyze literature and copy the pros. Comparison is used to make things stand out. It helps us understand new things by comparing them to things we already know. This is what analogies (common to all school curricula) are all about.

  Young writers should be on a constant lookout in their reading for examples of the writing skill that they are studying. Read examples of comparison to them. Speech makers and writers use comparison to emphasize a point.

  "Give me liberty or give me death." Patrick Henry

  "To err is human, to forgive divine." Alexander Pope

  Build class charts and require that they add the examples to their writer's notebook.

b) Flip books. Introduce comparison as a basis for expository writing by showing your young writers (all ages) how to create pocket-sized flip books.

To start, ask students to compare any two things. Help them brainstorm a list of things to compare. Ask them to refer back to field trips or thematic studies.

Sample comparison list

- duck and chicken
- fox and dog
- dinosaur and anole (lizard)
- horse and zebra
- nickel and quarter
- Snow White and Cinderella
- whales and fish
- skunks and raccoons
- manatees and dolphins
- doctor and veterinarian
- baseball and softball
- desert and forest habitat
- Venus and Mars
- pond and river
- frogs and toads (*Frog and Toad* by Lobel)
- Miss Nelson and Viola Swamp (*Miss Nelson* series by Harry Allard and James Marshall)
- Robert Frost and Walt Whitman.

To make a flip book,
Fold paper like a hot dog roll.

Fold that like a hamburger roll.

Fold that in half to look like a half a peanut butter sandwich.

Unfold paper so it looks like a roof.

Cut each fold line to the top of the roof on one side only.

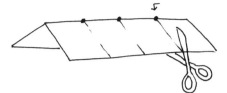

Younger students can use the booklet pages opened vertically for short comparison statement.

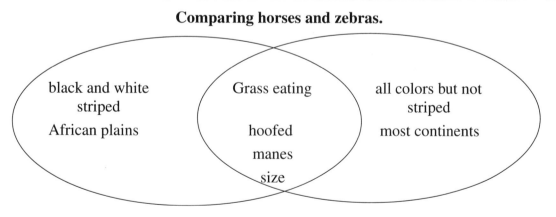

| Ducks have web feet. | Ducks quack. | Ducks swim. | Ducks lay eggs. |
| Chickens don't. | Chickens cluck. | Chickens don't. | Chickens do, too. |

Older students might want to use the booklet pages opening horizontally in order to write longer phrases or sentences.

c) Venn Diagrams. Show young writers how to make comparisons between objects and people using a Venn Diagram. A Venn Diagram is a graphic representation of the sets of attributes common to two or three entities showing the ones they share and the ones they do not. Venn diagrams, devised by John Venn (1834-1923), British logician, come from set theory.

You can show the use of a Venn Diagrams in a concrete graphic manner by using two large plastic hoops and a set of attribute cards for two things compared. Name the two characters, animals, or things to be compared. Place two hoops on the floor, one for each of the compared pair. Talk about the attributes of these. As you introduce an attribute, ask the students how you can overlap the hoops to represent what they share. Place the attribute card in that shared area.

Comparing horses and zebras.

black and white striped

African plains

Grass eating

hoofed

manes

size

all colors but not striped

most continents

Venn Diagram Practice

- science and writing — compare natural objects, and living things.
- reading and writing — compare books, characters, settings, and plots.

- music and writing — compare country western and rap.
- art and writing — compare painting and drawing.
- math and writing — compare adding and subtracting.
- social studies — compare Mohawks to Navajos.

d) <u>Making Comparisons</u>.

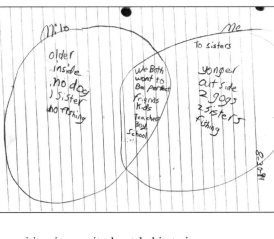

Marleen Wallace, Abel Elementary, Bradenton, Florida, makes comparison the basis for science writing in a unit about habitats in her third grade class. She models how to set up a paper for the class to compare two plants from differing habitats. The model paper is a vertical version of a Venn Diagram.

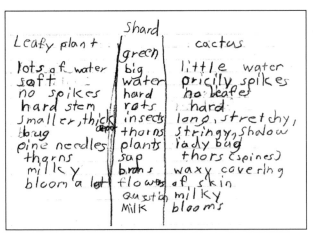

Next, peer partners select plants or animal from two differing habitats and build a comparable Venn Diagram. Their compositions consist of a statement or two at the bottom of the page about the differences or likenesses found. Wallace does not require that the children write reports about the two. Her goal is to familiarize them with the use of comparison and the graphic Venn Diagram.

Cohesive And Developed Paragraphs

Cohesive paragraphs are built from statements supported by substance. The writer introduces a subject and delivers the implicitly promised information. For example, if you write "Teeth are important," the reader expects to hear why they are important. Teach young writers not to let their readers down.

Cohesive paragraphs consist of

Statement: A declarative statement of opinion or fact, and
Substance to:

       clarify the statement,

       define the statement,

       illustrate with concrete examples,

       supply details,

       prove with examples,

       offer authoritative opinion,

       set forth self evident truths, and

       make comparisons.

Translated into young writer's language this means:

Statement: Say something you think or know, and
Substance:

What do you mean?

Give an example.

Prove it.

Who else says so?

Like what?

What else about it?

How?

Why?

"Write a topic sentence with supporting details." This is the most repeated phrase of all time in writing classes. But what does it mean? Young writers often have no idea. Help them by translating it into kid language such as:

- What is this paragraph going to be about?
- What are you going to say about this topic?
- What are you going to tell your reader in this paragraph?
- This paragraph is about another aspect of the main topic.
- This paragraph is about the......section of my web.

Young writers should write these questions and statements in their writer's notebooks.

What Works

1. **Start With a List.** Students select a topic and simply list words associated with the topic. After at least six or seven entries, ask your writers to star their favorite word. Now ask them to write a sentence about that word. Star another and write about it and so forth. This is a small first step in writing a paragraph on a single topic. The students find it is an easy task. Add to this the concept of keeping similar material close together, (see Chapter VI, Revision, Reorganization) and the students' paragraphs will start to show evidence of cohesion.

2. **What Does the Reader Expect?** Model for students how to deliver the information the reader expects. Write a sentence about something you would like to teach your student. Select the topic from science, history, or literature and kill two birds with one stone. For example,

Make a Statement: There are 206 bones in the human skeleton.

Ask your students: What information do you expect next? The name of some bones? What else the skeleton is made of? How the 206 bones are divided up into spine, arms, legs, feet?

Continue writing: The human skeleton is made up of 206 bones. The spine contains 34, and the arms and hands each contain 32.

Ask your students: What information do you expect next? Names, size, or function?

And so on.

Try this with several topics. Invite the students to try it out on a current study topic. Asking what the reader might next expect is another step toward writing cohesive paragraphs.

3. **One Thing Leads to Another.** Model a method of constructing a paragraph by following the first sentence with related information cued by the use of words in preceding sentences.

Find a word in the first sentence and write a sentence about that word. Find a word in that new sentence, or the preceding one, and write about it, and so on. This results in a paragraph of related sentences, another step in cohesive writing.

> Art class is my <u>favorite class</u>. I love it when the teacher shows us <u>how to illustrate our books</u>. He shows us how to do scenes, people, and <u>how to show things moving</u>. You can put straight lines behind someone who is running, or little black lines around something that is shaking.

4. **Copy the Pros.** Make a list of the ways that authors start paragraphs or whole articles. Have students look in *Ranger Rick*, and other magazines, science and social studies texts. Topic sentences fall into several categories. Give the students the following categories to enter in their writer's notebook.

- Author asks the reader a question.
- Author tells how he learned the information to follow.
- Author tells what interests him about the information to follow.
- Author defines what he will present.
- Author tells reader the importance of the topic.

Remind young writers that topic sentences are not always the first sentence of a paragraph. They can come at the end or follow an unusual introductory sentence. Have them find examples.

5. **Supporting Details.** Several years ago I tutored a high school student in writing who asked me at our first meeting, "What are supporting details? My teacher keeps putting that on my paper, and I don't know what she wants." Here's what we worked out.

For young writers, supporting details (substance) can be translated into the following. (Note that not all are applicable to every statement or topic sentence.)

- What do you mean?
- Prove it. Give a specific example.
- Why?
- How?
- Who says so?
- Compared to what?

Model how to use these kinds of details. (25 minutes)

- Invite young writers to make a statement about what they are good at. Model one of your own. Brainstorm with students briefly to come up with large range of activities, hobbies, skills. Write your statement, "I am good at quilting."

- Ask the students to Prove It. Any trophies, honors, compliments, prizes, products? Model yours: "I was invited to exhibit my quilts at my town's library. " Call for some sharing so the students who haven't come up with one can see the possibilities.

- Ask them how they got good at it. Model yours: "I have been making quilts and reading quilt books for many years." Share student examples to reveal possibilities.

- Ask them, "Who Says So?" Model yours: "My friends and family say my quilts are beautiful and ask me to make them one." Share student examples.

- Ask them to make a comparison. Model yours: "I'd rather make quilts than crochet." Share student examples such as the following from a fourth grader in Abel Elementary, Bradenton, Florida.

Student Example:
   I am good at Karate. It's a martial art sport. I have a black belt. I won a trophy last year. I take lessons and practice a lot. My coach says I earned my black belt fast. I am better at the kicks then the throw downs.

Make identifying elements of substance a target skill in peer conferences. Students should try to identify when the writer has used Who says so, A good example, How, Why, or Made a comparison. Peer responders identify the type, and compliment the author on its use.

Visual and concrete models.

a) The hand. For young writers in grades two to four who are still grappling with the concept of a paragraph, use a graphic involving their hand. Have students trace their hands on an unlined paper. Cut the tracing out and use it as a graphic planner for a single paragraph.

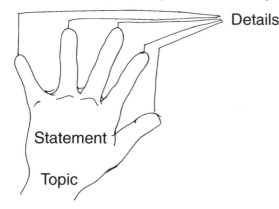

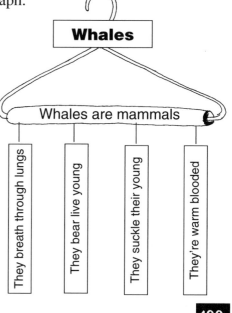

A clothes hanger. Construct mobiles from clothes hangers to show the relationship between topic, topic sentence, and details.

Unity Through Transitions

Transitions lead readers through paragraphs from one piece of information to another or, from one expository paragraph to another without awkward or abrupt pauses. They help to tie a piece together into a unified whole. (See also Chapter VII, Editing, Paragraphs.)

Make copies of the following list for the young writer's notebooks. (See **Reproducible #35**.)

> <u>Adding to:</u> and, also, or, along with, similarly, for instance, for example, for one thing, for another thing, especially, altogether, besides.
>
> <u>Summarizing:</u> at last, so, finally, all in all, and so, therefore, consequently, in short.
>
> <u>Establishing sequence:</u> later, until, not until, eventually, meanwhile, immediately, soon, no sooner, frequently, occasionally, always, sometimes, at last, never, now, then, afterward, when, usually, finally.
>
> <u>Linking cause and effect:</u> as a result, because, that caused, that resulted in, what happened was, that produced, naturally, therefore.
>
> <u>Comparing:</u> like, similarly, on the other hand, whereas, however, but.

Add transitions to the editing standards for expository pieces. Give students the opportunity to edit each other's work for this element of writing.

What Works

1. **Summaries.** Start with summary transitions because a summary can be applied to a piece of writing after the fact. This is easier than trying to incorporate it during drafting.

- Make a list of the summarizing transitions for your students to keep in their writer's notebooks. Start with: Finally... And so... The last thing... At last... So that is... Therefore...

- Make copies or project a transparency of the sample paragraphs about coins provided in **Reproducible #36**.

- Select one of the summarizing transition words and with the class make up an appropriate summarizing sentence to the coin piece. (Keep it to a one or two sentence summary paragraph to start.)

For example, a final paragraph might be:

> The last thing you should know is that the value of the coin does not depend on its size. The smaller dime is worth more than the larger nickel.

- Ask young writers to choose an expository piece from their collection of writing. Invite them to try to form a summarizing sentence using one of the transition phrases.

- Ask for volunteers to share theirs.

- Ask students to be on a lookout for examples in their reading, subject text books, magazines, and such. Add examples to the list in their notebooks.

Some categories and corresponding examples of ending strategies for entire expository pieces:

- reminder statements   Be sure to...
- summaries   No matter how you look at it...
- questions   Will we meet this challenge?
- quotes   "Let us all..."
- predictions   In no time you will be able...
- finalities   The last thing you need...

(Categories and examples are provided in **Reproducible #11**.)

2. **Adding Information.** Make a transparency of text you can use to model the transition vocabulary: *adding to*. Project it or one made from the sample paragraphs provided in **Reproducible #37**.

List the *adding to* transition words on the board or have students use the list in their writer's notebook. Show them how to add a piece of information by introducing it with one of these words.

Original text:

> Horses come in all sizes. They are measured in hands, which is the width of a man's hand, or about four inches. The measurement is taken from the front hoof to the top of the shoulder at the end of the mane.

Added information using the transition *For example*:

> For example, work horses are the largest, measuring about seventeen to twenty hands high.

Have students try a different transition word or phrase for the sample paragraphs in the transparency.

Ask students to look through their journal entries or informational expository pieces to find text they can revise by adding new information introduced by transitions.

3. **Cause and Effect.** Invite young writers to compose excuses for not turning in homework on time. Tell them to be as inventive as they choose. List the transitions linking cause and effect and ask them to use one of them between the cause of the lateness and the effect. Write a model for them first.

> Yesterday I had gymnastics class after school. I had my book bag with me. My home work assignment and math book were in it. When my mother picked me up, I left the book bag at gymnastics and she wouldn't take me back to get it.
>
> *As a result,* I wasn't able to do my math homework. And I don't have my math book either. I will get it tomorrow.

Have your students try out some cause and effect transition words on the sample paragraphs in **Reproducible #37**.

4. **Sequence.** If you have previously introduced your young writers to transitions of time sequence in narrative writing, they will find it easier to use them in expository pieces that require the reader to follow a step sequence.

Recipes, game directions, geographic directions, how to make something, and how a process works are all topics that lend themselves to the use of order and sequence transitions. Make sure students have a list of the transitions in front of them when they write directions. (See earlier in this chapter, Sequence in Organization, Expository Writing Content.)

5.   **Comparison.** After young writers have had experience with flip books and Venn diagrams, model sentences and short paragraphs using the transition vocabulary of comparison. They should try to use them within paragraphs to start. For example:

> Baseball and football both use balls, *but* they are different shapes. Football teams consist of eleven players, *whereas* baseball teams have nine. or,

> Dinosaurs were reptiles, and were *either* carnivores or herbivores. *Similarly*, modern day reptiles eat animal and plant material. Turtles eat plants *and* snakes eat animals.

Ask students to go back to one of their flip books of comparisons and add a transition word there. Have students work in peer partnerships to do this.

> Ducks quack, *but* chickens cluck. Ducks are birds, *just like* chickens are. Ducks have webbed feet, *whereas* chickens have separate toes.

It is best for young writers to practice a skill at a very simple level using very well known information. It makes the task easier. The objective is not quality writing, it is simple application.

Focus

Focus is one of the primary indicators of well written exposition. Most writing assessment procedures score student writing on how well the piece is focused.

Focus means simply that the writer sticks to the subject. Young writers often lose the focus of their piece. A new idea strikes them while they are writing and they follow it. Or, they may be anxious to write in quantity and throw everything they can think of into one piece.

It is natural for young writers to concentrate on including all the information they can. We encourage them to write in quantity because we want them to be fluent both mechanically and expressively. Developing writers will write *long* before they write *well*.

The time to begin training young writers to focus is after they are writing freely. Asking young writers who can squeak out only one or two sentences to concentrate on the focus of their piece is meaningless and counterproductive. Wait until you see some quantity and fluidity.

What Works

1.   **Label Each Page.** Ask writers to write a topic statement on the top of each sheet as they draft, for example, "This is about my gymnastics class." If your students are working in journals, have them write the statement at the top and at the bottom of the sheet.

2. **Refer Back to Their Plan.** Have your young writers color code each section of the original graphic plan. They should then read each sentence and mark it with the corresponding plan color. If their piece is about coins and the plan section on quarters is marked blue, they should mark each sentence about a quarter with blue. If, at the end, they see any unmarked sentences, they should ask themselves, "Do these sentences belong in the piece?"

Color coding each sentence will also help the students find where similar information became separated and how sentences will need to be moved and rejoined.

3. **Conference.** In both peer conferences and individual conferences, ask the writer to state what the piece is truly about. Make identifying where a writer wanders off the subject a target in peer conferences. Refer to the Paragraphing sub-section in Chapter VI, Revision, for discussions of non sequiturs and keeping similar information together. (See also Chapter IV, Drafting, for lessons about going from graphic plan to rough draft.)

Summary—Expository Writing

Encourage your young students to write a variety of expository pieces— not just reports but opinion papers, informational personal narratives, invitations, newsletters, science observations, literature responses, comparisons, attribute books. Help them with organization, using the concrete models presented in this chapter. Encourage their gathering of facts and data. Show them how the pros start and end their pieces. Integrate writing with science, history, geography, and math. Most of the writing they will do in their lives will be exposition.

Poetry

In the first year of my classroom writing process workshop, I faced my first conference with a writer presenting a poem. I nearly panicked. I knew little about poetry except that my college English experience had convinced me that the more obscure a poem was, the better. I figured that since I loved to hear Robert Frost's poems and could recite A. A. Milne's *Christopher Robin* from cover to cover, my taste in poetry was naive or, at best, downright unsophisticated. What could I possibly say to help this young writer?

I muddled through the conference. I had the student read her poetry aloud. I read it back to her. We clapped syllables. We heard some dissonance— some lines didn't seem to have the same rhythm. The writer had some clever rhymes. I complimented her for that. The poem reminded me of one of Milne's, and I told her that. I asked her if she found poetry easier than other genres and let her do the talking. I wondered if she noticed how ignorant I was about poetry.

Receiving Poetry

Years later, I was escorting poet Brod Bagert to a school's Young Author's Celebration and asked him how he handled conferences with young poets. He said he always asks the poet to perform the poem. He receives it and makes the following connections—allusion, aesthetics, and argument.

Allusion — comparing the child's poem to another known poet's work. Saying "This sounds like Shel Silverstein or Ogden Nash" tells the child he is in the company of poets, validating his work.

Aesthetics — remarking on some part of the poem— its rhyme, story, sound, choice of words, or imagery, encourages the writer.

Argument (questions) — asking what if, how about, why, did you notice tells the young poet you are actively interested in his opinion as a fellow writer.

Here is an example of a more recent conference by mail that I had with a fifth grader who gave me one of his poems and asked me to critique it. I tried to do as Brod Bagert advised in terms of allusion, aesthetics, and argument.

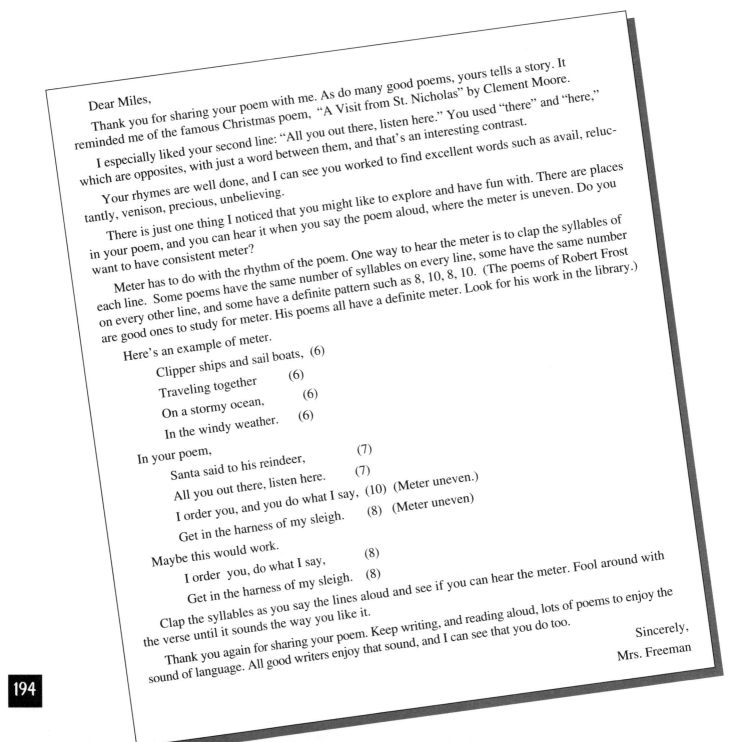

Dear Miles,

Thank you for sharing your poem with me. As do many good poems, yours tells a story. It reminded me of the famous Christmas poem, "A Visit from St. Nicholas" by Clement Moore.

I especially liked your second line: "All you out there, listen here." You used "there" and "here," which are opposites, with just a word between them, and that's an interesting contrast.

Your rhymes are well done, and I can see you worked to find excellent words such as avail, reluctantly, venison, precious, unbelieving.

There is just one thing I noticed that you might like to explore and have fun with. There are places in your poem, and you can hear it when you say the poem aloud, where the meter is uneven. Do you want to have consistent meter?

Meter has to do with the rhythm of the poem. One way to hear the meter is to clap the syllables of each line. Some poems have the same number of syllables on every line, some have the same number on every other line, and some have a definite pattern such as 8, 10, 8, 10. (The poems of Robert Frost are good ones to study for meter. His poems all have a definite meter. Look for his work in the library.)

Here's an example of meter.

Clipper ships and sail boats, (6)

Traveling together (6)

On a stormy ocean, (6)

In the windy weather. (6)

In your poem,

Santa said to his reindeer, (7)

All you out there, listen here. (7)

I order you, and you do what I say, (10) (Meter uneven.)

Get in the harness of my sleigh. (8) (Meter uneven)

Maybe this would work.

I order you, do what I say, (8)

Get in the harness of my sleigh. (8)

Clap the syllables as you say the lines aloud and see if you can hear the meter. Fool around with the verse until it sounds the way you like it.

Thank you again for sharing your poem. Keep writing, and reading aloud, lots of poems to enjoy the sound of language. All good writers enjoy that sound, and I can see that you do too.

Sincerely,

Mrs. Freeman

Poetry Instruction

Teaching young writers all the ways to enjoy poetry can be the focus of poetry study. Memorize and perform it, listen to it, make up rhymes. Genre study, the various forms poetry can take, may be part of it, but do not make that the heart of your instruction.

Poetry is an aural and oral art. The performance of poetry is appealing to young writers. Read poetry to them often.

Play records and recordings of poetry in the big voices of actors. To avoid the stereotypical reaction that poetry is for sissies, make sure the recordings feature male voices. Ask one of the male teachers on your staff, or a male PE teacher-coach to make a tape of amusing poems for your class.

Poetry instruction should focus on the sound of words, feelings, imagery, and action. Poems tell a story. Poems tell of people doing things. Read poetry that tells a story. Some good examples:

"The Midnight Ride of Paul Revere" and

"Hiawatha's Childhood" by Henry Wadsworth Longfellow

"Stopping by Woods on a Snowy Evening," by Robert Frost

"Washington," by Nancy Byrd Turner

"A Visit From St. Nicholas," by Clement Clarke Moore

"The Star Spangled Banner," by Francis Scott Key

"The Landing of The Pilgrim Fathers," by Felicia Dorothea Hemans

"Pocahontas," by William Makepeace Thackeray

"Lochinvar," by Sir Walter Scott

"The Dorchester Giant," by Oliver Wendell Holmes

"Daniel Boone," by Arthur Gutterman.

Poems that tell stories of famous Americans or events are one way children learn history.

What Works

1. **Table Top Performance.**

Jennifer Howard, Palmetto Elementary, Palmetto, Florida, invites her second graders to recite or read their favorite poems standing on the top of a table as if it were a stage. Children ask for an audience and every few days they take turns on the table top. It is a favorite activity. The poems are copied from books and magazines. Howard keeps a collection of poetry for children in her class library and reads poetry aloud often.

I am convinced that we don't sufficiently take advantage of young children's ability to memorize. Used wisely, memorization is a powerful learning tool. In addition, the things we learn as children stay with us forever. All proficient musicians start at an early age. Poetry, with its rich vocabulary, rhythm, and meter is easily memorized and will develop young writers' ear for language.

2. **Rhyme Lists.** Here's another listing activity. For fun and practice, have young writers list words that rhyme. The urge to inventory is satisfied, and it is an easy task. Some children may use their list to write poems. Others won't. Rhyming, not writing a poem, is the object of the exercise. Vocabulary building is an additional benefit of the exercise.

Your students might start their list with color words. Pink, think, wink, link, rink, mink, sink. White, bite, mite, site, kite.

Orange will be tough. Folk singer Arlo Guthrie once told an audience interested in song writing that he had found only two words that rhymed with orange: door hinge.

Number-word rhyming will be familiar to children who know the old favorite: "One, two, buckle my shoe. Three, four, shut the door..."

3. **Take a Poem Out to Lunch.** Ask your young writers to find a favorite poem. Have them copy it on a card, hang it from their neck with soft yarn and wear it for a day. Give them time to report what happens. Copying the poem also provides handwriting practice, killing two birds with one stone.

4. **Meter.** Poetry is literature written in meter or verse. The meter of poetry can be analyzed by clapping syllables. Syllabication is an important reading decoding and spelling skill. Practice it in poetry. From simple rope skipping chants to the iambic pentameter of Shakespeare's sonnets, the meter can be counted in syllables.

The meter in poetry is varied — every line with the same number of syllables; a pattern, as in limericks; combinations of patterns, as in sonnets; or no pattern at all (free verse).

A favorite example of metered poetry from Mother Goose can be used as a model. Let the students tap on their desks at first, then use their fingers to get the syllable count.

> Pease porridge hot,
> Pease porridge cold,
> Pease porridge in the pot five days old.
> Some like it hot,
> Some like it cold,
> Some like it in the pot five days old.

When students write poems, ask them if they have tried to produce meter. Most poems that young children hear and love have strong meter — strong rhythm. Help them figure out how theirs are constructed. Find places where the pattern breaks down. Revision will require that they consider synonyms and fool around with word order and organization. Most of the young writers I have worked with on meter are intrigued by it and like to revise their work until, as one young poet I worked with concluded, "It sounds like a song!"

5. **Poetry Anthologies.**

Beth Severson's third graders at Palmetto Elementary in Palmetto, Florida, keep a scrapbook — an anthology of poems they collect from their reading and the poems she reads to them. The children copy some of their favorites into their anthology scrapbook (handwriting practice). Severson reproduces some poems for children to paste in their scrapbook. The class reads them chorally and memorizes them. Severson asks them to highlight words in the poem that fit certain patterns:

- Can you find a word in the first verse in which the author dropped the *y* when he added *ed?*
- Who can find a word in the second verse that has a long 'e' sound?
- Highlight a word in the first verse that mean the same thing as huge.
- Highlight the words in which a consonant was doubled because of adding a suffix.

Two children are invited to make up a highlight word. They ask, "Who can find a word...?"

On one of my visits to her class, the students were working on two poems about spaghetti. After they finished reciting and highlighting, Severson sent two students to the cafeteria, and they returned with a pot of spaghetti. Great care was taken with the procedure of waiters and waitresses serving students who had placed their forks and napkins on their desk in a place setting. Children said, "Please," and "Thank you," and politely asked for seconds. I overheard one child tell another that he had sauce on his chin and he might want to wipe it off before they went to recess. This writing community pulls together all day long.

6. **Rap.** Interest in rap music can be tapped by asking young writers (grades four and up) to put one of their favorite stories into the metered rap cadence. Textless tapes of the rap cadence are available. Ask your music teacher for a source. A clever college professor summarized Hamlet and chanted it to a rap cadence on America's Funniest Home Videos. (See also Chapter II, The Writing Process Classroom, Daily Writing.)

7. **Shape Poems.** Haiku and diamente are two poetry forms that not only have a specific meter but a definite form. Haiku is an Oriental poetry form made up of three unrhymed lines of 5, 7, and 5 syllables respectively, about an aspect of nature or the seasons. The word *hai,* meaning amusement, and *ku,* meaning sentence, are from Chinese.

> The sun is setting.
>
> My light comes from deep within.
>
> I need no starlight.

Diamente is a shape poem consisting of a single noun line (the focus), a double adjective line, a sentence about the noun, another double adjective line, and the noun again. It takes a diamond shape.

Snow
Chilled crystalline
Snow decorates the cold ground.
Sparkling glittering
Snow

The study of this poetry form offers an opportunity to teach young writers the parts of speech — nouns, adjectives, verbs, adverbs, pronouns.

Young writers can construct these types of poems after they have seen models. Limericks are much harder and should be postponed until middle school or high school.

Literary devices

Literary devices are patterns of word usage and figures of speech that create an effect beyond the basic meaning of the words. Some create sound, rhythm, or emphasis. Others create a picture by comparison. They are an integral part of an author's style and charm.

Some young authors use them intuitively, having an innate feeling for language and words. All developing writers can be introduced to them and encouraged to add them to their repertoire of writers' tools.

Some Literary Devices

- Alliteration
- Personification
- Anthropomorphism
- Metaphor
- Simile
- Anadiplosis
- Hyperbole
- Oxymoron
- Onomatopoeia

a) <u>Alliteration</u> is a repetition of the starting consonant, consonant blend, end consonant, or first syllable in two or more adjacent or near by words.

> <u>M</u>ickey <u>M</u>ouse, <u>d</u>affy <u>D</u>onald <u>D</u>uck, <u>r</u>eally <u>r</u>eluctant, <u>b</u>old <u>b</u>owman, <u>pay</u> <u>day</u>, they were <u>w</u>orried and <u>w</u>atchful.

b) <u>Anthropomorphism</u> is attributing human characteristics, thoughts, and feelings to inanimate objects or, more commonly, animals. An-thro-po-mor-phism (invite the children to say this big word, they love it) is the basis of all the wonderful books in which animal characters talk and act like us. Young writers enjoy writing these kind of stories and are usually familiar with them through reading. Some well known examples of this genre:

> *Dominic* by William Steig
>
> *Charlotte's Web* by E. B. White
>
> *The Cricket in Times Square* by George Selden
>
> *Peter Rabbit* by Beatrix Potter

c) <u>Simile</u> is a figure of speech in which two basically unlike things are compared based on a common trait or characteristic. It takes the form: as —————as ——————-, or uses the helping word *like*.

> She is as strong as a Sumi wrestler.
>
> My cousin walks like a duck.
>
> Its teeth were like daggers.
>
> Her fur was as silky as thistle down.

d) <u>Hyperbole</u> is a figure of speech in which over-exaggeration is used for emphasis or effect. Mothers excel at hyperbole.

> "I've told you a billion times to close that door tightly."

e) <u>Onomatopoeia</u> is a creation or use of words, such as buzz or splash, that imitates the sounds associated with the object or action to which they apply. Often they are written in capital letters.

> SPLISH, SPLASH. The twins were playing with the hose again.
>
> The bottle opened with a loud POP.

f) <u>Personification</u> is a figure of speech in which inanimate objects or abstractions are given human qualities or described in human form.

> The leaves danced across the lawn.
>
> The lawn chair did a back flip in the wind.
>
> Fatigue crept up on the runner.

g) <u>Metaphor</u> is a figure of speech in which a word or phrase that usually designates one thing is used to designate another, forcing a comparison, or a picture in the mind of the reader or listener.

> The man was an ox.
>
> The kid was a shrimp.
>
> They were lost in a sea of troubles.
>
> That mocking bird is a regular Mozart!

h) <u>Anadiplosis</u> is a repetition, at the start of a phrase, of the word or phrase with which the previous group of words ended. It is used for emphasis by speechmakers as well as writers.

> He was busy, busy as a bee.
>
> They were attacked by hunger, hunger so deep they could feel it in their bones.

i) <u>Oxymoron</u> is a figure of speech constructed of two contradictory terms.

> A deafening silence, jumbo shrimp, burning cold, a depressed optimist

Literary devices can be added to a manuscript in the response and revision stage of the writing process, to the extent that they have not been included naturally in the drafting stage. Gifted writers use them without thinking because they have a feeling for the sound and impact of language that most of us don't. They are the Michael Jordans of writing (metaphor).

To use literary devices, young writers need to know how to construct them and what words they replace. Bear in mind that metaphor is a more abstract concept than simile, personification more abstract than anthropomorphism, anadiplosis more difficult to construct than hyperbole, and that alliteration and onomatopoeia are the most common to their reading experience.

What Works

Use the techniques described in Chapter II, The Writing Process Classroom, Lesson Models to introduce each literary device. Select the ones appropriate to your writers' needs.

- Read from children's literature to show examples of the literary devices you introduce. (See bibliography at end of this section.) When you read to the class, stop to point out how the author used one of the devices.

- Build a class entry chart for each literary device and encourage young writers to make entries from their independent reading.

- Have students set up pages in their writer's notebooks for each literary device you introduce and have them add examples they find in their independent reading.

- Give a minilesson on the construction and use of the device.

- Invite the young writers to try it and to overuse it.

- Call for its use as a target skill in the piece on which they are working.

- Designate its identification as a target skill for peer conferences.

- Compliment writers publicly when you see or hear them using literary devices.

- Record evidence of this skill use in the student's record for reference at parent conferences.

1. **Alliteration.** Alliteration is a good choice for introducing literary devices because it is so commonly used in environmental print—advertising, TV, cartoons. There are several levels of alliteration. Start with the easiest.

   a) Same starting consonant or consonant sound. This can be applied to names, and constructed of adjective-noun combinations.

   > Mickey Mouse, Donald Duck, Gerald Giraffe, Peter Piper, Mike Mulligan. Cute cat, rude rabbit, furry fox, elegant eagle, careless camel, lost llama, polite postman, talkative telephone operator, sleek submarine.

   b) Verb combinations, and verb-adverb combinations using the starting consonant.

   > Running and romping, talking and taking pictures, doodling and drawing, kept calling.

   > Sewing secretly, went wearily, walk willingly, carefully carving.

   c) Same starting sound—consonant blends, consonant and vowel combinations. This is more difficult than simple starting consonant. Again, it can be applied to names, adjective-noun combinations, verbs, and adverb-verb combinations. The alliterative words may be separated by a word or two.

   > Clyde Clausen, blue blouse, frozen with fright, the squirrel let out a squeal.

   > tired tiger, poky polecat.

   > picked tomatoes and picnicked afterward

   > called cautiously.

   d) First sound and descriptive connection—This is the most difficult level of alliteration. The choice of alliterative adjective for the noun must convey a meaning consistent with the noun.

   > Slippery, slithery, slug; wallowing whale.

Ask young writers to find animals, people, and objects in their stories and then find a descriptive word they could add starting with the same letter or sound. Encourage them to help one another. Invite them to go overboard, using as much alliteration as possible. Some will immediately construct tongue twisters—recognizing what tongue twisters are all about—alliteration.

> Verb-adverb combinations of this kind should be used carefully because there frequently is a specific and wonderful verb that means the same thing and is the preferred style. Example: crept cautiously = sneaked. More advanced writers should be aware of this.

2. **Simile.** Young writers can apply similes when they use adjectives and verbs. Using comparisons are the mark of good descriptive writing and avoids hitting your reader over the head as well. (See Chapter IV, Drafting, Expanding Ideas.)

Either form of similes, as......as, or like....., are acceptable. Start with making comparisons as an oral exercise. Use a list of adjectives you might find in an English text book or have the young writers brainstorm a list of their own. From this list, model some similes and invite your young writers to construct some to share orally.

Now ask the young writers to search through a manuscript of their own and find a place they described something. Encourage them to share the description with the class. Brainstorm similes that fit the description. Invite the writer to revise. Invite everyone to find one place where they might use a simile. Students should start to listen for them in each other's manuscripts.

On a later occasion try the same with verbs. For example: swam like a fish, walked like a duck, jumped like a kangaroo.

3. **Hyperbole.** Mothers and fishermen are naturally prone to hyperbole. So are kids. This is an easy device for them to use. The cue words to look for are numbers in their manuscripts, superlatives, repetitive things, things occurring in quantity, or quality.

He ran faster than an Olympic sprinter, instead of, He ran very fast.

She had a billion freckles, instead of, She had a lot of freckles.

4. **Onomatopoeia.** The word that mimics the sound of an action is used for emphasis and may be used with exclamation points. Repeated, they may be separated by commas or a period. Often all the letters of the word are capitalized.

BOING, BOING! Karen hopped along on her pogo stick.

The babbling brook cut across the glade.

Try a class practice piece that describes a busy and noisy scene. Brainstorm all the sounds and words that can be used to add to the description. Make up some of the sound words. Add them to lists and charts.

5. **Personification.** Read Clement Moore's, "A Visit From Saint Nicholas" and the Mother Goose rhyme, "High Diddle, Diddle," to your students. They are filled with examples of personification. Brainstorm a list of objects with your class and imagine the objects as alive and acting like humans. Invite

students to make up some sentences about the objects using verbs that apply to human beings. For example:

> house—The house held us safe in its arms.
>
> stars—The stars winked at us from a black sky.
>
> leaves—The leaves whispered in the breeze.

Point out examples of personification to young writers when reading to them. Add them to lists and charts.

6.   **Metaphor.** The difference between simile and metaphor is that in metaphor an object or person is not compared to another but is called the other. Not: He *is as strong as an ox.* But, He is *an ox.* Specific words in our literary heritage and culture represent concepts. A Pandora's box represents a potential source of many problems, an ox represents strength, a snail represents slowness. When you substitute the word for the concept you use metaphor.

> What a Scrooge you are, counting every penny, nickel, and dime!
>
> The girls all vied for his attention. He was an Adonis.
>
> Hurry up, you snail!

You and students can be on the look out for examples of this literary device and share them with the class. Add them to lists and charts.

This example is from a fourth grader's descriptive practice write.

The Building

> I stand in the city beside a building surrounded by a *fence* of other buildings. This building is exceptionally special. It has a cross section of a triangle and is nine stories high. The smell of fumes is in the air and a flag sways up above my head. With the cars zooming by and the people in suits holding briefcases you really get the feeling you are in a city.

7.   **Anthropomorphism.** This is not only a literary device, it is also a genre. Cartoonist Gary Larson of "The Far Side" has made a living based on anthropomorphism. The advantage of this approach is the increased role imagination plays in the process. Children and adults alike are fascinated with animals. Do they talk to each other? Do they have feelings and experience pain, happiness, love, fear? Do they think?

When young writers use this genre, encourage them to think about the similarities of animals to people. Refer back to the information and lessons about Character Traits in this chapter.

8.   **Anadiplosis and oxymoron.** These are literary devices for the advanced writer. I have included them primarily for your information. If you have some advanced writers, you might like to introduce them to these devices. Certainly compliment any young writer who uses them intuitively. Gifted writers need confirmation and encouragement and are pleased to learn the vocabulary of the writing craft.

Literary Devices Bibliography

Hall, Susan. *Using Picture Storybooks to Teach Literary Devices.* Phoenix, AZ: Oryx Press, 1990.

Alliteration

Kellogg, Steven. *Aster Aardvark's Alphabet Adventures.* NY: Morton, 1987.

Hyperbole

Terban, Marvin. *It Figures: fun figures of speech.* NY Clarion Books, 1993.

Simile

Hanson, Joan. *More Similes: roar like a lion.* Minneapolis, MN: Lerner Publications Co., 1979.

Juster, Norton. *As: a surfeit of similes.* NY: Morrow Junior Books, 1989.

Onomatapoeia

Spier, Peter. *Crash! Bang! Boom!* Garden City, NY: Doubleday and Company, Inc., 1972.

Chapter X

Evaluation and Portfolios

Parents want to know how their children are doing. Principals want to know how children and teachers are doing. You want to know how the children are doing. Everyone wants to know how the children are doing. Are they progressing, are they on grade level, are they achieving as much as they can?

Teachers need to demonstrate and document student growth in the writing craft. You most probably are required to calculate and record a grade that students have earned in writing. A young writer's body of writing, the curriculum you follow, and your records of the writing workshop will provide the material you need to document and grade progress.

A writing grade should reflect a student's knowledge and use of the writing process — progress and achievement in topic choice, genre range, planning techniques, use of response mechanisms, revision techniques, independent editing practices, and publishing. It should include the student's knowledge of writing content — genre characteristics, composing skills, and convention use.

Preliminary planning will greatly ease the task. Start by looking at curriculum. What skills will you introduce and reinforce? What criteria will you use for evaluating work in writing workshop and assessing student writing? These will provide a framework against which you can evaluate the anecdotal information you extract from your workshop records and student writing examples.

Do not evaluate and grade every piece of writing a student undertakes. That will inevitably turn off the flow of writing you are trying to achieve in your classroom writing community. Young writers need a good deal of practice and opportunity to experiment and take risks. Alert them when you need to evaluate and explain the criteria you will be using. Let them help select the pieces to be evaluated.

If your young writers are building writing portfolios, it is absolutely necessary for them to have a large volume of practice writing and finished pieces to self-evaluate. They will want to choose not only their best pieces for the portfolio but those that show a range of genre and skills. They will want to demonstrate their use of the writing process. They, should, therefore include the planning, rough draft, responses, revisions, editing, and the final copy of some of their pieces. They should write justification statements such as, "I included this piece in my portfolio because..."

Evaluating Writing Process Progress

Use your class Commitment Statement records and your reading of student manuscripts to make some judgments about the progress a child is making in the writing process. During Commitment Statements, writers declare what type of graphic planner they used, how they chose their topic, what good responses they got, what they revised as a result of the responses, who helped them edit, etc. You can use the Commitment Statement form to enter anecdotal notes about skills and progress from conferences as well. If you take a Commitment Statement at least once every two weeks and the children keep personal Commitment Statements, you will have sufficient information to verify their progress.

Take information from their manuscripts to augment Commitment Statement information. This includes such things as evidence of revision, topic choice, the plan they used, who gave them comments, and editing evidence.

Here are the areas in which you should look for student growth in the writing process.

- Topic Choice
- Planning Techniques
- Revision
- Editing

I. Topic Choice Progressions

Children make progress in the strategies they use to choose writing topics. Young writers with a strong sense of self make wise and independent choices from the start. Less confident writers, writers who have not been allowed choice, or writers who have been given story starters in the past will work their way through several of the strategies listed below before they find their own best strategy to initiate topics.

Early on, young writers may

- Ask teacher for ideas.
- Choose a topic of which they have little knowledge.
- Copy other children's choices.
- Use movies or TV programs, and write their own version.

As they gain experience and confidence in making choices, young writers may

- Choose a topic of high interest to their peers or classmates.
- Use an interest survey.
- Write repetitively on one topic.
- Choose a topic based on reading.
- Use classroom work, pictures, stories, and tapes for ideas.
- Choose a topic of high interest to themselves.
- Choose a topic about they have a good deal of knowledge or feeling.

The last seven strategies are not arranged in a hierarchy. All are equally valid choices for young writers.

II. Planning Techniques

Young writers' growth in planning techniques is demonstrated by the degree of elaboration within their plans and the usefulness of the plan in their writing. The listed graphic planners are not arranged in a strict hierarchy. Within planner types, however, there is a progression — lists turn into outlines, webs go from 'wheels' or 'pin cushions' to webs with sub-topics and sub-sub-topics. The choice of plan type is usually based on individual thinking styles and preferences.

Early plans might include

- pictures
- simple word lists
- assisted (dictated) list of events
- webs that look like a pin cushion
- three element fiction planners (character, setting, problem),

and grow to include

- coded lists or lists with connections
- webs with sub-topics
- storyboards
- fiction planners including setbacks, resolution
- outlines
- timelines.

III. Revision Progressions

Young writers progress in revision type and sophistication as they advance in their writing abilities. Here are the types of revision and the progressions that young writers make.

Emerging Writers (K-1)
Additions

- Another element to their picture
- Another label on their picture
- More coloring
- Another letter(s) per word
- Another word to their message
- Action in their pictures
- Feelings

Developing Writers (Grades 1 and up)
Additions: (K -1) additions plus

- Another word
- Another sentence

- Another idea
- Feelings
- Adjectives and adverbs
- Explanations
- Specific nouns
- Sound effects
- Literary devices — alliteration, simile, hyperbole, metaphor, etc.
- Dialogue

Substitutions
- Words
- Phrases
- Sentences
- Verb tense
- Point of view

Developing Writers (Grades 3, 4, 5, and up) The preceding, plus:
Reorganization

- Move words, sentences, and paragraphs.
- Change beginnings or endings.
- Change point of view.
- Paragraphing.
- Deletions.
- Divide a long piece into chapters.

IV. Editing Progressions

(Grades K-1)

- Put capital letter at the start of the piece.
- Put period at the end of the piece.
- Put name on the paper.

(Grades 1-4)   K-1 edits, plus:

- Use capitals at start of sentences.
- Use capitals for people's names and 'I.'
- Use end punctuation — period, question mark, and exclamation.
- Correct spelling of a predetermined percent of Dolch Primary words, colors, days of week, other environmental classroom text, and content words.

(Grades 2-5) Grades 1-4 edits, plus:

- Use capitals for titles, yelling, and selection of names.
- Use quotation marks around what came out of the speaker's mouth.
- Correct percent of Dolch words, content words, and words spelled as they sound, such as banana, blip, crab, tent, splendid, limit, watermelon.

(Grades 4-6) Grades 2-5 edits, plus:

- Punctuate series commas.
- Use capitals for all proper nouns.
- Indent for paragraphs in narration with transitions of time and place.
- Correct percent of misspelling using variety of resources.

Evaluating Content Achievement

Your content curriculum for the marking period, your conference notes, and your assessment of student manuscripts will provide the basis for your evaluation of achievement in content knowledge and skill use. Assessment of content achievement includes the student's knowledge of genre characteristics, composing skills, and convention use. Reading children's manuscripts is the best way to assess their growth and achievement in these areas.

You might want to develop additional, and more specific, sets of criteria for the different styles — personal narrative, fiction, expository, and persuasive writing.

I. Composing Progressions

Young writers will progress in organization, development of ideas, and the focus of their writing if they are shown how and are given sufficient information. They find their style through experimentation and by mimicking professional authors. They will develop their writer's voice if they are given the opportunity and sufficient time to practice.

Children's early writing considerations are focused on giving information and on correctness. Later they begin to experiment with the tone, purpose, and impact of their word choice on the audience. You might hear a young writer say, "I want show how he felt when he....." or, "I want to make this scarier." or, "Do you think they will understand this part?" This represents real progress.

Here are some typical composing progressions young writers make in response to lessons and models of the sort enumerated in this book.

Organization

Personal Narrative
- use chronological order, start at breakfast and end at bedtime
- use chronological order with transitions of time and place
- focus on one event or character
- list details
- integrate details with main idea
- create tone or atmosphere
- include description of feelings and emotion
- design beginning and endings to hook and satisfy reader

Fiction
- single dimension characters, abrupt endings, graceless starts, inconsistent point of view, may not have a plot.

- develop characters, use dialogue, have consistent point of view, reveal plot and bring it to resolution.
- use setbacks to increase tension; dialogue to present information,
- reveal character, advance plot

Expository

- have single idea, no order of information
- clump some similar information together
- present important information first
- show evidence of focus
- build cohesive paragraphs, use concrete device to indicate indent.
- use transitions to establish sequence, link cause and effect, refer back, and summarize
- identify left field sentences, information out of order, breaks in the focus.
- use detail to advance purpose of writing
- indent paragraphs.

Description

- describe with single attribute.
- list attributes — visual predominates, use adjectives predominantly.
- use multiple attributes, other senses appealed to.
- use verbs, nouns, and adverbs.
- use comparative attributes, similes.
- create imagery through a variety of means, use literary devices.
- use descriptive form — foreground to back, center outward, left to right, physical to personality traits.

Word Usage And Order

- use general nouns, common verbs.
- use specific nouns, active verbs.
- use simple sentence construction.
- use more complex sentences, add phrases.
- use literary devices. Normal progression — personification in the form of anthropomorphism, alliteration, simile, onomatopoeia, hyperbole, metaphor, personification, anadiplosis.
- go from inconsistent use of verb tense to consistently correct tense.
- select words for impact, pattern, sound, rhythm.
- select style appropriate for audience and genre.

Voice

- have no clear voice.
- are aware of audience.
- make up expressions, talk directly to reader.
- use language designed to influence audience's response to writing.

II. Writing Conventions

Writing conventions are discussed under Editing Progressions earlier in this chapter. Writing conventions are best taught in conjunction with editing —which is the writing process stage when writers need them.

III. Dialogue Convention Progressions

Dialogue format is one convention that develops in stages. Young writers progress in their use of the various stages of dialogue convention. That progress can be noted when you analyze their manuscripts. The conventions of dialogue include quotation marks, commas, capitalization, and paragraphing (See Chapter VII, Editing.)

Assessing Student Manuscripts

You can assess student manuscripts for achievement in writing content elements, conventions, and specific skill use based on work during the grading period. You can also assess the manuscripts for overall quality. Common assessment criteria are: clarity of purpose and voice, focus, details or development, and conventions (grammar, usage, punctuation, capitalization, and spelling).

What Works

1. **Analytical Assessment.** In analytical assessment, a manuscript is examined for each of the criteria and a judgment is made based on how well the writer demonstrates use and knowledge of that criteria. Scoring language might be: consistently, frequently, sometimes, and never.

Some common criteria for assessing writing are purpose, organization, focus, details or support, and conventions.

> **Purpose** refers to how well the author establishes intent and maintains it through the piece. The author may demonstrate awareness of audience.
>
> **Organization** refers to the coherence and unity of the piece — how well sentences are logically and clearly related to one another and if appropriate transitions move the reader forward.
>
> **Focus** refers to how well the writer stays on the topic.
>
> **Details or Support** refers to how well details contribute to the development of ideas, provide information, clarify content, and evoke images. Details should advance the purpose of the piece and should not simply be listed.
>
> **Conventions** refer to grammar, punctuation, capitalization, and spelling. Look for patterns. Repetitive errors should be counted as one error.

Example assessment of a Grade 2 manuscript.

My cat fuzzy

I got my cat for my birthday and I was sevin. I got her at the spca. she is gray and wite and a long tail my cat is little. She plas hide an seek with me and my bruther pete in hides in the door and waches tv. I feed her nine lives cat chow to her. She had 2 shots at the vetadniens so she wont get sick.

Criteria	Consistently	Frequently	Sometimes	Never
Purpose	X			
Organization	X			
Focus	X			
Details		X		
Conventions			X	

Purpose: Presents information about author's cat.

Organization: Logic to arrangement of information and keeps similar information together. (when and where got cat — seven and spca; looks like — white, tail, little; what cat does — plays, TV; care — eat, a shot).

Focus: All information is about the cat and author.

Details: Advance the purpose but are limited.

Conventions: Capitalized most starts of sentences and 'I.' End punctuation inconsistent. Uses inventive spelling, which is close phonetically.

You can see from the assessment that this writer is ready for lessons in description, varying the form of sentences using phrases, editing by ear for periods, capitalization of names rule, and to focus on identifying content words and correcting their spelling.

Practice using an assessment technique such as the one above on some of your young writers' manuscripts. You will be able to use the results immediately for diagnosing student needs and you will be able to document growth as you compare assessments made throughout the year.

2. **Holistic Assessment.** In holistic assessment, the criteria may be the same as for analytical assessment. The scoring, however, is based on an average number from all the criteria, each of which is each rated from 1 to 4 (or any range you prefer). The grade two manuscript in the preceding paragraph, for example, might receive a 4 each in Purpose, Organization, and Focus, a 3 in Details, and a 2 in conventions for an average rating of 3.4.

Many states are assessing children's writing at various grade levels. If your jurisdiction does not, write to the state departments of education in Vermont, Maine, New York, Florida, or others, to request information about their scoring rubrics.

3. **Assign Element Requirements For Assessing Writing.** Tell your writers that you want to assess their writing. Select a style or genre. For example,

give them a time limit in which to write a new narrative or rework one they already have drafted. Inform them that this assessment will look only at their application of skills. List those skills for them.

Assign maximum points per each element you list. The grade points you allot will be based not only on the inclusion of the skill but on its quality and sophistication. A list in fourth grade for a narrative piece might be the following.

10 points	Use of alliteration.
5 points	Use of one set of series commas.
10 points	Use of two time transitions.
20 points	Use of a compound sentence.
20 points	Use of verbs in description.
10 points	Their graphic planner.
10 points	Content words spelled correctly.
10 points	'Snake-ate-rat' shape to their story. (See Chapter IX, Narration.)
5 points	Manuscript turned in on time.
100 points	

The evaluation of quality and sophistication must be appropriate to the student's development level. For example, if you are assessing the use of alliteration at the fourth grade level, a starting consonant repetition such as *Leo Lion* would earn a 7 out of the 10, while the use of a blend and verb-adverb combination as in *frequently frightened* would earn the full 10 points.

Requiring specific literary elements in a given piece of writing is a writing workshop technique that keeps writers aware of writing curriculum content. They can base their self-evaluation on how well they meet these requirements.

4. **Give a Quiz in Writing.** Design a quiz that tests young writers' knowledge of the style and genre characteristics, composing skills, and writing conventions on which they have worked in the marking period.

Sample questions:

a. Name three ways a writer can let readers know what the main character is like.

b. What do you need to do to help a reader recognize a list in the middle of some writing?

c. Explain the literary device onomatopoeia using an example.

d. How many times do you need to revise?

e. Name two ways to present a book recommendation to another reader.

f. Use a Venn Diagram to compare the characters X and Y (from class shared reading).

g. Where do quotation marks go in dialogue?

h. Name two kinds of setbacks that an author might use in fiction.

Evaluation and Portfolios

Student Self-Evaluation

When young writers come to us with the question, "Is this good?" we need to mimic the therapists who throw questions back at the patient — What do you think of it? How do you feel about it? Do you think it's good? Why?

Good teachers do not take on the task of rewarding everything a student does. They do not set themselves up as the only judge of quality in the classroom. They let students share the responsibility of making decisions about quality control. As a result, students gain the self-esteem that comes from self-satisfaction.

If children know evaluation criteria and have an opportunity to excel, they can answer the question, "Is this good?" for themselves.

All students should have a copy of the tentative curriculum for the year. Young writers should be encouraged to keep track of the skills they think they can use independently, the ones they need help with, and the ones they are working on currently. Writers can make a personal list on their writing folder or in their writer's notebook. They can monitor skills they are working on, checking off those they have mastered and entering new ones.

Writing evaluation can and should include children's self-evaluation. Bringing young writers into the evaluation process accomplishes several positive things.

- Develops a sense of responsibility.
- Reinforces the notion that a grade is earned.
- Directs their attention to the objectives of the writing program.
- Develops their ability to make comparisons based on criteria.
- Develops a sense of accomplishment.

Young writers need to know that some of their work will be good and some will, quite frankly, stink. This is the case for all writers. Help your writers develop the criteria on which to base their evaluations.

What Works

1. **What is Good Writing in Our Classroom?** (20 minutes) Brainstorm with your young writers what they think makes a piece of writing good. Make a list entertaining all suggestions. Add your suggestions, too. They should reflect the skills you have been emphasizing.

A sample list from emerging writers might include

- It's got lots of action.
- It's funny. The other writers laughed when I read it.
- The picture is good.
- The picture is all colored in.
- It sounds good.
- It has finger spaces.
- It's about me.

213

A sample list from developing writers might include

- It's long.
- It's short.
- It's got lots of action.
- It is funny. The other writers laughed when I read it.
- It has pictures.
- There is good imagery.
- The characters talk.
- The ending is a surprise.
- I replaced some of the *saids* with other words like *whisper.*
- It has paragraphs.
- It's neat.
- All the spelling is correct.
- It gave all the information we needed.
- It makes the reader keep reading.
- There is lots of detail.
- It's interesting.
- There are lots of revisions.
- It's easy to follow.
- The verbs are all in the same tense.
- It sounds good.
- I used alliteration.
- There were lots of comparisons.
- The author really stretched his imagination.
- There was so much feeling in it.
- You feel like you are in the story.
- The writer stayed on the topic.
- You can tell the writer really knows what he is talking about.

Have your young writers sort the list into broad categories of organization, content considerations, composing skills, conventions, and aesthetics. Publish the list and give a copy to your writers to keep in their writer's notebook.

2. **Pick Your Best.** (30 minutes) Ask your writers to select three or four pieces of writing. These can be from journals and folders, from science, math, social studies writings, and can be rough drafts or published pieces. Have them read their manuscripts over, with an eye to selecting the best one of the batch. Ask them to put the criteria they are using to evaluate their manuscripts on the top of the paper as they read. When they have made their choice, ask them to write the reason for that choice on the back of the best paper. Model one for them on the board or chart paper, such as the following.

> November. This is the best piece I wrote since school started. It is the most interesting because I gave lots of details, like the one about the fish having a hook inside it when I cleaned it. Most of the words are spelled right and I used series commas which we have been studying.

3. **List or Inventory Writing Skills.** At the end of each marking period ask your young writers to make an inventory of the writing skills they use. Post a

list of the skills you introduced during the marking period. It should contain style, genre, composing, and convention skills. Have the students look through their writing for examples of these and any others they have been practicing. Students can use the notes they keep on their folder covers. (See Chapter II, Materials.) They can use their curriculum scope and sequence chart. They can use a rating system of always, frequently, occasionally, rarely, and never to indicate their skill use.

4. **Writer's Notebook Evaluation.** Ask your young writers to suggest the grade they feel they have earned in keeping up their writer's notebook. Review with the class the required ingredients for the marking period — hand outs, note taking, practice writes. Have them color code the required entries (assign a different color for each marking period). Add bonuses for their own pages and entries. Give students the opportunity to obtain missing hand outs and missing notes from their peers. Collect the notebooks and record grades.

Many teachers use the upkeep of the writer's notebook for a grade ingredient in the first half of the year, before the students are writing prolifically and have a body of writing to assess for progress.

5. **Compare early and current writing.** Young writers should be given the opportunity, and encouraged, to compare current writing and writing done early in the year. The practice writes they did in lessons and models will provide examples of their use of skills. Descriptive paragraphs are often excellent pieces to compare. Have students analyze the way they present attributes, whether they use adjectives or verbs, what literary device they employ in each piece. Students need to recognize the progress they make.

It is helpful to introduce some of your lessons and models with reminders such as this, "Remember when you were in first grade and you described your dog like this... " (write a description of a dog in four word sentences limited to the use of simple adjectives). "Let me show you how more fluent writers tackle description." Without criticizing young writers for simple adjective use, you encourage them to describe as fluent writers do.

The most exciting comparison young writers will make is the comparison between their kindergarten, first and second grade writing and their fifth and sixth grade writing when they review the contents of their grade school writing portfolios during graduation activities.

Portfolios

A portfolio is a resume. It is autobiographical, chronicling a young writer's progress, showing, by examples, development in range and style. It belongs to the young writers and they should keep the contents when they leave school.

Don't send elementary student portfolios to the middle school or junior high unless the portfolio process continues there. Instead, have the student select a few samples to go to the writing teacher at the next school, and keep the remainder. Invite students to bring their portfolios to their next school if they'd like.

What Works

1. **Contents of a Portfolio.** A portfolio might include
    *   A table of contents.
    *   Entry log with the writer's justification for inclusion.
    *   Entire process of some manuscripts—graphic planner, draft showing peer response and questions, revision, editing, and the final copy.
    *   Rough drafts as well as finished work.
    *   The writing class's required range of genre.
    *   Assessments of some manuscripts by you and student, using rubrics.

2. **Entry Log.** Students should maintain a log of entries in their portfolios. When they add a piece, they log it in. If they replace a piece, they log it out and the replacement in. The log contains the justification for inclusion and replacement of manuscripts.

    Help your young writers design their own form for a portfolio entry log. It should include the name of the piece, the genre, the date, and the reason they include it.

3. **Folio Media.** Use legal files, the red-brown expandable files with a cover flap and a rubber band around them, for the physical portfolio. Invite a law firm into a business partnership with the school to underwrite the portfolio process by providing the legal file folders.

4. **Kids Who Compose and Edit on a Word Processor.** To construct a portfolio of students' work through the writing process, and at same time allow them to work on a computer:

    *   Require a print out of each of the steps—a graphic scheme comparable to the handwritten webbing of the topic or a story map, the first draft after a revision session, and the final copy.

    *   Students should have an opportunity to receive peer responses to the earliest drafts to revise for clarity, purpose, and interests. The peer responses should be attached to a print out of the draft to which the responses were made. They should be initials by the students who heard the draft, with comments noted on the draft or on a separate piece of paper.

    *   Students must incorporate the writing skills you teach during the construction of the piece. For example, if a student is working on cohesive paragraphs, metaphor, quotation marks, and transitional devices, the use of these elements is required in the piece. That is not to say that young writers will have perfected the skill, but an

attempt must be made to try it out. A later piece can be evaluated for those skills at the instigation of the student writers, or by a deadline set by you. This should follow a period of sufficient practice in the skill.

Summary

Don't wait until portfolios are mandated by your district or state. Experiment with portfolios, using them for your conferences and for accountability. Contact other school faculties who have worked on portfolios and ask them for help. Work with other teachers in your school to design a useful set of guidelines for the portfolio.

Chapter XI

Meeting Common Challenges

While you are working to build a classroom writing community you will be faced with challenges on a daily basis. Teachers enumerate them for me at workshops, during classroom coaching, and over lunch. I have faced them myself. They can all be met — and the rewards of doing so are substantial.

Here are the most common challenges and some ways to handle them. (The chapter references are where you will find relevant information.)

Young writers who start many pieces and finish none. This is an important cycle to break because it may become chronic. It usually reflects an underlying lack of confidence.

- Review planning techniques (Chapter III) with students.
- Have students select the piece they think is their best. See where they are stuck. If they have lost the focus of the piece, have them tell you what they started out to do. Have them look back at their original plan.
- If an ending is the problem, review with them the categories of endings for the genre (Chapter IX). Have them write two endings and choose the best.
- Suggest a different, shorter genre. Success with a short piece will build confidence.
- Try the assisted outlining technique (Chapter III).
- Make sure the students have sufficient prewriting time to tell the whole story to a peer.
- Review topic choice strategies (Chapter III). The writers may be choosing topics of low personal interest and background knowledge.

Loss of edits between draft and published copy with the appearance of new mistakes. This is a common occurrence with very young, developing writers.

- Archive the draft for proof of the editing.
- Determine whether the goal for the piece has been met.
- Make corrections for the students if they want you to.
- Enlist volunteers to help type children's work. If pieces are usually short, you might be able to type a few each day yourself.

- Require revising and editing work without publishing.
- Reduce publishing copying-over-time to small increments.
- Ask students to underline, in color, the edits and revisions they have made on their drafts, in order to make them more conspicuous at copy time.
- Mask mistakes with liquid erasure or labels and let the author rewrite.

Writer has a very long piece. It's been revised and edited, but he won't publish. Don't be surprised. Publishing a long manuscript is a large task.

- Help the authors plan pictures and text page layouts. Determine how much text will be on a page. Make it a paragraph or two. Mark with a crayon each page's length. The students should only publish that much a day.
- Arrange to have a volunteer type students' manuscripts.
- Have the writers hire a scribe.

"How do you spell…?" (Chapter VII) If writers, during their emerging stage, are in an environment that emphasizes spelling, you will have to invest time in modeling and promoting inventive spelling so that they can get on with their writing development.

- Train young writers to ask, "How do you write…?"
- Make environmental print and theme vocabulary accessible.
- Add a Dolch word to each student's folders.
- Advise students to ask another writer for spelling help.
- Suggest that the student put just the first letter, or a blank, and continue writing.
- Establish personal dictionaries, word banks, and procedures to get spellings.
- Designate spellers to help each day.

Spelling fanatics. Many children become so focused on spelling — often by excelling on spelling tests, or by comparing their writing to and competing with the authors of the literature they read — that they will not write fluently during drafting. They stop to verify the spelling of the words they write. They will not take risks and often write use only the words they can spell.

- Encourage them to be freer in their choice of words and to use inventive or temporary spelling.
- Ask them to work with an emerging writer in their class. Ask them to say, as you do when that child asks for words, "Make a stab at it, put down as many letters as you hear, or circle it and come back to it later." Working with a classmate in this fashion often leads spelling fanatics to apply the same technique to their writing.
- Ask them to be designated spellers for the entire class for a week at a time. After suffering the numerous interruptions inherent in

this job they often see the value of the inventive spelling technique, especially when you provide the hint.

Poor spellers. (Chapter VII)

- Mark *SP* in the margin of the line containing the misspelled word if you do the final edit and let the writer find the word.
- Encourage oral presentations, taping the manuscript.
- Show these young writers that you value what they have to say.

Coping with the volume of writing generated by the class. (Chapter V)

- Don't read it all. Check off only that it's done.
- Read for specific, writer designated elements.
- Model and promote peer conferences.
- Evaluate designated pieces. Let the rest remain practice writing.
- Publish only 10-20 percent of work.
- Have young writers self-evaluate their work.
- Respond to only 10-20 percent of each writer's work.

Young writers who want to publish everything they write. (Chapter VIII)

- Establish and review editing standards for publishing.
- Require that a manuscript must pass inspection by the class editing committee.
- Require that a classmate of the author be able to read the piece to you before the author publishes it.
- Furnish hand-publishing booklets and materials for publishing.
- Invite children to publish at home.
- Have the author publish one book of a collection of pieces, an anthology. Construct it so pieces may be added and deleted as the author works.

Young writers can't find incomplete sentences.

- Invest time in choral reading training using Big Books.
- Work only with a group of students who share that problem.
- Have children locate who and what happened in the sentences.

Manually inept, dyslexic, or learning impaired students. The physical act of writing is difficult for some students. It takes them forever. They may say they hate to write. The writing process classroom is ideal for them. They can take part in many of the writing process procedures, models, and lessons using oral and aural skills. Require that they participate in as many of the process techniques as they can manage.

- Have them dictate their piece to a scribe.
- Arrange that they revise by talking to scribe, who will do the rewriting. They will be able to read it because it's their own words.
- Put them to work as peer responders and editors unless they are

hearing impaired.

- Encourage them to publish large print books for kindergarten children — attribute books, alphabet, and counting books.
- Have them audio tape their stories.
- Invite them to use unlined paper.
- Encourage the use of inventive spelling.

The results of working through problems for this special group can be rewarding.

> A manually inept student who had difficulty writing told me about his poker games with his grandfather. I brought him a deck of cards, and he wrote a book about the hierarchy of combinations in poker. Each page contained a single sentence and the cards glued to form the combination. He went through each stage of the writing process.
>
> He planned it, organized it, put card hands together, wrote single sentences per page on another sheet, read it to a peer and changed a few words, showed it to his grandfather who corrected the order of value on one of the hands, typed the pages on a computer, and assembled the pages. I took dictation as he described himself for the About The Author section. The project took him eight days. During that time, he also acted as a peer responder and helped another child plan a book. The writing process is accessible to all students.

Very young students, or those whose primary language is not English.

- Have these students tell their story to you. Write in large block print and have the student trace over the letters and write it below.
- Take dictation and have the students type the piece or enter into a computer. Print it out and help the students read it back. Ask them to illustrate their pieces to remind them of the content. Keep a collection of these printed stories for the students to practice reading. It is their own text and will be easier than other material.

Students who write repetitively on one topic. Where would Stephen King or Walter Farley of *The Black Stallion* fame be if they had been told to get off their repetitive topics? Young writers may select a topic repetitively because of the high engagement they have with it, or because it serves as a security blanket. Do not discourage the choice of repetitive topics. Do, however, discourage the rewriting of the same piece.

- Make sure the writer works on different target skills in each of the pieces on the same topic. Ten well written and developing pieces about cats, Power Rangers, or fishing are better than ten poorly written pieces on a variety of topics.
- Encourage writing on the topic but presented through a different genre.

Dependent writers who needs reassurance at every turn.

- Team them with partner writers.
- Remodel what to do when the teacher is busy and the options a writer has when needing help.

- Encourage writing short pieces until the writer's confidence is established.

Writers who won't read their piece in Author's Chair.

- Allow the writers to ask a peer to read the piece.
- Invite them to read only a portion.
- Use a microphone for Author's Chair
- Ask all authors how it feels to be in Author's Chair.

Copious output of low quality. (Chapter VI)

- Celebrate that the writers are engaged in writing.
- When they are in Author's Chair and conferences, ask the students to identify the best parts and places they utilized the target skill.
- Encourage publishing and let the consumer market (classroom audience) judge the quality.
- Encourage multiple reading by authors. They may discover the weakness in their writing on their own.
- Give lessons in left field sentences, dialogue that advances the plot and reveals character, staying focused, and underlining content words.

Plagiarism of encyclopedia and CD-ROM material in reports. We invite copying from references when we ask young writers to write about things they don't know.

- Develop all the precursor skills needed in report writing (**Chapter IX**).
- Start with small informational pieces based on a topic with which the student is already familiar. These may require searching for specific additional information.
- Direct all students, grades three and up, to start their research with easy-to-read children's illustrated texts—they should read them without taking notes. This will give them an overall view of the topic. From there, they can focus on the part of the topic that interests them and move on to grade level materials.

"I won't write." Mainly a first week challenge. When children see the success other writers have, they will usually join in. Until they do,

- Send them on a clipboard trip (**Chapter III**).
- Suggest that they make a list of all the things they hate about writing.
- Include the students in all the other process stages, lessons, etc.
- Avoid confrontation. Remain friendly and encourage them in other areas.
- Have them tell you a story—draw them out orally. React to their stories and ask questions to let them know you are interested in what they have to say.

Discuss your challenges with other teachers. Have faith that the writing community you build ultimately will provide the answer to most of these challenges.

Appendix

A. Plan of Attack

Developing writers—Grades one and Up

If you are new to the writing process workshop, this overview of a year's plan and some sample days in the life of a classroom writing community may help you get started. Note carefully the structures that are to be set in place for your young writers, as well as the areas of freedom with responsibility.

General Strategies and Tactics

1. **Schedule a block time for writing workshop every day.** It must be consistent and almost inviolate. At least four times a week all year is best. Alternatively, you might schedule writing workshop daily for a block of four weeks every two months. A 30-minute period, with room to grow to 45 minutes or more, is ideal. This will give you an opportunity to integrate writing with other subjects in the latter half of the year.

2. **List the styles and genres you plan to study.** Check with the previous grade level to avoid duplication. If a style or genre you select is being introduced in the lower grade, find out how far that grade will go in the genre. You can build on it.

For instance, if you are a third grade teacher, you might select descriptive narrative, literature response, opinion papers, personal letters, and fiction. (Notice that this list includes both narrative and expository writing.) These do not have to be the only styles and genres your writers may choose, but you can require that they have an example of each of these five in their portfolios by the end of the year. Concentrate your teaching in these target areas. Most of the skills you teach while focusing on a given genre will be applicable to others.

List the features for each of the selected styles and genres. You will model these and provide lessons about them for your young writers. For example: literature response features would include the following instructions and models—Title of book, author, main characters, setting, and plot (problem, struggle, or conflict), comparison to another book, finding similarities between the reader and the main character.

Collect professional and student examples of the selected genre. Involve the children in the collecting process. Use these examples to analyze the genre.

3. **List the writing skills you must teach.** Check the prior grade level's curriculum and build on it. Include genre features and composing skills as well as conventions. For example:

- descriptive attributes
- making comparisons/similes
- personal letter conventions
- cohesive paragraphs (See **Chapter IX**)
- paragraph indenting in narratives for time and place changes, using a concrete marker
- capitalize book titles, underlines book titles, capitalize authors' names
- series commas
- content word spell checks

4. **List the books you will read with the children to illustrate these skills.** For example:

Sarah Plain and Tall, Patricia MacLachlan — personal letter

Dear Mr. Henshaw, Beverly Cleary — personal letter and journal

What's Your Story? Marion Dane Bauer — fiction

5. **Look through multiple-copy book sets** or your basal reader and identify passages you can use to illustrate the genres and skills you intend to teach. Bookmark them with a note or enter them in your lesson plans.

6. **Start your writing workshop on the first day of school.** Let the children know they will be writing every day. Give them a writing folder with some greenbar paper, or paper marked to use every other line, and a writer's notebook (loose-leaf notebook). As a model, write your own short personal narrative on an overhead transparency or on the board. Read it to the class. Ask others to share their narratives. Tell children they will write tomorrow at the same time.

7. **Establish the use of writer's notebooks.** Students use the notebooks to record topic and story ideas, make observations, ask questions, and to gather information on a topic they are considering. They also use them for collections such as first lines and names. Finally, they use them for practice writing during lessons.

8. **Publish early.** Your students will begin to talk and act like authors as soon as they publish. You can encourage them to read like writers, looking at the author's style and noting how he accomplished something. Display your young writers' published work and read it to the class. It does not have to be perfect, but it should have been edited for some basic conventions that young writers know and can edit for independently. Show the class how their fellow authors have solved problems or have done something unusual.

Determine a tentative class publishing schedule with your class. Set modest publishing goals that can be augmented rather than cut back.

- how many or what percentage of their drafts?

- how often?
- how many responses per manuscript?
- what kind of revision?
- what kind of editing?
- what percentage of misspelled words corrected?
- what forms of publication (bulletin board, book, mounted on construction paper, foldered)?

9. **Begin to model all the writing workshop strategies you will need to create a cooperative and productive class.** Give short minilessons (approximately one each week to the whole class, and, while others write, one or two per week to a needs group). Start some sessions by reading professional literature to the class and discussing how the author hooked his readers, helped them picture the scene, or made them laugh. Start some sessions with Commitment Statement.

10. **Conference on a roving basis or conduct short scheduled conferences.** Use Author's Chair to model compliments and how to remember responses calling for revision. Model class edits, and publishing modes.

Learn how to conference efficiently with your writers. Focus on one thing at a time. Focus early on content and then move gradually to considerations of process, composing problems, and lastly, mechanics. Schedule conferences (three or four of them) following submission of drafts for your overnight reading. Have writers specify the problem or area they want to discuss. Confine the conference to that consideration.

11. **Be demanding when it comes to editing, but always model first.** Try Editing by Ear. Remember, it is always easier to edit someone else's paper. Edit for one item at a time, and use multiple edit sessions. Establish classroom publishing editing standards with your young writers. What share will they have to do? And how much will you do?

12. **Learn what interests your writers.** Keep records of the children's pieces through the Commitment Statement, conferences, and their folder records. Carry a clipboard with sticker labels for each student and write brief anecdotes about the children's writing progress as you rove, encourage, and conference. Place these anecdotes in young writers' portfolios and refer to them during parent conferencing.

Examples of sticker anecdotes:

> "Karen requested peer conference and received two suggestions. She revised by adding information."

> "Tom turned back to his graphic planner to decide what to write next in his piece about snakes."

> "Daryl using dialogue in his latest piece. Asked how to show yelling. Karen told him, Capitals."

13. **Set up portfolios** and ask students to select and place some of their manuscripts in the portfolio with all the stages of the manuscript attached. These may be a graphic planner, the draft with responses and responders initials, revisions made, editors' initials, edits, and a Xerox copy of the final neatly written or typed

piece, or the original if the child wants to keep that in the portfolio.

14. **Teach young writers to evaluate their own writing** and have them select additional pieces based on criteria for good writing established by the class. They should put as many of these in their portfolio as they wish, accompanied by a short note telling why they selected them.

15. **Let parents know about your writing program.** Tell them about editing standards and the spelling strategies used, about response and revision, about the skills their children are practicing. Encourage them to receive their children's published works in the same spirit as they do their children's dance recital, school band performance, or athletic performance.

16. **Keep a record of the things that work best for you.** Build on them. Discard the things that don't work. Don't try to do too much at first. Remember, children need to write (compose) every day if you want them to write well.

B. Sample Writing Workshop Weeks

The sample weeks presented here will give you a feeling of how the writing workshop is managed and conducted. The first sample set is for a class of young developing writers, grades one and two. The second is for a class of more advanced developing writers, grades three to six. Each set includes five consecutive days at the start of the year and another five days at mid-year. The samples make reference to the procedures and practices detailed in this book. They are meant to provide a possibility, not a prescription.

Sample for Grades One and Two.

These writers have some sound-to-symbol connections (including some vowels), can write most upper and lower case letters, may separate words into discrete units, and, most importantly, can read today what they wrote yesterday.

Your immediate objectives are to establish the writing workshop routine, focus on personal narrative writing, encourage sharing and self-evaluation, and publish early. Your long range plans include descriptive personal writing both narrative and expository, expansion of ideas, establishing editing standards, and maintaining a writing community.

Beginning of the Year

Day One
Requirements:

- twenty minutes
- greenbar paper, unlined paper, and primary paper (blank with two lines at the bottom of page) or coiled bound notebooks for journals
- pencils and crayons
- laminated alphabet strip for each student or attached to tables or desks.
- package of small Post-It notes

- samples of construction paper covered and stapled class collection books
- writing folders with the skill list of the owner attached to the back of the folder (You make these using the student's writing portfolio from the previous year).

Example Skill List:

> "I can make all my lower case letters."
> "I write stories with action in them."

1. **Introduce the writing workshop** with the expectation that everyone will be writing, including you. Tell the children they may write about anything they like.

2. **Assemble the children, and model writing** on an easel, overhead or blackboard. Tell your story as you write, using inventive spelling. Make it a short personal narrative. Also draw a picture for the emerging writers you will have in the group.

3. **Send children off in pairs to talk about their story, draw, and write.** Let them choose paper type as some may not choose to draw a picture.

4. **Rove and encourage writers.** Talk to them about their content, ask questions to help them focus, take dictation of a sentence or two for emerging writers who request it. Write the sentences in large letters and ask the student to trace over it.

5. **If students ask how to spell** a word, repeat and reword the request — How do you write 'friend?' Have you asked your partner? Can you help me write it? Do you hear any letter sounds? Sound it out and write it on a Post-It note, and tell children to put it on their desk or table and share it with someone.

6. **If students say they can't write**, have them tell their partners about their picture or story, or watch other writers.

7. **End the session by asking partnerships** to read their stories to one another before they put it in their folder. Designate the place for sharing.

8. **Place work in folders and folders in class storage container.**

9. **Tell the students they will be writing** every day and to be thinking tonight about what they might write about tomorrow.

Day Two (You might repeat this several times.)
Requirements:

- twenty-five minutes
- writing materials
- class names — record keeping sheet
- a special chair marked Author's Chair.

1. **Gather the class for a short discussion** about topic choice. Ask those who wrote yesterday what they wrote about. How did they come up with their idea?

2. **Send pairs off to draw and write.** Those students who have no ideas should stay with you for brainstorming and discussion. Send them to write as

they come up with ideas. The emerging writers in your group will draw. Encourage them to label their drawings with the starting consonants of the words. Note who these students are and pair them up for the next sessions with a developing writer.

3. **Gather students in ten to fifteen minutes after you have roved and encouraged.**

4. **Model Author's Chair.** Model the assembling procedure. Have three children who wrote personal narratives share their work. Receive their writing enthusiastically but do not say, "That's good." Instead, react to the content. Then model for the children how to react to the content. You might introduce the idea that the author tell the genre of his piece — "This is a story, a narrative." Or, "You will learn something from this piece." Later you will coach some of them to say, "This is an information piece, it's expository." Thank writers. Record who had a turn in Author's Chair, and tell the children you will keep track for them so everyone will get a chance.

5. **Tell students to read their piece** to another child before they put their writing away. Tell them to think of what they will write tomorrow. Ask them, "Will you add more to your piece?"

6. **Later look over the writing and start to diagnose needs and to note skills.**

Day Three

1. **Start workshop with a short discussion.** Use your story from the day before or a selected student's work, to show young writers that they can add to the piece they started yesterday. Read and talk about your piece or have the volunteer read and encourage him to talk about what he might do next. Send kids off to write — to start anew or add to yesterday's piece.

2. **Rove and encourage, help emerging writers.** If you have students who have not written a word, gather them together and show them picture-prompted writing samples. Invite them to select a picture from the class file to paste on their paper and to write about the picture contents.

3. **Call finished writers for a fifteen-minute group share.** Tell those who are absorbed in their writing that they can continue working. Sit in a circle and ask for volunteers to read their pieces. Select four to six, including emerging writers. Talk about writing — What do they like about it? What is hard? What is easy? Then have all the writers form pairs and read to each other before they put their writing away.

4. **Have writers put their work in folders** and remind them they will write again tomorrow and that they may write in their free time during the day.

Day Four

1. **Start the workshop with a few comments** about some of the good things you see writers doing. Meet with the group of children who are having trouble selecting topics and take them through one of the techniques in Chapter III, Prewriting. Focus on personal narrative.

2. **Create a word bank wall and introduce your young writers to it.**

Before class starts, choose ten to twenty common words from their stories. Write them in block print on large index cards—laminate them in the future. Place the cards on the wall. Show your writers how they can take the words from the wall to their desks to copy, putting them back afterward. Read the words with the children. Ask them to help each other find the words they need for their stories.

3.   **Rove and encourage.** Especially encourage the children to help one another.

4.   **Remind students to read to a partner before putting their writing away.**

Day Five

1.   **Start the workshop by showing students hand-published class collection books.** Invite them to select their best piece to publish in a class collection book. It must be one they can read to their partner. Exempt emerging writers who may simply pick the drawing they like best. Explain that when writers publish, they must help the reader by starting the piece with a capital letter, and putting a period at the end. They will want to have their names on their work. Emerging writers can do this, too.

2.   **Have all the writers take their work out of their folders** and work with their partner to find their best piece, put their name on it, and make sure there is a capital at the start and a period at the end. Suggest they might want to color more of their picture or add one if they did not have one. If they rip them from coiled book you can trim them. Add one of your pieces to the class collection as well.

3.   **Devote the writing session to this activity.** If a child wants to continue writing or finish a piece, let him.

4.   **Assemble the book for them after class,** and on the following days invite authors to read their contribution to another child.

What you have accomplished in the opening week:
- Children know they will be writing everyday on topic(s) of their choice.
- Personal narrative has been modeled and discussed.
- One group has been introduced to a topic choice strategy.
- Author's Chair has been modeled.
- You have used the vocabulary of the writing craft.
- Children have heard their writing and have shared with another writer every day.
- Children see that you are not going to listen to all their writing, that they will be using peers for an audience and for help..
- You have introduced the concept of editing in preparation for publishing.
- Writers have been introduced to self-evaluation.

Mid-Year

Day One
Review target skills for peer conferences. Meet with a group who need a brief lesson about expanding their ideas. Rove, help, and encourage. Have everyone share with a peer before putting away their work.

Day Two
Have students write while you rove, help, and encourage. After fifteen minutes, call a Knee to Knee modeling session (See Chapter V) to introduce questions that lead to additive revision. After the model, ask all peer partners to try. Ask some students to tell what good questions they received from their partner.

Day Three
Read a literature example of description using sounds. Show and discuss Peter Spier's onomatopoeic book, *Crash! Bang! Boom!* Ask writers to freeze and listen carefully to the sounds of the school. Have young writers practice in their notebook making up a sentence that uses a sound word. Ask writers to make that the target skill in their current piece. While they write, you rove, help, and encourage. Have everyone read his piece to a partner before putting his work away.

Day Four
Conduct Author's Chair for two or three writers with compliments, questions, and stickers. Focus on descriptive writing in general and sounds specifically. Some writers may have used a sound reference. Who heard it? Compliment the author's use of the skill. Use the remaining time for writing.

Day Five
Conduct a class exchange edit of a journal entry or short piece for periods and caps, using the Edit By Ear technique. Have students write for the remainder of workshop while you rove, help, and encourage, or conduct two individual conferences.

What you have accomplished:
- Introduced another descriptive element (sound).
- Remodeled Knee to Knee, introducing the element of questions. During prior weeks, Knee to Knee would have been modeled for repeating back, reacting to content, and compliments.
- Introduced a group to the expanding ideas technique.
- Reinforced editing by ear, for periods and capitals at the start of a sentence.
- Reinforced sharing with peers.
- Used Author's Chair for target skill identification and complimenting.

Sample for Developing Writers Grades Three to Six

These writers may be at the same level of development in their writing as first and second graders, but they will be older, bigger, have a larger vocabulary, and have more background knowledge and life experiences. They may be a mix of non-writers, inexperienced (in the writing process workshop environment) developing writers, experienced developing writers, and some fluent writers.

Your immediate objectives are to establish the writing workshop routine, focus on personal narrative and expository writing, encourage sharing and self-evaluation, and publish early. Your long range plans include descriptive personal writing both narrative and expository, expansion of ideas into cohesive paragraphs, studying the genres of book reviews-literature response, personal letters, and fiction, establishing editing standards, and maintaining a writing community.

Beginning of the Year

Day One
Requirements:

- twenty minutes
- greenbar paper, unlined paper, and coiled bound notebooks for journals
- pencils, markers, crayons
- package of small Post-It notes
- class collection book samples (construction paper covered and stapled) and some hand-publishing ready-made books with pictures on their covers
- writing folders with a few sheets of greenbar paper inside and a sheet listing the writing skills of the owner attached to back of folder (made from the student's writing portfolio from the previous year).
- Labeled writing folder container for file style storage.

1. **Introduce the writing workshop** with the expectation that everyone will be writing, including you. Tell the students they may write about anything they like. Qualify that statement with the rider, "You may write anything in this classroom except something that would make your grandmother blush or would hurt someone's feelings."

Explain the use of greenbar paper. Ask students to write on every other line. Let them choose whether to write in the coiled notebook or on greenbar paper. Write in your own coiled journal notebook. Write on an everyday topic — making your lunch, the traffic on the way to school, your plans for vacation.

2. **After ten minutes close your book** and ask if any writers have gotten started. Ask them to tell the topic they are writing about. Tell what you are writing about. Discuss how writers find ideas and ask the starters how they did it. Encourage the children who didn't get started by telling them that writers often need to think for a while before they are ready to write.

3. **Read your draft** to illustrate that writers can write about ordinary events and experiences. Invite a student to share his or her draft. Remind all students to put their work in their folders. Invite them to read their skill list to see if you left any off. Invite students to write additional skills on their list.

Ask two students to pick up folders and place them in a box, plastic tub, or such.

Examples of folder skill entries:

I describe scenes with more than adjectives.

I write stories with action in them.

I capitalize names of people, pets, parks, schools, states, cities.

I use alliteration.

4. **Close the workshop by reminding your students** that they will be writing again tomorrow and to be thinking of a topic. Give out a parent letter that explains your program for the year. Invite your students to read it before putting it in their backpack or homework bag.

Day Two
Requirements:

- Interest Inventory (**Reproducible # 2**).

1. **Start the writing workshop** by asking two students to give out folders and two more students to hand out the Interest Inventory. Read it with the students and ask them to fill it out. Have them star any item that interests them and which might be the source of an idea for their writing. Begin writing. Remind them to skip lines. Tell the students you are going to model a rough draft on the board and they can watch or write.

2. **Model a one-two paragraph personal narrative**, talking to yourself as you write about what you will include or say next. Skip lines, leave a blank for a word you don't know, circle a possible misspelling, read it back to yourself every few sentences, add a word or two by using a caret (^).

3. **Rove around the room encouraging writers** or gather the students who have not started and interview them with their interest sheets for possible narrative or expository ideas.

4. **After twenty minutes call a halt to writing** and invite writers to name their topic or read a bit of their manuscripts. React to content only. Show them your model and the things you have done in the rough draft. Ask if any others did some of these things. Invite all writers to read their piece to the student next to them or across from them. Go through closing procedure: students placing writing in folders, collection and storage; reminding they will have writing workshop again tomorrow.

Day Three
Requirements:

- Loose-leaf writer's notebooks with large label on spine for each child including greenbar paper, dividers
- the second Dolch list of nouns, verbs, and common words, or the 240 Most Common Words list
- the curriculum scope and sequence for developing writers.

1. **Set up the procedure for weekly rotation** of student pairs to distribute folders. Tell young writers that they may write in any of their free or indepen-

dent work time, but they are responsible for refiling their folder.

2. **Describe the workshop procedures** about what to do when you're finished or when you need help or a word.

3. **Give a Writer's Notebook to each student**. Begin the writing workshop with a lesson about descriptive attributes. They will copy some things into their notebooks in a Style and Genre section (they can label one of the dividers). Or you may give them a handout with holes already punched to put in the same section and to which they can add their own notes from the lesson. They may do some practice writing during the lesson in another section called Practice Writes. Tell them about the notebook and the part it will play in the grade they earn in Writing.

4. **Close the workshop with the collection and storage procedure.** Before the next class read what they have produced so far. Note the non-starters.

Day Four

1. **Open the session with compliments** and encouraging comments about things you saw in their writing when you read it last night. Discuss topics chosen and where writers are in the writing process. Ask to meet with any students who have finished their draft. While they read their drafts to each other at a table or gathering area, settle the rest of the class to writing. Ask non-starters to make a clipboard trip or to join the group who are meeting with you.

2. **In the group of students who have finished their first piece**, have one volunteer read his aloud. Ask the others to be thinking of a compliment for something they really liked — a word, a phrase, the topic. Hear two more then have the remainder read their piece to another writer. When they finish, talk about what they think they learned while they worked on it and what they plan to do next. Ask them if they need help. Do not act as if they are finished. Do not ask them to turn the writing in to you. Send them back to their desk and call the entire class to attention.

3. **Tell the class that tomorrow you will be modeling a peer conference** that will help writers improve their pieces. Ask them to read over their own writing and anticipate what their peer partner might compliment or ask about. Close the workshop.

Day Five

1. **Model a peer conference.** Talk about target skills and use the descriptive attributes list as a guide to listen for use of descriptive words.

2. **After the model, take a Commitment Statement** to find out where your writers are in the process. Plan the next few day accordingly. A lesson, an editing model, more work with students who are having difficulty starting, or peer conferencing, may be the work of the next week.

3. **Close the workshop session**. After class, read student work, learn what interests each student, and diagnose needs.

What you have accomplished:

• Students expect to write daily.

- Readied an Interest Survey for topic choice guidance.
- Established a procedure for starting and ending the writing workshop.
- Given a lesson in descriptive attributes.
- Modeled drafting.
- Demonstrated the use of Writer's Notebooks.
- Encouraged your young writers to write, share, and help each other.

Mid-Year

Day One
1. **Start the workshop with a Commitment statement** or ask students to write on a personal commitment statement and display it on the corner of their deak. Set up peer conferences, meet with a group for lesson, editing or publishing help, then rove to help and encourage.

Day Two
1. **Conduct a class discussion about book reviews and recommendations.** Make notes on the board for students to enter in their Writer's Notebook; show young writers different presentation examples produced by other students. Ask writers to be thinking of how they will present theirs.

2. **Ask students to select a book for their first review** by checking through the Literature Response journaling, earlier W. E. B ("We Enjoy Books") independent selections, or a book the whole class has read. Tell what elements are required and give the due date.

Day Three
1. **Start writing workshop with a reminder of the ingredients** of a book review and comparative descriptive writing they have in the year.

2. **Conduct two pre-scheduled individual conferences.**

3. **Before the close of workshop, ask some students** to describe to the class what they have planned for their book recommendation or review.

Day Four
1. **Start the writing session with a Commitment Statement** or have students enter their commitment on their own record sheet at their desks. Students continue writing. Meet with individual or groups of students with similar needs.

2. **Before the end of the session, review with the class** some of the descriptive writing and fiction genre elements they have worked on in the past. Ask them how they might apply them to the book review. Call for partner sharing before they put their writing away.

Day Five
1. **Conduct an Author's Chair for two writers** who are ready to present their book review drafts and direct the listeners' attention to elements dis-

cussed on the prior day. Use stickers for compliments and questions. Use the remainder of time to meet with a group working on editing.

2. **Assign Homework Response for students** latest manuscripts. Post the target skill(s).

What you have accomplished:

- Reinforced Commitment Statement.
- Introduced book reviews and elements of the genre.
- Continued to work with individuals and groups on all stages of writing and skills.
- Reviewed some descriptive and fiction elements.
- Conducted an Author's Chair and reinforced compliments and questions.
- Allowed writers their choice of presentation for their book review while establishing the essential ingredients.
- Used Homework Response mechanism for response and revision.

The described writing workshops are only representative. My hope is that they provide you with an image of how you can use the techniques and procedures presented in this book to help build a community of writers in your classroom. You can see that the early days of the school year are spent establishing structure and process procedures while your young writers focus on personal writing. Later in the year, you can concentrate more on teaching writing content as the earlier established framework continues to support and sustain your writers.

Reproducibles

TITLE	STAGE OF PROCESS **P**: PLAN **D**: DRAFT **R**: RESPONSE/ REVISION **E/P**: EDIT/PUBL	MODE OF SHARING **PC**: Peer Confer. **AC**: Author's Chair **G** : Group Confer. **H**: Homework Response **TC**: Teacher conf.	TARGET SKILLS AND SKILLS USED	DATE

NAME: _____

COMMITMENT STATEMENT

NAME:_____ DATE:_____

I have been to a:

❏ zoo	❏ airport	❏ park
❏ circus	❏ desert	❏ fair
❏ farm	❏ forest	❏ amusement park
❏ marineland	❏ museum	❏ waterfall
❏ mountain	❏ city	❏ lake
❏ beach	❏ stadium	❏ _____
❏ parade	❏ swamp	❏ _____

I can:

❏ sing	❏ braid	❏ run a computer
❏ swim	❏ ride a bike	❏ cook an egg
❏ draw	❏ saw wood	❏ recite a poem
❏ ski	❏ dance	❏ subtract
❏ whistle	❏ jump rope	❏ sew
❏ skip	❏ tell a story	❏ play music
❏ _____	❏ _____	❏ _____
❏ _____	❏ _____	❏ _____

My favorite kind of books are:

❏ mysteries	❏ history	❏ _____
❏ adventures	❏ science	❏ _____
❏ poems	❏ fairy tales	
❏ biographies	❏ science fiction	

People I know:

❏ veterinarian	❏ sheriff	❏ coach
❏ dentist	❏ cousin	❏ cheer leader
❏ teacher	❏ plumber	❏ computer ace
❏ carpenter	❏ rancher	❏ lab technician
❏ singer	❏ banker	❏ grandmother
❏ math whiz	❏ drummer	❏ mechanic
❏ baby-sitter	❏ truck driver	❏ writer
❏ librarian	❏ doctor	❏ artist
❏ postman	❏ waitress	❏ dry cleaner
❏ dancer	❏ cook	❏ grandfather
❏ fisherman	❏ secretary	❏ architect

Story Board

First

Next

After that

Later

Then

After that

Soon

Finally

Star the most important part or the most exiting event in the narative.

Maupin House © 1995, Building a Writing Community: A Practical Guide
by Marcia S. Freeman

STORY TIMELINE

OUR FIELD TRIP TO THE ZOO

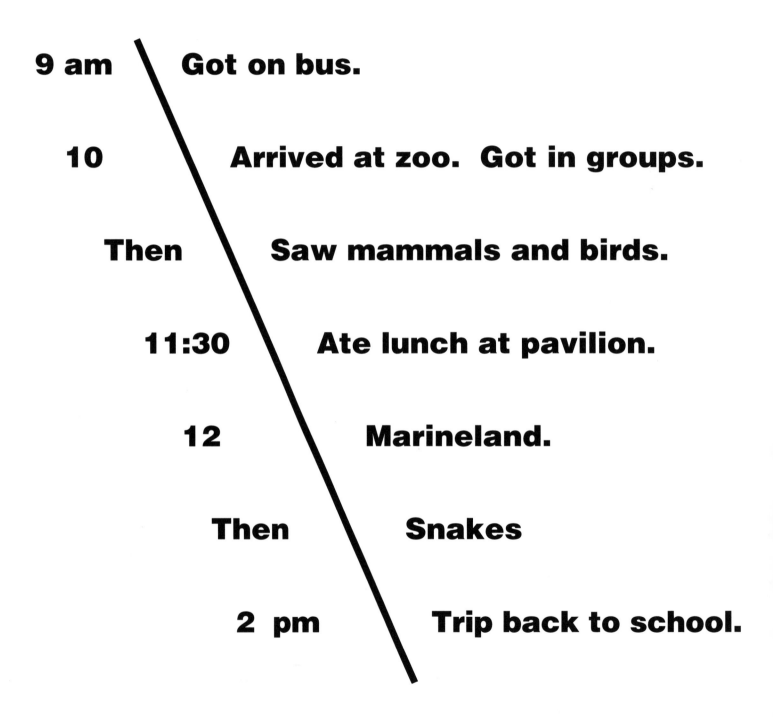

9 am — Got on bus.

10 — Arrived at zoo. Got in groups.

Then — Saw mammals and birds.

11:30 — Ate lunch at pavilion.

12 — Marineland.

Then — Snakes

2 pm — Trip back to school.

WATER

All living things need water.

Water dissolves sugar and salt.

People can not drink sea water.

Water is a liquid which takes the shape of its container.

Our bodies are 96% water.

Water is a compound made of hydrogen and oxygen.

Animals obtain water by drinking and from their food.

Water is colorless.

Water occurs in 3 forms: gas, liquid, and solid.

A person should drink several glasses of water a day.

A fish gets its oxygen from water through its gills.

Plants obtain water from the soil through their roots.

Seeds need water to sprout and grow.

Water turns into ice at 32 degrees Fahrenheit.

Rabbits

Rabbits are furry mammals.

Rabbits live in burrows or under brush piles.

Rabbits eat plants.

Baby rabbits are born live.

Rabbits have especially long ears.

Rabbits live in almost any climate.

Rabbits have whiskers.

Rabbits live in the desert.

Rabbits change their fur color to camouflage themselves.

Rabbits have powerful hind legs.

Rabbits are warm blooded animals.

Arctic rabbits turn white in the winter.

Rabbits line their burrows with grass and fur they pull from their body.

WEB PLAN

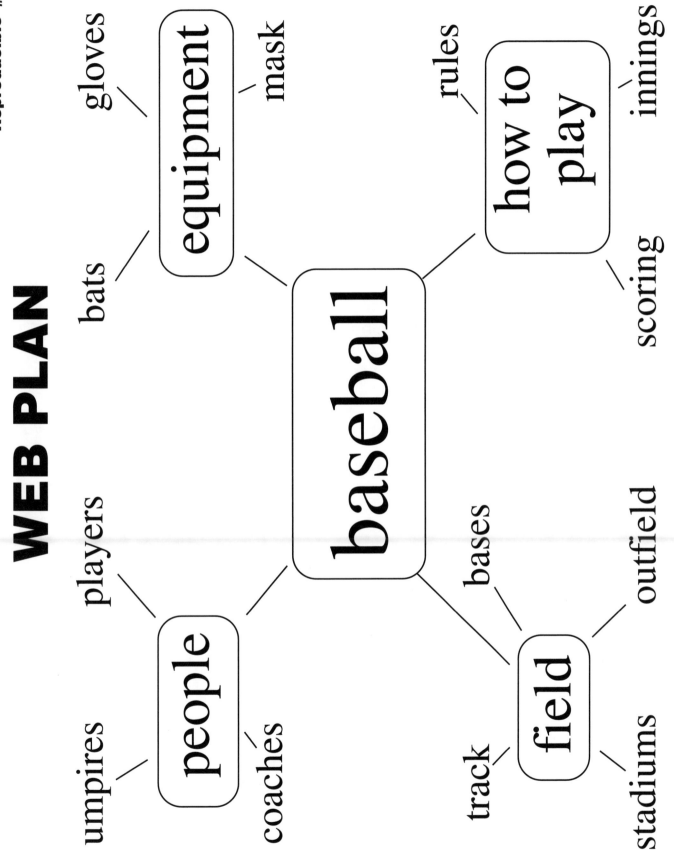

gloves

equipment

mask

bats

rules

how to play

innings

scoring

players

baseball

bases

people

coaches

umpires

field

outfield

track

stadiums

FICTION PLANNER

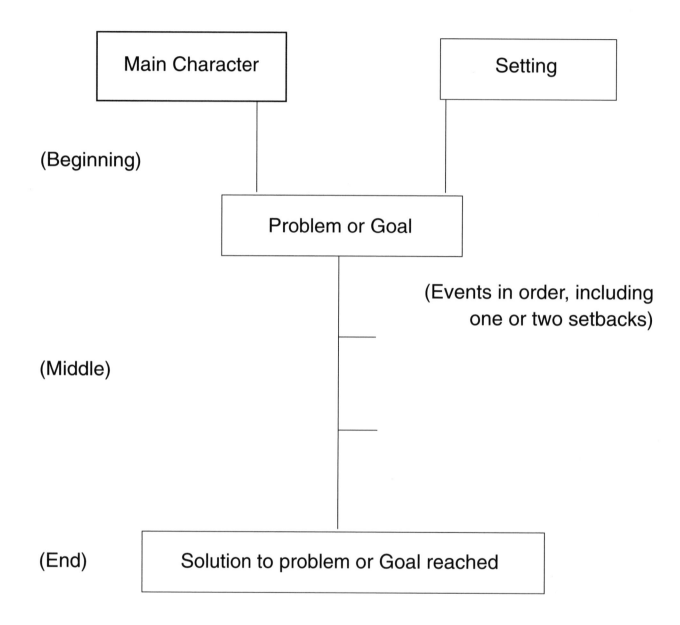

Main Character

Setting

(Beginning)

Problem or Goal

(Events in order, including
one or two setbacks)

(Middle)

(End)   Solution to problem or Goal reached

SOME CATEGORIES OF BEGINNINGS
(add some of your own)

Fiction

The main characters are talking.

The time and place setting are described.

The main character is introduced by description.

The main characters are doing something.

Some action is taking place.

- _____

Personal Narratives

Author describes the time and place.

Author describes a situation or event.

Author asks a question.

- _____

Expository

Author asks a question.

Author defines the topic word.

Author tells of personal involvement with the subject.

- _____

Biography

Author establishes the time of the introductory event or the start of person's life.

Author describes the person.

Author introduces the subject with which the person is closely associated (Civil War—Abraham Lincoln, Radium—Marie Curie, Basketball—Michael Jordan).

- _____

Vocabulary of Feelings

Joyful:	**Sad:**	**Mad:**
glad	lonely	angry
happy	miserable	furious
excited	depressed	hurt
energetic	bashful	hostile
playful	unhappy	rage
aware	guilty	frustrated
creative	down	hateful
elated	stupid	irritated
delighted	hurt	annoyed
cheerful	pitiful	jealous
daring	teary	irate
amused	riled	up
_____	_____	_____
_____	_____	_____

Scared:	**Peaceful:**	**Proud:**
anxious	serene	esteemed
afraid	calm	satisfied
weak	content	valuable
embarrassed	relaxed	worthwhile
bewildered	thoughtful	confident
confused	loved	appreciated
insecure	trusted	intelligent
foolish	thankful	important
helpless	cozy	faithful
ashamed	safe	
_____	_____	_____
_____	_____	_____

Expository and Non-fiction Narrative Endings

Reminder statements:
> Be sure to ...
> Remember that...
> So, if you...
> The next time you...

Finally, eventually:
> The last thing you need to know...
> The last thing to do is...

A quotation concerning the whole topic:
> "Let us all join in preserving the ..."
> "I owe my success to ..."
> "I hope..."

Feelings about the event:
> The best part about...
> I knew then...
> This valuable information helped me...

Predictions:
> The next time you will know...
> In no time you will be able...

Summary statements:
> To survive, they must ..., ..., and ...
> And they all...
> No matter how you look at it...
> For more details about...

Homework Response Format

1. Responder must be older than writer.

2. Writer holds and reads the manuscript. Responder listens to the text.

3. Writer asks responder to listen to the manuscript for what the author did well and to give a compliment.

4. Writer describes the target skill he is trying to use in the piece and asks the responder to:
   - Listen to the manuscript for evidence of the skill or for a place to apply the skill.
   - Offer help with using the target skill.

5. Writer revises the manuscript using the responder's help.

6. Responder signs name to Homework Response Form or manuscript.

Homework Response Form

WRITER:_____RESPONDER:_____

TITLE:_____

TARGET SKILL:_____

COMPLIMENT:_____

COMMENT:_____

Roving Conference Cue Card

React to content—relate to text and the author's knowledge.

Compliment— I like the way...
                   I noticed you...

Ask— What are you trying to do in this piece?
           What do you want your reader to learn?
           What writing skill are you working on in this piece?

Help—Do you need any? Provide resource or help.

ADDING SINGLE WORDS OR SENTENCES

Sometimes we forget and leave a word out of our writing. Sometimes we even leave out whole sentences or think of something later that we would like ^ include at the start of ^ piece.

Adding a word or two is easy. You just put a ^ where you want to add the word(s). Then write the new word(s) above the ^.

Adding words or whole sentences is easy too, if we skip lines as we write. Some writers even skip two lines. Maybe they are the kind of writers who find lots more to say after they think about their piece for a few days.

*<u>For instance, I would like to add the following sentence between the first and second sentence in the first paragraph:</u>

The reason we leave out words is because our brain goes faster than our pencil.

BUSCH GARDENS

When we were at the water fountain in Busch Gardens we left my little brother Miles at the water fountain. And when we came back to our senses we all panicked and started walking around in circles nervously. My Dad went back to look for Miles at the water fountain and he found Miles. After we found Miles we got ice cream and looked at the crocodiles. "Did you know that one of the crocodiles died because he had over two pounds of pennies in his body?"

(fourth grader)

SAMPLE PARAGRAPHS

My mom took my brother and me swimming. We went to the Arlington Park Pool. I rode in the front seat. The park has a pool that has black lines painted on the bottom. That helps you swim in a straight line, but only if you can open your eyes under the water.

* * * * *

Everyone in my family is tall. My Uncle Tom is the tallest. He can touch the ceiling in our house. My Dad is the next tallest. He can touch the ceiling if he stands on tiptoes. The ceiling is made of that popcorn stuff. When my brother gets a little older he might be able to touch the ceiling, too. Now he can, if he stands on a milk crate.

* * * * *

Baby lions are called kittens. They follow their mother everywhere. They learn to hunt by watching her. They are mammals. They practice pouncing on insects and lizards.

* * * * *

The team was ready to play. The pitcher yelled in to the catcher to watch out for the next hitter. The catcher threw the ball to the first basemen. He threw it to the short stop. Then the pitcher got it. He pitched the ball. Strike One. The hitter got ready. The left fielder was chewing gum. The pitcher threw another strike.

Keeping Like Information Together

Camels have long eyelashes that catch blowing sand. If some sand gets into the eye, a camel has an extra eyelid to get it out. The camel is designed to cope with desert winds. Like a windshield wiper, the extra eyelid moves side to side and wipes the sand away.

* * * * *

There are many kinds of bears. Polar bears are white and very big. Grizzly bears are dark brown or gray and have long claws. They are taller than a man. Polar bears eat seals and fish. Black bears are smaller than grizzly bears and not as dangerous. They are frequently scavengers at rural garbage dumps.

* * * * *

The school cafeteria will be closed today. The maintenance people will be painting the tables and benches. You will have to take your lunch outside and eat on the playground. You may get drinks from the vending machines or from the cafeteria staff who will be selling milk. The tables will be painted red and blue and the benches will be yellow. Thank you for your patience while this project is underway.

Practice Writing

Setting

Micky Mouse is at
a big ~~park~~ all his friends
are there. ~~Igopecialie~~ his girl friend
Where is this place they are
taking pichers with kids

Last week on monday I took my

dog bruno ~~for~~ with me when I

went to baseball. I alwasy take him
and he
watches us play. Its at
jefferson park. next to where my

dad works.

Narrative piece:

Excerpt from a cat story.

One evening, in the town of Dorset, a small cat crept out from under an old house. She was thin and black and covered with dust.

Suddenly, she crouched and twitched her ears back and forth. An eerie noise came from the yard behind the house.

"Who's there?" she whispered. No one answered. She waited and waited.

After a few minutes, she bounded across a dark stretch of grass and leaped into a tree. Up she climbed until she perched safely on a large branch.

A light flashed on at the back of the house. The cat could hear the clump, clump, clump of someone crossing the porch. The screen door opened with a loud screeching. A beam of light swept the back lawn.

Across the yard, a swing set threw out bars of shadow as the swing moved slowly back and forth. Back and forth.

Expository Piece:

Ant Lion

Ant lions are a curious insect. The interesting thing we notice first about them is the traps they build. These traps are funnel-like structures that you might find in dry soil under shrubs and edges of buildings. They are about two to three inches in diameter and an inch deep. The ant lion is hiding in the bottom of the trap.

The ant lion feeds on small crawling insects who wander into their traps. These might be ants, small caterpillars, and beetles. When a small insect falls into the trap, the ant lion flings soil up to keep the insect from escaping. It grabs the insect and eats it.

The ant lion is the larva of a dragon fly type of insect. As a larva, it is the size of a lentil bean. The body is segmented and the small head has a large set of pincer jaws. These pincers work like arms and help it build the trap and grab the insect prey.

When to Paragraph

- Start of every piece.

- Every change of place.

- Every change of time.

- Every substantial change in the action.

- Start of a new topic or sub-topic (every new section of your web).

- Every change of speaker (a speaker gets his own paragraph).

- Every 5-7 lines if none of the above. Give your reader a break!

SAMPLER OF REPETITIVE WORDS

And Then, So:

I went to the mall with my friends. And then we all went to the music store. We bought some tapes and then we went to the food court. We saw some of our other friends from school so then we all went to the movie. Then when we came out we went into the game arcade. And then we hung around at the fountain waiting for my dad. And then I went home.

And:

I have a cat and it is white and black and purrs. Her name is Tammy and she is nice and she plays with me. And she goes in a paper bag and makes it move and knocks it over.

Said:

Mom said, "Don't forget to send your grandmother a note."

"I won't," I said as I went out the door.

Mom said, "You forgot your lunch. Come back!"

"Now I'm really going to be late," I said, huffing and puffing.

I:

I had a terrifying experience yesterday. I was riding my bike along Prospect Avenue. I was on the side walk because the road is narrow. I heard a dog give a ferocious growl. I looked over my shoulder and saw an enormous Pit Bull sail over the low hedge along the side walk. I could see he was dragging a chain. I got scared and rode the bike off the sidewalk in my panic. I almost got hit by a car.

Character's name:

Miles went to Epcot Center with his friend, Josh. Miles and Josh were with Miles' mom and his sister. Miles wanted to go to The Living Sea with Josh but his sister wanted to start at the Into the Future exhibit. Miles asked his mom if he and Josh could go alone and meet them after. His mom told Miles no.

Content Words

Climate is the average weather over the whole year. A climate may be warm and humid, or cold and dry. Some climates have lots of rain and some have periods of drought. Some climates have precipitation in the form of snow.

or

Kittens are baby cats. They purr. They have fur and whiskers. They have pads on their paws and they have claws that they can pull back in.

* *

For writer's practice locating and correcting content words.

Softball is my favorite sporte. I am the pichur. I can through a fast ball and a courve ball. Maria, who is my best friend, is the chacher when we play on the team on our street. When I play on the reck-reashun team another cacher is Kelsey. She is good at taging runners out at home plat.

DESCRIPTIVE ATTRIBUTES

- size: nine by twelve inches, one hundred yards; comparative—larger, as big as...

- color: purple, green, pale yellow; comparative—reddish, sea green,...

- shape: round, oval, cubic, square, columnar, tubular, triangular,...

- movement or action: gliding, slithering, flapping, explosive; comparative—faster, more frenzied,...

- symmetry: horizontal, vertical, radial

- texture: smooth, rough, bumpy, lumpy, soft, fuzzy, slippery; comparative—stickier, slickest,....

- number: fourteen, a thousand; non-specific—many, some, several; comparative—more than, fewer,...

- composition: wooden, metal, plastic, cloth, glass, concrete, cardboard, paper,..

- smell: smoky, putrid, floral, acrid, burnt, sweet; comparative—like smoke

- taste: sweet, salty, acidic;comparative—like licorice, fruitier,...

- function: use

- location: inanimate objects—place, time

- habitat: living things: underground, den, water, ocean, desert,...

- direction: left, right, up, down, backward, forward,...

- orientation: horizontal, vertical, parallel, perpendicular,...

- state: liquid, solid, gas.

- temperature: forty- six degrees, three below zero; non-specific—broiling, freezing; comparative—hotter than, coldest,...

- weight: ten pounds, seven grams; non-specific—heavy, light; comparative—as heavy as, the lightest,...

- age: five years old, eighteen months old; nonspecific—old, new, ancient, antique; comparative—older than Methuselah,...

- special features: writing, designs, knobs, buttons,...

DESCRIPTIVE STRUCTURE

Choice of Elements and Attributes (based on the five senses and memory)

- People and objects seen—who, what, number, position, age, condition, size, shapes, features, all attributes.
- What is happening—people, animal, and object movements, weather conditions.
- Sounds heard—type, source, magnitude.
- What it feels like—textures, mood, atmosphere, ambiance.
- Smells—types, source, magnitude.
- What you are reminded of—other places, other people.

Form And Presentation Order.

- Scenic—From left to right, from top to bottom, from foreground to background, from center to perimeter. The choice of order depends on the nature of the scene described but a writer must be consistent.
- Events—Chronological order.
- Portrait—No prescribed order although visual attributes and motion usually are presented first.
- Comparison—Help your readers picture what you observe by using comparisons through simile and metaphor.
- Follow the "Don't Hit Your Reader Over the Head" principle (see Expanding and Developing Ideas in Chapter IV, Drafting). Instead of My dog is very big, try, My dog barely fits in the front seat of our car.

Character Traits

PHYSICAL

Looks: height, weight, hair color and style, eye color, brows, freckles, scars, glasses, teeth, hands, ...

Clothing: occupation related, casual, formal, style, new, old, color coordinated, random, ...

Habitual gestures: squint, twitch, bite lip, crack knuckles, chew on braid, push glasses back on nose, hum, shrug, ...

Speech patterns: speed of speech, speech crutches such as "er" "like" "you know", pitch of voice, drawl, regional idioms, ...

PSYCHOLOGICAL

Emotional: happy, sad, optimistic, pessimistic, loud, shy, quarrelsome, placid, hyper, secure, insecure, cautious, ...

Intellectual: curious, smart, uninteresting, dull, inquiring, boring, inventive, ingenious, creative, ...

SOCIAL

Group behavior: bossy, reserved, overbearing, cooperative, uncooperative, leader, follower, ...

dentist	veterinarian	swimmer
florist	tennis player	soldier
minister	ballet dancer	mechanic
police officer	coach	teacher
dog trainer	singer	mail carrier

nurse
baseball player
telephone operator
librarian
pianist

bank teller	rancher	detective
realtor	hairdresser	farmer
astronaut	waitress	truck driver
	doctor	plumber
		artist

track meet	Marineland	fishing pier
restaurant	hospital	tennis court
Disney World	cafeteria	farm
space center	ranch	boat dock
dance	circus	zoo

	library
	Home Depot
	florist
	state fair
	concert

skating rink	mall	campground	football game
beach	airport	dentist	fireworks
bank	bakery	movie theater	video arcade
basketball game	swamp	haunted house	hockey game
day care	soccer camp	desert	rain forest

PLOTS

Here are six basic plots that have been used by all writers from Shakespeare to Judy Bloom. They are in the public domain and young writers may use them freely.

Expressed in Problem/Solution form they are:

- Lost and Found— person or object is lost and recovered.

- Character Versus Nature—character survives a natural calamity.

- Character With Personal Problem or Goal—character solves it, reaches goal, changes attitude or feelings.

- Good Guys Versus Bad Guys—good guys usually win unless author plans to write a sequel.

- Crime and Punishment or Mystery and Solution—Characters solve the mystery or crime and culprit caught.

- Boy meets Girl, problems or misunderstandings arise—characters solve differences or clear up misunderstandings.

These plots may be used singly or in combination.

Timeline For a Fable
The Boy Who Cried Wolf

A young shepherd tended his flock of sheep. Each day he herded them up into the hills, watched over them, and brought them back down to the village in the evening. He grew bored of his task and one day decided to create some excitement.

"Wolf, Wolf!" he cried. The people in the village hurried up the hill, carrying their sticks to drive off the wolf and save their sheep.

"He has run away," the boy told them when they gathered around him. "He was big and ugly. My shouting must have scared him away." The villagers praised the boy, making a big fuss over him.

The next day the shepherd boy, again growing tired of his work, shouted, "Wolf, Wolf!" Again, the villagers hurried up the hill. Again, he told them the wolf had run away. The shepherd boy enjoyed the stir. Some of the villagers praised him but some of them looked skeptical.

On the third day, a large gray wolf crept into the herd and killed a lamb. The boy cried, "Wolf, Wolf!" The villagers looked up from their work and said to each other, "It's that foolish shepherd boy, trying to get us to run up the hill again to see a wolf that ran away. Ignore him." And so the village lost many lambs that day while the foolish shepherd boy cried "Wolf."

Timeline:

POINT OF VIEW

Joy Thomas lost her dog, Trooper, on Saturday. She searched the neighborhood all day with no success. No one had seen Trooper since Joy had walked him early that morning.

By Sunday, Joy was frantic. She called the police. They advised her to call Animal Control on Monday. Joy thought this was not particularly helpful.

¤¤¤¤¤

The other contestants all looked bigger and stronger than I was. I wondered if I had the slightest chance to place in the Martial Arts Regional Tournament. My coach, Auggie Morrison, had told me not to worry about my opponent's size, that my speed and agility would compensate for my smallness.

I waited for my match to be called. Twice I checked my belt to see if it was tied correctly. I stretched for the tenth time. It seemed like hours before the announcer called my name.

FICTION FIRST LINE CATEGORIES

- **The author introduces the main character by name.**

- **The main character, named, is thinking or doing something.**

- **The author describes the setting-place.**

- **The author tells the setting-time.**

- **The author sets up the conflict in the first sentence.**

- **The character is talking.**

- **An event is in progress.**

- **Combinations of any of these.**

- **A letter or note.**

- **A prologue telling of an event in past that sets up the story.**

TRANSITION WORDS FOR EXPOSITORY WRITING

Adding to—and, also, or, along with, similarly, for instance, for example, for one thing, for another thing, especially, altogether, besides...

Summarizing—at last, so, finally, all in all, and so, therefore, consequently, in short ....

Establishing Sequence—first, last, now, then, later, afterward, when, until, not until, eventually, meanwhile, immediately, soon, at last, finally, ...

Establishing Incidence— always, usually, frequently, occasionally, sometimes, never.

Linking Cause and Effect—as a result, because, which caused, that resulted in, what happened was, which produced, naturally, therefore...

Comparing—like, similarly, on the other hand, whereas, however, but...

U. S. Coins

There are four basic United States coins. They are the penny, the nickel, the dime, and the quarter. All but the penny are made of a silvery metal. The penny is copper.

The coins are worth different amounts. The quarter is worth twenty-five cents, the dime is worth ten cents, the nickel five cents, and the penny one cent.

You can tell all the coins apart just by feeling them. The quarter and dime have ridges along the edge, but the dime is thinner and smaller. The nickel and penny have smooth edges, but the penny is thinner and smaller.

Additive Transitions in Expository Writing

<u>Adding to:</u> and, also, or, along with, similarly, for instance, for example, for one thing, for another thing, especially, altogether, besides...

Horses come in all sizes They are measured in hands, which is the width of a man's hand or about 4 inches. The measurement is taken from the front hoof to the top of the shoulder at the end of the mane.

(Using an additive transition : *For example*)

For example, work horses are the largest, measuring are about 17-20 hands high. Thoroughbreds measure 16-17, western quarter horses, 14-15 hands, and ponies, 10-12 hands.

* * * *

The school playground is divided into several areas. The kindergarten area is filled with sand. The little kids play on slides and climbing equipment. Their swings seats are made of canvas.
(start another paragraph using a transition word or phrase from the list above)

* * * *

My mom is always telling me how much harder school was when she was a kid. First, there was a long walk to school because there were no school buses. And of course the weather was worse in the old days.
(start another paragraph using a transition word or phrase from the list above)

I've read your book and like the part...

Mail to: Marcia Freeman
c/o Maupin House Publishing
P.O. Box 90148
Gainesville, FL 32607 USA

About the Author

Marcia Freeman is an author and writing consultant specializing in the practical aspects of creating a classroom writing community. She was educated in Woodford Hollow School, a non-room school in rural Vermont, the Bennington Free Library, and Cornell University. Marcia taught high school science before pausing to raise a family. Later, she taught second, fourth, and combination fourth/fifth grades in Caldwell, New Jersey. A meeting with educator Donald Graves and subsequent workshops with Lucy Calkins in New York City led her to embrace the writing process approach and to begin a second career in writing education.

Following a move to Florida in 1986, Marcia became involved in various activities related to writing and the public schools. She has taught creative writing in the Sarasota County Library System, co-produced the University of South Florida-Sarasota Suncoast Young Author's Conference, served as an instructor in Language Arts at the University of South Florida, and conducted writing process staff development workshops in Sarasota and Manatee counties. She currently serves as a writing consultant to elementary schools.

If you enjoyed *Building a Writing Community: a practical guide*, try these language arts resources from Maupin House.

Caught'ya! Grammar with a Giggle

by Jane Bell Kiester

Hairy Beast and Friends, Romeo and Juliet at the Mall, and The Magic Umbrella help teachers of students in grades 2-12 teach writing skills in just ten minutes a day! Save valuable planning and classroom time while effectively teaching grammar, usage, and mechanics with a whole language twist. These humorous, kid-tested soap opera plots written by a teacher turn the sentence-a-day approach into an intriguing and fun skill-builder. Tens of thousands of public, private and home school teachers tell us enthusiastically that this technique works. There are enough sentences, with board corrections, for three years! Machine-gradeable tests and keys, plot outlines, and spin-off activities make this a winner.

$14.95 • Whole Language • 227 pages • 7 x 10 • 0-929895-04-5

Caught'ya Again! More Grammar with a Giggle

by Jane Bell Kiester

Holy Moldy Bread contest! Kiester strikes again, this time with four more stories plus mini-lessons, writing workshops, and a complete grammar primer. Once again, this zany, creative educator gives teachers solid, classroom-proven techniques that turn students into better writers. As always, the techniques and stories can be used with students in grades 2-12. Teacher keys, tests and special notes for the home school teacher are included. A real time saver that works!

$19.95 • Whole Language • 314 pages • 6 x 9 • 0-929895-6

Nurturing Your Child's Natural Literacy

by H. Thompson Fillmer and William Cliett

Follow these easy home-based ideas and help your child along the road to a lifelong love of books and learning. Educators Fillmer and Cliett teach an easy, child-centered technique based on key vocabulary that encourages reading at the child's readiness level. Included are tips to help you choose a literacy-wise pre-school. An enriching and insightful book for parents, pre-school teachers, and literacy agencies.

$9.95 • Parenting • 127 pages • 6 x 9 • 0-929895-07-X

Maupin House
P. O. Box 90148
Gainesville, FL 32607

1-800-524-0634

Scope and Sequence
Model

See Foldout